POLITICAL CONSIDERATIONS
ON
COUPS D'ÉTAT

CONSIDERATIONS
POLITIQVES
SVR LES
COVPS D'ESTAT

Par G. N. P.

A ROME.

M. DC. XXXIX.

GABRIEL NAUDÉ

POLITICAL CONSIDERATIONS ON COUPS D'ÉTAT

EDITED, TRANSLATED AND WITH A PREFACE BY
SIMONA DRAGHICI, PhD

PLUTARCH PRESS
CORVALLIS, OR

This translation first published in the United States of America by Plutarch Press, Corvallis, Oregon, in 2006.

Complete English translation of Gabriel Naudé's *Considerations Politiques sur les Coups D'Estat*, Rome, 1639.

This English translation, Preface, Short Bibliography, Chronology, Notes and Index of Names Copyright © 2006 by Simona Draghici.

For information address the publisher:
PLUTARCH PRESS
P.O. Box 195
Corvallis, OR 97339-0195, USA

Library of Congress Cataloging-in-Publication Data

Naudé, Gabriel, 1600-1653.
   [Considérations politiques sur les coups d'État. English]
   Political considerations on coups d'etat / Gabriel Naudé ; edited, translated and with a
preface by Simona Draghici.
     p. cm.
   Includes bibliographical references and index.
   ISBN 0-943045-23-1 (pbk. : alk. paper)
   1. Political science—Early works to 1800. I. Draghici, Simona, 1937- II. Title.

JC155.N3913 2006
321.09--dc22

                                   2006050876

Manufactured in the United States of America.
Book design and cover by JAY.

TABLE OF CONTENTS

POLITICAL CONSIDERATIONS ON COUPS D'ÉTAT

PREFACE

'Nous entrons
dans l'avenir à reculons'
PAUL VALÉRY

There are two books, both entitled 'Coup d'État', of which I am aware, and both published last century: one, in 1931,[1] and the other, in 1968, with a second edition in 1979. I am referring to Curzio Malaparte's and Edward Luttwak's, respectively. The former is the work of a journalist and writer, turned memorialist, who lived through the European turmoil precipitated by the Great War, the resulting collapse of three empires and the various attempts to fill the power vacuum thus created. The latter book, on the other hand, bears the subtitle 'A Practical Handbook', and is the work of a political scientist, educated at the London School of Economics and Political Science,[2] and interested mostly in the political events of the so-called Third World in the aftermath of WWII, which he examines empirically, from a distance, as he looks for regularities that are then set in patterns. (Hence his rather provocative Preface to the first edition, in which he congratulates himself for making the techniques of seizing power within a state accessible to everybody, and so democratizing the coup.) Notwithstanding, both authors consider the coup d'état a technique, politically neutral, for the seizure of power from a formal government or administration inside a state. In both works, secrecy, planning and surprise are the main ingredients of the action for the disablement of any government.

These three factors also happen to be mentioned in our author's own discussion of the coup d'état, consigned to paper some three hundred years before. The most obvious difference, though, is one of perspective: for Naudé, the techniques used to seize power may be as useful for the preservation of that power, and it is on this aspect that he concentrates in his book.

VI

Naudé's choice of perspective had been determined by the purpose of his work, which is more or less the equivalent of a modern business plan to be submitted to potential investors in order to obtain the needed financing, and in his particular case, that would have been a position at the French royal court, in Cardinal Richelieu's chancellery, or at least, an ecclesiastical benefice for life. Indeed, he belonged to a category of people known in France as *donneurs d'avis* or *brasseurs d'affairs* (advice-givers and go-getters, respectively). It emerged in the 16th century and continued in the 17th, was put on stage by Molière and written about by Daniel Defoe in his '*Essay on Projects*': mostly urbanites of humble origin or empoverished gentry, swarming at the gates of the royal palace, and teeming in the Place de Change in Paris. One of the luckiest was a certain Théophraste Renaudot, a native of Loudun, who became one of Richelieu's amanuenses and director of the Bureau d'Adresses, which combined the services of a labour exchange, an intelligence department, and a charitable institution, referring the poor who were sick to physicians willing to treat them for free. Under Richelieu's patronage, he later founded the first French newspaper, a weekly sheet, with the title LA GAZETTE DE FRANCE.

On the other hand, born in 1600, with limited intellectual resources and slender family means, Naudé was one of the eight children of a bailiff at the Paris Bureau of Finances, and of his illiterate wife. Two of his brothers would become merchants, and the other two, petty officials, while his three sisters would marry, one a goldsmith, another a haberdasher, and the third a prosecutor at the criminal court of Paris. He himself allegedly attended several prestigious colleges, and his passion for name-dropping to enhance his self-importance takes an ironic turn when of all his teachers, only those of rhetoric, logic and metaphysics are singled out by name,[3] the very disciplines of which he showed a poor command in his subsequent writings. Then at the age of twenty, he went to medical school from which he dropped two years later, probably realizing the difficulties which the acquisition of knowledge in the field involved, alongside the length of training and high expenses, and all that with no other prospect but an uncertain future. He was an ambitious young man, determined to arrive, but like many of his kind, he thought speed and economy of effort to be essential to the fulfilment of one's dreams when capital was in short supply. His next step was to become a librarian in the employ of Henri de Mesme, President of the Paris Parliament and owner of the then famous Bibliotheca Memmiana, probably little suspecting that there he would find the occupation of his life. Or rather his double occupation, the second never mentioned by any scholar as far as I know, namely of colporteur of books and manuscripts. The collections of the various libraries in which he worked, or had access to, served him not only to cultivate himself but were a source of personal income: he could copy rare books from them and sell or trade the result, he could round up the price of new acquisitions, sell better editions and replace them with cheaper ones, and also from the shelter of those libraries carry on a trade in illicit books, very lucrative though full of risks. (Wouldn't the son of his friend Guy Patin be imprisoned for that very kind of trade?) With an interruption of several months which he spent at Padua allegedly to study medicine and ingratiate himself with some of the luminaries of the University there, Naudé remained with President de Mesme until the end of 1630, some eight years in all.To catch the public eye and win the goodwill of potential benefactors he had already at the age of twenty compiled and printed a pamphlet under the title LE MARFORE, OR DISCOURSE AGAINST LIBELS, unlikely to have created a stir in a market flooded by pro and con pamphlets. But for him, it had been an occasion to set himself up as the defender of the calumniated, role that with him would become a second nature. Then, while in the employ of President de Mesme, he compiled another pamphlet, INSTRUCTION TO FRANCE ON THE TRUTH OF THE HISTORY OF THE ROSICRUCIAN BROTHERS (1623), avowal of his patriotism and loyalty to the official church of the country. It was followed by quite a long treatise, by which in fact he was teaching his master, as chief justice of the court of the Paris Parliament, how to deal with those books and authors accused of heresy and of the practice of magic, all the more useful as heresy trials had shifted from the Church to the secular courts of the regional parliaments. Under the title APOLOGY TO THE GREAT PERSONAGES FALSELY SUSPECTED OF MAGIC, it was published in 1625 and dedicated to de Mesme, who was also the dedicatee of ADVICE ON ESTABLISHING A LIBRARY, printed two years later. Both are prose centones like the present work, and whoever has read the English translation of the ADVICE would find himself on familiar ground as regards style and structure when reading the POLITICAL CONSIDERATIONS. The APOLOGY allowed Naudé to claim expertise in esoterica and books on alchemy and various types of magic, while the ADVICE, the title of professional librarian, although people in the know, such as Jacques Dupuy, future royal librarian, and the gentleman scholar Nicolas Claude Fabri de Peiresc were less enthusiastic about it (and I share the latter's observation that 'This Naudé makes it too obvious that he has not perceived clarity but through a hole...'[4]). Indeed, what is frustrating about Naudé's expositions is his inability to argue logically, to organize his material in a coherent whole and to carry through his incipient classifications (his excuse that in his own digressions, he only followed Montaigne could please but himself). His is the prolixity of the smatterer who wants to impress at all costs, which was not unusual in those times. Two maxims were current then: one, that men of lowly status can never manage to reach high rank without ruse, and the other, that courtiers are of three kinds — flatterers, projectors and informers. A parish priest of the times described the urge most eloquently in his confession: the ambition of attaining the state of being well thought of in the world and particularly by respectable people. He called it one of the two temptations that tormented him. The other was that of the flesh, which Naudé seems to have had under control, not only because it was costly and risky, but also because it interfered with his achievement of the former. Eventually both Peiresc and the Dupuy brothers allowed themselves to be cultivated by him several months later, when prevailing upon his teacher at the Medical School, René Moreau, Naudé was allowed to deliver the commencement speech for the 1628 class of graduates. The text of his speech not only earned him a medical degree but also opened him the doors of the cabinet of the Dupuy brothers at the famous De Thou library. His next book was ADDITION TO THE HISTORY OF LOUIS XI, published in 1630. It is a curiosity book aimed at drawing royal and public attention to the importance of books from all fields, of writers of books and of the centres of learning, and to awaken interest in them he produces a brief history of book-writing and book-printing and provides a catalogue of various books worth collecting. To add weight to his argument, he focusses on King Louis XI as positive example to emulate, and adds an impressive index to the work. Ultimately, the book or its index won him a job in the retinue of the Papal Nuncio who was making ready to return to Rome. The Dupuy brothers seem to have acted as intermediaries, presenting Cardinal Bagni with a copy of the ADDITION that made the hoped-for good impression. It is my suspicion that the Dupuy were eager to get rid of Naudé who after the publication of the ADVICE might have nourished the ambition of becoming a royal librarian or at least a De Thou librarian, and so endanger the position and future prospects of the brothers. At the time, Naudé was known as a bibliographer only, whose ambitions could not be curtailed but from the outside. Arriving in Rome in 1631, he became a zealous caller on Tommaso Campanella who had been released from the two-year long detention at the Sacred College to the care of the Roman chapter of his Dominican order, where he kept thinking his thoughts and writing his books. Naudé had heard of the Calabrian monk from the latter's visitors in the Neapolitan prisons, and perhaps even more from Campanella's writings, printed mainly in Germany. Once in Rome, however, Naudé had, and took, the opportunity to insinuate himself in Campanella's favour, earn his confidence, worm ideas out of him, pocket his notes and manuscripts, pretending to act as his ardent admirer, self-appointed literary agent, secretary and expert in French matters. That was made easy by Campanella's growing interest in French power politics as he was witnessing the gradual demise of Spanish imperialism. He had already written AVVERTIMENTI AL RE DI FRANCIA (1628), which was followed by a political dialogue between a Venetian, a Spaniard and a Frenchman. Moreover, the year 1631 had seen the publication of Campanella's important work ATHEISMUS TRIUMPHATUS [The Atheism Prevailed upon], to which Naudé had access and likely served him as a source of inspiration for his own book, POLITICAL CONSIDERATIONS ON THE COUPS D'ÉTAT. His rather disreputable conduct towards Campanella was common practice among ambitious young scholars aspiring to a fast career on the capital painstakingly accumulated by politically and socially vulnerable masters lacking dependable, powerful patrons, in a period characterized by moral anarchy and a crisis of authority.[5] He was going to do the same by Grotius in France, later on. Nevertheless, Naudé's plans to become a full-time professional politician in France seem to have collapsed with Campanella's flight to Paris, which Naudé had not anticipated. He apparently had worked assidiously on his CONSIDERATIONS during the first two years of his stay in Italy with the intent of presenting the work to Louis XIII's first minister or to the king himself, but it happened that Campanella got there first, thus inadvertently forfeiting his opportunity, and so the POLITICAL CONSIDERATIONS was set aside in expectation of another occasion. Instead, he had another book of his printed in Venice in 1633, namely, BIBLIOGRAPHIA POLITICA, a compromise between his acknowledged status of bibliographer and his political aspirations, less riskier than the CONSIDERATIONS which quoted as authorities books on the Index list. An example suffices: in the POLITICAL CONSIDERATIONS, Justus Lipsius is quoted as one of the authorities, whereas in the BIBLIOGRAPHIA, he is dismissed as a mere stylist, given that Lipsius' POLITICA had been on the Index list since its publication in 1589. Besides, it was less time-consuming and also more lucrative to compile a bibliography for the French book-lovers, not only because there was no small number of them in circulation in Italy, but also because he must have had access to the lists of recommended and forbidden books of the Sacred Congregation and to their reviews by its official censors. There was also a practical aspect to it for Naudé, the book and manuscript colporteur, who thus armed himself with a catalogue of authors and titles of his own to go by in his trade. It was also easy to carry around and hide, with its 4⅛ in. by 2⅛ format, its hundred pages with very narrow margins and the type block cramped with lower-case black letters, without spaces for paragraphs, hard to read and so discouraging prying eyes. It is more likely that its dedicatee, Monseigneur Gafarel, the Papal protonotary and a Frenchman who had been part of the Dupuy brothers' circle and so was known to Naudé, together with the French ambassador to Venice, was instrumental in obtaining an honorary title of court physician from Louis XIII for Naudé, rather than Cardinal Bagni, his master. The event led to Naudé's address delivered before the faculty of the University of Padua, which as a result, granted him the title of doctor of philosophy and medicine in the same year.

Another five years had to pass, though, before POLITICAL CONSIDERATIONS was taken out of the drawer and re-edited, its author desperately anxious not to let so much intellectual effort on his part go to waste. The flattering terms in which he had referred to the French king and to Cardinal Richelieu in it, and the fact that it was written in French and not Latin, and French incidents and history were mentioned with a sense of tacit concurrence, all this inclines me to think that originally, as already said, Naudé had intended to dedicate it to the French king and/or to his first minister. The French historian René Pintard suggests that Naudé resumed work on the CONSIDERATIONS in 1638, and it is possible that it was at that time that he rewrote parts of it to accommodate its rededication to Cardinal Bagni, who was then object of machinations started in the wings of the Curia by the French to elect him as successor to Pope Urban VIII. Naudé might have seen in that a new

opportunity for his book, and implicitly for himself.
Consequently, he rewrote its opening to present Cardinal
Bagni, the new dedicatee, as the inspiration and mundane
wisdom behind its realization, whom he went on to
glorify in the concluding pages as pontiff of a universal
church, while reserving for himself, according to the
stereotyped formula of the time, the privilege of presenting Bagni with another book, commensurate with the
new office. Naudé's wishes did not come true, however,
because Cardinal Bagni became increasingly ill, had to
give up the work in his diocese, and in 1639, returned to
Rome for a short while, only to leave it in 1640 for San
Marco in the South, where he stayed with the Frangipani
and where he died on 25 July 1641. The funeral in Rome
became another public relations event for Naudé who had
been willed librarian to Cardinal Barberini. He wrote a
panegyric for the occasion, had it printed, and handed it
with the votive candle to each of those attending the
burial.

Meanwhile, Campanella had died in Paris, in February 1639, and so Naudé had nothing more to fear from
that side any longer: no more accusations of theft and
plagiarism from the old Dominican. On the other hand,
Bagni was unlikely to give attention to Naudé's writings
when he returned to Rome from Rieti: his illness and his
peace with the Creator were closer concerns of his.
Whether Naudé printed the CONSIDERATIONS in that
year, as impressed on its front-page, or simply antedated
it is a moot point. Personally, I suspect that it went into
production, so to speak, after Bagni's death, when Naudé
was making plans to return to France, and capitalize on it
there; that Bagni never saw it in the final form: he might
have prevented its distribution and castigated its author
for misrepresentation, abuse of trust and perjury, as he
had been shifting on the Cardinal the responsibility for
its contents and even for the initiative. He had to date
the printed book '1639', the year his master was still
alive and in Rome, and his name could be invoked to
serve as protection for him and his ideas. A stratagem
that was repeated with regard to Campanella and Pope
Urban VIII, when Naudé composed and antedated by

several years a eulogy of none other but the Pope, a Barberini, describing in flattering and mendacious words among the Pope's many feats and acts of generosity, the rescue of Campanella from the Spanish dungeons, his 'liberation'. Campanella had been in fact kidnapped by the Inquisition and brought under arrest to Rome in 1629, after having been freed from jail by the Spanish authorities in Naples. He printed it in Paris in 1644, probably soon after the Pope's death, who most likely had been unaware of its existence. In that way, Naudé contrived to appropriate some of the prestige of the two for himself, and so claim for himself the role of Campanella's literary executor in France.

Naudé's is a case study for a category of people who wanted to come on top but lacked a supporting tradition and inheritance, as well as a network of socially significant relations, in a world in which the old institutions had given way and new ones were still in a fluid stage, as war and civil strife kept smouldering. As already said, and also seen from Naudé's efforts, it was by ruse that anyone of humble and not so humble origin could make it in the world. That implied contempt of fellowman and even hatred of the populace from which the like of Naudé struggled to dissociate themselves, and utilitarianism and cynicism in their social intercourse. To live by one's wits in cases like Naudé's also meant the suspension of any religious creed outside its politically utilitarian value: it was a luxury he could ill afford because it would have narrowed considerably any opportunity to better himself at a time when the formula *cujus regio ejus religio* was imposing itself as a principle of state. Ambiguity of language and equivocality of action, alongside interest, both individual and collective, characteristic of any crisis of mores and authority in the modern world, were the parameters of his conduct and his occasionalism, which in his writings assume an aspect that has been identified as political realism. It is the concomitant absence of any sanctimoniousness from his discourse that kept the interest in the POLITICAL CONSIDERATIONS alive for a century, only to be rekindled in our age, torn by similar uncertainties and a persistent penchant for self-destruction as their doubtful solution.

Naudé was one of the first to use the phrase 'coup d'état', which was given currency in France, in the first half of the 17th century. Deriving from the Latin *status*, the term 'état' (state) had come to be used in Italy as 'stato' during the Renaissance, and to mean a community in which the public interest, as distinct from the private, was the rallying factor. One comes across it in Machiavelli's vocabulary, for instance. With the secularization of the body politic, it spread gradually over the Italian boundaries, and found an equivalent in England in the terms 'commonweal' or 'commonwealth'. On the other hand, the term 'coup', derived from the Greek *kolaphos*, meaning blow, came to designate a sudden action, its violence consisting in the speed or suddenness with which it was carried out, rather than physical harm, as 'd'état' was its qualifier; in other words, it came to mean a sudden action, carried out in the public interest, at a propitious moment, by the head of the body politic, after consultation with his closest advisers, when the laws of the land were unable to deal with the particular situation.

The secularization of politics operated in Renaissance Italy and in England, through the expansion of the class of lay lawyers and the affirmation of natural law at the expense of the canon law, coincided with a febrile search for answers and solutions in the pre-ecclesiastical literature, and particularly that of the Roman civilization. It meant not only the emancipation of politics from the precepts of religion and canon law, but even something more drastic, namely, the submission of religion to politics, in a deliberate effort to restore order and authority. That was possible, as Naudé shows, because of the premise of the relativity of all things, which as the basis of politics, made of the present its only active concern — it served to legitimise the efforts to slow down the demise of any power structure by making the best of the moment. The welfare of future generations was outside its boundaries.

On the other hand, morality, which had been the monopoly of the church, had come to be considered more of an individual matter, separate from the affairs of the state, and secondary to them, as laconically conveyed by the saying *somo Venetiani dopo Chrestiani* (we are Venetians first, and Christians only afterwards). It is this renewed awareness of the conflict between individual interests and the welfare of the whole that became the quandary which Louis XIV solved by deciding 'L'État c'est Moi', with ruinous consequences for his country, but which has remained the crux of practical politics to this day. (It is interesting to note here that the Americans became aware of it early in the 19th century, if not even before that, and tried to solve the crux by distinguishing between statecraft and politics, and disparaging the latter as self-seeking, and so, inadvertently, granting a licence for the abuse of political power by those entrusted with it. Even now, when members of the Congress and the President of the Republic talk contemptously of the 'politicians in Washington DC', do they really want their audiences to forget that they are those very politicians?). The difference between politics and morality, even when the latter was considered the product of natural law and not of the church, resided in their specific object: morality regulated the relations between the members of the community in keeping with customary law, whereas politics was expected to deal with those issues that affected the community as a whole, and was willing to sacrifice individual interests for the sake of the common good, when the reason of state[6] made it necessary. Furthermore, it was by its *result* that the morality of a political action was judged, as Machiavelli himself had been reminding his readers. (The modern dictum that the end, in the sense of goal, aspiration, justifies the means shifts the perspective and replaces the result as criterion of acceptability by a projection into an elusive future, and so insinuates a moralist creed into politics, making the requirement of the palpable success redundant.) The notion that politics is different and separate from other spheres of human action, and has its own rules and regulations, has been the main gain which the 16th century contributed to political thinking in the West and Lipsius was one of its advocates, closely followed by Charron. It is made apparent in Naudé's choice of the Massacre on St Bartholomew's Day, as Julien Freund remarks: 'by using an example which was unanimously condemned both by the Protestants *and* the Catholics alike, Naudé was sure to provoke reactions that would demonstrate the autonomy of politics, which in their criticism both the Protestants and the Catholics had played down.' In the context of the 16th- and 17th-century religious wars, however, it remained one of the horrors, despite the legitimacy of its intention, namely of putting an end to those wars in France, and that because politically it failed to attain its aim. The coups d'état, however, were the exception in politics which made wider use of maxims and stratagems that practically exploited the ambivalence of any action and the ambiguity of expression, without making of secrecy a necessity. The filibuster in a legislative assembly is an example that comes easily to mind.

Naudé's merit in this matter is to have laid stress on the particular role of politics in social life in relation to justice: politics deals with those cases that are not justiciable, that is, when appropriate rules or laws for their resolution do not exist, and in that manner, it also paves the way for further legislation that *normalizes* similar events that might occur subsequently and brings them into the domain of justice. In the 20th century, Max Weber, the German sociologist, focussed on the link between power[7] and decision in politics, considering the former its characteristic means. When power is in short supply for lack of authority as well as of material coercive forces, such as police and army, it compensates by secrecy, surprise and speed (or to use Naudé's vocabulary, through the coup d'état) in the implementation of the decision.

The resolution of emergency situations as the essence of politics was only incidental in Naudé's outlook, which itself was much narrower and determined by self-interest. Hence his conventional attempts to disarm any criticism of his undertaking by anticipating it, and bypass, so to speak, censorship which was as active in Rome as it was in France. They take most of the first chapter of the book, the advertisment and the dedication. It is only towards the end of the first chapter that Naudé confesses that it was Bodin's remark about the absence of any study of secrets of domination or secrets of princes that emboldened him to concentrate on their examination in his own book (p.20). His dismissal of Clapmar's work on the subject as lacking any merit betrays Naudé's inability to distinguish between two different approaches: Clapmar's, which was nomothetical, and his own, which was empirical, possibly reinforced by his commerce with Schoppe and the latter's little book on Machiavelli that was circulating in manuscript. (By the way, Machiavelli's PRINCE and all his other writings had been on the Index list since 1552.).

Naudé resumes his criticism of Clapmar in the second chapter of his POLITICAL CONSIDERATIONS. What he accuses Clapmar of may be reduced to two points: one, etymological, is Clapmar's alleged misuse of the term 'secret' by associating it with all the stratagems and maxims of politics, whereas in Naudé's opinion, he should have reserved it only for coups d'état, and the other, Clapmar's division of the coups into those for the defence of the common good, and those carried out by rulers in order to maintain themselves in power, division which Naudé's considers superfluous. It was safe to talk disparagingly about the religiously non-committed Clapmar who had died in 1604 and whose DE ARCANIS RERUMPUBLICARUM LIBRI SEX was hard to come by outside the northern countries of Europe where it was a best-seller, while at the same time freely borrowing from it.

What Clapmar, a jurist teaching at a Protestant university, had done was to try and construct legal concepts for a public law, distinct from private law, and not bound by religious rules, aiming to regulate the relations among the German principalities and the Hanseatic free towns with different forms of government and religious creeds. He had started from the concept of dominion in his other book CONCLUSIONES DE JURE PUBLICO, which gave the ruler the right to set himself above common law in the interest of public good, but only on special occasions. Its abuse, he considered criminal, and called it *flagitia*. From the law of dominion, he derived the general methods of public affairs, that is the way and means by which public good might be realized, and then divided them into two subgroups: one, the methods aimed at maintaining the forms of the state, and the other, those aimed at maintaining the ruling in power. He defined the latter methods as rightful and secret privilege to conserve dominion, assumed and practised for the cause of the public good. The term 'arcanum' was given a special function in his work, namely, of setting apart the private from the public sphere, the modus operandi of which was knowable only to a few, the initate, who were familiar with the affairs of state as distinct from private affairs that were the concern of the individual, subject to common law. He had learnt from the social disruptions during the early stages of the Reformation, from the Knights' War and the Peasants' War and their consequences, to assume the premiss that deception was a method indispensable to statecraft, allowing him to introduce alongside *arcana*, the *simulacra* (dissimulations) or stratagems/maxims, which exploited the equivoque in each act or message without any accompanying violence or infringement of common law. His intention had been to produce a code for rational and purposive action in politics, as a separate sphere from that of everyday life. The difficulty of which he had been aware was that of keeping apart in legal practice the ruler's actions prompted by personal interests from those envisaging the common good.

It is Naudé who creates confusion by playing at semantics, as he deliberately overlooks the fact that both the coups (arcana) and the stratagems (simulacra) resort to secrecy. In the case of the coups, it enwraps the whole process, and sometimes even the result, while in the case of the stratagems, the intention alone is kept under wraps. Lipsius, another source of inspiration both for Clapmar and Naudé, had a different approach, which does not effectuate a complete separation between politics and religion-inspired morality. In his POLITICA (1589), he presents three categories of deceit in politics, on a sliding scale and in terms of virtue, a moral concept with religious undertones. They range from a slight departure from virtue and with 'a drop of malice' to an increasing deviation that verges on sin. In his third category, which represents solid malice and deviates not only from virtue but from laws as well, he places breach of faith and injustice. He condemns it as much as he tolerates and even recommends the first two. He defines injustice as furthering one's interests against rights and the law in wicked rather than cunning ways, such as assassination, and quotes Tacitus in support of the idea that periods of power transfer are more propitious for coups. In practice, though, he comes to concede that common good or reason of state, alongside necessity, expediency and a successful outcome, makes such actions not only permissible but honourable. [8]

Despite everything, Naudé manages to gather together all the elements that make of a political action a coup d'état, or as we call it nowadays, the state of exception, and to provide a satisfactory definition in terms of political realism, in the second chapter of the POLITICAL CONSIDERATIONS. Here it is: *daring and extraordinary actions, which princes are constrained to carry out against common law when faced with difficult and seemingly desperate situations, without regard for any order or form of justice, risking the interest of the private person for the sake of the public good* (p.39). It is after this definition that he makes the difference between stratagems and coups in terms of judicial process, which in the case of the former precedes the resolution, itself presented as the logical consequence of a public judicial process, while in the case of the coups d'état, the resolution is said to precede the public judicial process. Nonetheless, Naudé is guilty of what he accuses Clapmar of, namely inconsistency in the use of terms. Indeed, as one cannot dilate upon coups d'état, once their definition is given, not only because they are secret and rare but also because they refer to unique situations, and examples to ellucidate them are not easily detectable in history unless the coups have happened to fail. All others are simply reconstitutions. So in order to pad out his

book, he goes on to mix Botero's ragion di stato, stratagems, maxims and coups, as without warning, he shifts
to Charron's two-pronged division of deceit into intelligence gathering and tricks of state. In that way, he
produces the third chapter, the longest in his book.

It starts with a review of Charron's list of the conditions that warrant a coup: absolute necessity, public
interest, defence, qualified by moderation and discretion.[9] He then proceeds to illustrate the types of
deception mentioned both by Lipsius and Charron,
beginning with those occasioned by the emergence of new
political entities, followed by others, connected with
internal strife, and furthermore, with unrest among one's
neighbours. Priority is given to what we now call
foundation myths, in which civic religion, combining fact
and legend, plays on people's fears and credulity. Then
he turns to the stratagems practised with a view to the
conservation and restoration of states, followed by
others meant to restrict or abolish certain privileges of
particular subjects, to go on and illustrate those that may
be used for the enforcement of new rules and regulations, as well as for the elimination of subversive forces
on one's territory, with special reference to the Massacre
on St Bartholomew's Day, and from them to turn to
foreign policy and the weakening of powerful neighbours
so as to attain a balance of powers.

Chapter IV expands on the ideological background
against which the political actions and decisions occur
during a period of transition, and in which duplicity,
rediscovered in the 16th century and resorted to thereafter, is pivotal in any scheme or enterprise — the same
action may be good or bad, depending on the angle from
which it is considered. Hence the relativity of all things,
and the hazardous character of the relationship between
cause and effect. Religion, the unifying factor, is being
undermined by the secularization of social and political
thinking, the irruption of the crowd into the political
arena, as a force to be reckoned with, all the more so
when taking into account its unpredictability, short attention span, and its openness to manipulation by
fanatics, in a world unravelled by religious wars. Naudé

concentrates only on the communal aspect of religion, the apparent and the formal, as an instrument of authority, and implicitly of compliance, as the populace is by nature superstitious and impressed only by the apparent. The spiritual aspect of religion is an individual quality, and so it is outside the sphere of the political which deals with the *public* good, and consequently is of no interest to Naudé in this context.

The last chapter follows Lipsius's Book III of POLITICA, with its division of a prince's helpers into executive ministers and counsellors, that is, secret advisers, the latter all the more necessary to supplement the ruler's lack of political acuity and information, to which his isolated position condemns him. Naudé has the time of his life defining the relationship of the secret adviser and his prince in terms of status, duties and obligations, and in more than one way, he reverses the traditional order, as he lists the qualities which a prince needs to have to be a ruler, only after those to be looked for in his secret councillor, and in terms of his conduct towards the latter. He reserves three main virtues to his councillor: staying power, fairness and prudence, and makes it the duty of the prince to see that they are culti- vated and requited to his own ultimate benefit, both personal and as caretaker of the commonwealth. The last pages complete the circle begun with the dedication, and in the same mood of mixed humility, impertience, self- satisfaction and flattery. Content as he is with his completed book, Naudé declares himself ready for greater feats to honour his high-placed dedicatee.

Naudé's is neither a teach-yourself book, nor a memoir, not even a mirror-for-princes, but an attempt to appropriate the legal concept of coupt d'état for political science, a branch of knowledge on the rise since Machiavelli, and present it in a book that has the hybrid form of a prose cento. In other words, his is a book made up of fragments, occasionally paraphrased, ex- tracted from other works, not his, as well as from commonplace books, fashionable at a time when printed books were still rare and expensive, and on occasion, even forbidden. It reflects the eagerness to accumulate as much knowledge, and as fast, as the social mobility required, in order to impress and improve one's social status. To his sources should be added the collections of proverbs or adagia, pithy aphorisms in imitation of the ancients, that scattered all over the text enhance the desired effect of ostentation. It is possible that many of the errors of attribution, name-spelling and quotation originated in the commonplace books consulted in the process of compilation. One should not be too ready to attribute them to faulty memory on the part of a Naudé or other compilers of centones. Moreover, the prose cento of his time accommodated a 'twofold reading': one, called 'naive', cursive and paying no attention to attributions, and the other, a 'savant' reading, deconstructivist, that took the collage apart, reset and corrected the quotations and the attributions, replacing some and adding others. That Naudé tried to present his work as recondite should not surprise anybody: he had been making of mystery and conspiracy a dimension, however imaginary, of his rather pedestrian existence. Nevertheless, it would be a mistake to consider his work a ciphered book: the 'naive' reading of it suffices. He did not expect his readers to be savants, particularly as he nourished an unapologetic distrust and contempt of higher-ups and thought most princes dim-witted. His claim that he merely wanted to offer them a divertissment was not only a ruse to cover his tracks from the prying eyes of the censors. The prose cento, moreover, required the treatment of ideas and events inserted in it in a timeless and absolute sense, as implicitly, human nature was held to remain unchanged. Its universalism, as old as the Bible, reappeared in the Hellenistic culture, was taken over by Imperial Rome, borrowed by the Church, was finding its secular reaffirmation in the natural law inspired by the rediscovered Roman culture. It paved the way for the doctrine of mechanism which came to inform not only the conception of the universe but also politics as such. (Curiously enough there is a tendency nowadays to do the same, despite the development of historicism in the interval.)

The fact that the book was originally printed in a

dozen copies and quasi-anonymously, with the author's initials (G.N.P.) only, and without any mention of a publisher, allowed its dissemination in France and wherever French was spoken, through pirated copies, whole or fragmentary, most likely hand-written and circulated underhand until another printed edition was brought out posthumously in 1667, with the author's name in full but without any location. In his opening remarks, its publisher presented the book as a curiosity, probably to protect himself from the adverse reactions of some churchmen. Like Charron's OF WISDOM, it had been subject of debate to the extent its political realism recalled the morally reprehensible Machiavellism. It was as a platform for debate that interest in it was sustained until 1752, when the accumulated commentary made of the POLITICAL CONSIDERATIONS a three-volume work.

Naudé's contribution to the science of politics is to have brought together in his book some of the most pertinent ideas in that field that had emerged in the 16th century, and on which the Age of Reason would build its own political science and international law. That no other edition was printed in the 19th century and until very late in the 20th, is mainly due to a shift in interest from politics and morality to politics and economy. It is the failure to produce a perfect match between the latter two, in spite of the desperate efforts of so many luminaries of the 19th and early 20th centuries, that has rekindled the interest in Naudé's original text. Nevertheless, it was only in 1989, this time in Paris, that the 1667 edition was reprinted with its French translations of the Latin quotations, but the latter were ommitted: for a 'naive' reading of the book, who needs the Latin, anyhow! What its editors did, however, was to painstakingly identify the characters mentioned in the book, while reproducing Naudé's sparse marginal notes between brakets, within the body of the text, without any additional commentary. It is true that with very few exceptions, Naudé did use his quotations simply as a mannerist embellishment, and so they may be easily left out altogether without serious prejudice to the contents. Lipsius, a scholar, was careful to identify his sources correctly as far as the works he had been quoting from and their authors were concerned, but not so Naudé who even by the standards of his day was a mediocre editor. His quotations, which make the work of any editor problematic, are of several kinds: accurate both as regards transcription and authorship; accurate but misattributed; altered, which may or may not be correctly attributed; invented by him and without attribution or with spurious attribution, and finally sayings or proverbs from the public domain. As a result, work on any of Naudé's texts may be quite frustrating. The editors of the modern English version of ADVICE ON ESTABLISHING A LIBRARY have had their experience, and as a result, warn readers that the sources of Naudé's numerous quotations have been given to the extent they were able to find them. I too have done my best with what I have at my disposal, which in practical terms means that quite a number of sources have remained unidentified. There is more to identification than editorial pedantry, and in such cases as Naudé's, it may help to see which were the books that he had direct access to, as distinct from such sources as commonplace books, although most of this kind of work remains conjectural. An example suffices: his correct reproduction of Lipsius's opinion of Machiavelli, as it was printed in the first edition of the POLITICA, which was a forbidden book, shows that he had access to that very edition. Unfortunately, no copy of Alessandro Piazzi's annotated edition of the POLITICAL CONSIDERATIONS, brought out in Milan in 1992, was available in the States. To a limited degree, the work in this direction of Françoise Charles-Daubert was helpful, particularly as regards post-classical sources, as she seems to have had access to many hard-to-find printed editions. Her elucidations are acknowledged in the notes. Dr William King's English edition of 1711, printed in London and dedicated to a scion of the Beaufort family, Duke Henry, on the occasion of his appointment to Queen Anne's Council, reveals some cuts and abbreviations in Naudé's text of 1667, and a rewritten ending to suit the position of his own dedicatee. The interventions are cogent and reduce considerably Naudé's long-windedness. The English of the translation is that of the Enlightenment (one of King's friends was Jonathan Swift). It reflects another age, so much unlike the belated mannerism of the Frenchman's. Dr King accompanied the Latin quotations by English renditions, often taken from translations by established authors, such as Dryden. Having read it through in the rare-book reading room of the British Library, in its old quarters at the British Museum, I decided upon a new translation, closer to the original (and more congenial to our times), which would signal Dr King's editorial interventions in the notes only. On the other hand, I borrowed from the 1989 French edition the idea of leaving out the Latin of the quotations and incorporating their translation in the body of the text in a cursive way, without respect to the blanks, the central positioning and the versification in the original Roman copy. The translation of the quotations, however, is mine, and not that of the 1667 edition or Dr King's. Otherwise, the text of the 1639 quarto (Call No. E826) from the rare-book collections of the Bibliothèque Nationale in Paris has been used for the present edition. Rebound in 1963, it had once belonged to the French Royal Library, as the seal on it showed. It was collated with a copy of the 1667 edition in 8vo, made available a floor below, in the Hémicycle, by librarians as gracious and helpful. There are very few textual differences, and they too are signalled in the notes of the present edition.

I started work on it in the Spring of 1989, but the business of identifying sources was consuming a time which I could hardly afford, and so I was forced to set it aside. I was able to resume it only in the Summer of 2004, but away from any comprehesive library of 16th- and 17th-century books. The Library of Congress and its most obliging staff have smoothed over many of the difficulties.

Notwithstanding, the effort has been worthwhile not in the least for the fact that Naudé manages in spite of himself to remind us that any act may be good or bad, depending on the angle from which it is considered, and that each sphere of human activity has its own rules by which it must be judged and which define its identity.

Thus politics should not be mistaken for religion nor the latter, say, for economy, in spite of the contradictions at play in them that reflect that very relativity. Yet for that very reason the distinction is not absolute nor could it be blotted out by a moralism with universal claims that endangers human existence as such. If some of the concepts such as 'state' and 'sovereignty', that once were essential to political thinking and made possible the definition of human communities and of the relations between them, have lost their meaning, a second look at such works as Naudé's, Machiavelli's, Campanella's or of a Lipsius may help us recover the will for a positive political thinking and in that way refuse to be victimized by the all-oppressive cant in an overflowing world.

January-March 2006   *SIMONA DRAGHICI, PhD*

NOTES

1. Actually the original title of the book which happened to be written in French is *Technique du Coup d'État*. On the other hand, the title of its English translation, *Coup d'État: the Technique of Revolution* contradicts the author's thesis, and so the contents of the book, by equating coup d'état with revolution.

2. Later on, he joined the Center of Strategic and International Studies of Georgetown University in Washington DC, and is now Senior Fellow of the Center.

3. See Phillip Wolfe's Introduction (p.8) to his edition of *Lettres de Gabriel Naudé à Jacques Dupuy*, Edmonton, 1982. The same information is repeated in Annexe I (Biographie de Gabriel Naudé), p.199 of the 1989 Paris edition of *Considerations politiques sur les Coups d'État*, to which the present editor is indebted for the details about Naudé's family.

4. See Phillip Wolfe, op. cit., p.9, who quotes from *Lettres de Peiresc* I, pp.412-413 and p.874.

5. Naudé had a famous precedent in this respect in Lipsius who was accused by the French humanist Marc-Antoine Muret (Muretus), an authority on Aristotle, Cicero, Catullus, etc., with a special interest in Tacitus, and professor at La Sapienza University in Rome, of having plagiarized his work on the Tacitus manuscripts during his stay in Rome.

6. The phrase 'reason of state' knew a rather rapid metamorphosis in a couple of decades at the turn of the 17th century. Thus for Botero, it meant the *measures for founding, preserving and expanding dominion* (p.36), while by Naudé's time it came to mean the authority in the name of which various steps were taken. Unfortunately, Naudé is inconsistent in making this distinction.

XXVII

7. Justus Lipsius (1547–1606) had a different notion of power which he defined as *the command of means useful for preserving one's own goods and obtaining other people's goods* (*Politica*, IV.x.5). It reflected the outlook that preceded the era of state centralization.

8. See *Politica*, IV.xiv. Lipsius contradicts himself here, as he attempts to blur his ideas about the relationship between religious morality and practical politics, in order to elude any accusations of heresy.

9. See *Of Wisdom* (ET 1729), Book III, 2, pp. 1023–1025.

SHORT BIBLIOGRAPHY

Naudé, Gabriel, *Advice on Establishing a Library*, intr. Archer Taylor, Westport CT, 1976, c1950.

Naudé, Gabriel, *Addition à l'Histoire de Louys II/ Contenant plusieurs Recherches/ curieuses sur diverses matières*, Paris, 1630.

Naudé, Gabriel, *Apologie pour tous les grands personnages qui ont été faussement soupçonnés de magie*, ed. Jacques Prévot, in LIBERTINS DU XVIIe SIÈCLE, vol. I, Paris, 1998.

Naudé, Gabriel, *Bibliographia Politica*, Venice, 1633.

Naudé, Gabriel, *Bibliographia Politica* [the expanded 1642 Leiden edition], Latin and Italian, ed. Domenico Bosco, Rome, 1997.

Naudé, Gabriel [G.N.P.], *Considerations politiques sur les coups d'Estat*, a Rome, M.DC.XXXIX.

Naudé, Gabriel [G.N.P.], *Considerations politiques sur les coups d'Estat*, avec une introduction et notes par Françoise Charles-Daubert, Hildesheim, 1993.

Naudé, Gabriel [Gabriel Naudé, Parisien], *Considerations Politiques sur les coups d'Estat*. Sur la copie de Rome, n.l., 1667.

Naudé, Gabriel, *Considérations politiques sur les coups d'État* [1667 ed.], Preface par Louis Marin. Notes, etc. par Frédérique Marin et Marie-Odile Perulli, Paris, 1988.

Naudé, Gabriel, *Considérations politiques sur les coups d'État* [reprint of 1988 edition], *précédée de 'Gabriel Naudé' par Sainte-Beuve et suivie par 'Naudæana'*, Paris, 2004.

Naudé, Gabriel, *Lettres de Gabriel Naudé à Jacques Dupuy (1632-1652)*, ed. Phillip Wolfe, Edmonton, 1982.

Naudé, Gabriel, *Political Considerations upon Refined Politicks and the Master-Strokes of State as Practised by the Ancients and Moderns*, tr. Dr. King, London, 1711.

XXIX

Peiresc, Nicolas Claude Fabri de, *Lettres à Gabriel Naudé, 1629-1637*, ed. Phillip Wolfe, Seattle and Tübingen, 1983.

Adam, Antoine, *Les libertins au XVIIe siècle*, Paris, 1964.

Allen, J.W., *A History of Political Thought in the 16th Century*, London, 1957, c1928.

Baldini, A. Enzo, ed., *Aristotelismo Politico et Ragion di Stato*, Florence, 1995.

Bodin, Jean, *Method for the Easy Comprehension of History*, tr. Beatrice Reynolds, New York, 1945.

Botero, Giovanni, *The Reason of State*, tr. P.J. and D.P. Waley, London, 1956.

Briggs, Robin, *Early Modern France 1560-1715*, Oxford, 1977.

Burckhardt, Carl J., *Richelieu and His Age*, 3 vols., London, 1967-1971.

Campanella, Tommaso, *Aforismi Politici*, ed. Luigi Firpo, Torino, 1941.

Cardan, Jerome, *The Book of My Life*, tr. Jean Stoner, New York, 1930.

Cardano, Girolamo, *Arcana politica, sive de Prudentia Civili liber singularis*, Leiden, 1635.

Cardano, Girolamo, *Opera Omnia*, 10 vols., Stuttgart, 1966, facsimile reprint of the 1663 Lyons edition.

Charbonnel, J.-Roger, *La Pensée italienne au XVIe siècle et le courant libertin*, Paris, 1969, c1919.

Charron, Jean Daniel, *The 'WISDOM' of Pierre Charron - An Original and Orthodox Code of Morality*, Chapel Hill, 1960.

Charron, Pierre, *Of Wisdom: Three Books*, tr. George Stanhope, 3rd ed., London, 1729.

Church, William, F., *Richelieu and Reason of State*, Princeton, 1972.

Clapmar, Arnold, *Conclusiones de jure publico*, Frankfurt, 1617

Clapmar, Arnold, *De arcanis rerumpublicarum libri sex*, Frankfurt, 1624.

Clark, G.N., *The Seventeenth Century*, 2nd ed., Oxford, 1947

Clarke, Jack A., *Gabriel Naudé 1600-1653*, Hamden CT., 1970.

Crouset, D., *Les guerriers de Dieu. La violence au temps de troubles de religion (vers 1525-1610)*, Champ Vallon, 1990.

D'Addio, Mario, *Il pensiero politico di Gaspare Scioppio e il machiavellismo del Seicento*, Milan 1962.

Ferrari, Giuseppe, *Histoire de la raison d'État*, Paris, 1992.

Freund, Julien, 'La situation exceptionnelles comme justification de la raison d'État chez Gabriel Naudé,' pp. 141-164 in *Staatsräson, Studien zur Geschichte eines politischen Begriffs*, ed. Roman Schnur, Berlin 1975.

Guicciardini, Francesco, *Ricordi*, tr. Mario Domandi, New York, 1965.

Godard de Douville, Louise, *Le libertin des origines à 1665: un produit des apologètes*, Paris and Seattle, 1989.

Lipsius, Justus, *Of Constancie, Two Books*, tr. John Stradling, New Brunswick NJ, 1939 [facsimile reprint of the 1594 London edition].

Lipsius, Justus, *Politica* [*Politicorum sive Civilis Doctrinæ libri sex*], ed. and tr. Jan Wasznik, Assen, 2004.

Mann, Golo, *Wallenstein, His Life Narrated by...*, tr. Charles Kessler, New York, 1976.

Mattei, R. de, *La politica di Campanella*, Rome, 1927.

Meinecke, Friedrich, *Machiavellism*, tr. Douglas Scott, New Haven, 1957.

Mousnier, Roland, *Les XVIe et XVIIe siècles: la grande mutation intellectuelle de l'humanité, l'advénement de la science moderne et l'expansion de l'Europe*, 5th ed., Paris 1967.

Mousnier, Roland, *Social Hierarchies, 1450 to the present*, tr. Peter Evans. ed. Margaret Clarke, New York, 1973.

The New Cambridge Modern History, Vols. II, III, IV, Cambridge, 1957.

Palingène, *Le zodiaque de la vie* [Zodiacus Vitae] *XII livres*, ed.& tr. Jacques Chomarat, Geneva, 1996.

XXXI

Pintard, René, *Le libertinage érudit dans la première moitié du XVIIe siècle*, Genève-Paris, 1993, c1943.

Ranum, Orest, *Richelieu and the Councillors of Louis XIII; a study of the Secretaries of State and Superintendents of Finance in the Ministry of Richelieu, 1635-1642*, Oxford, 1963.

Rice, James V., *Gabriel Naudé, 1600-1653*. Baltimore Md. and Paris, 1939.

Scioppio, Gaspar, *Paedia politices*, ed. Hermann Conring, Helmstedt, 1663. [The volume also includes: *De studio politico* by Christophorus Colerus, and *Bibliographia politica* by Gabriel Naudé.]

Solomon, H.M., *Public Welfare, Science and Propaganda in the 17th-Century France*, Princeton, 1972.

Tapié, Victor-L., *France in the Age of Louis XIII and Richelieu*, tr. and ed. D. McN. Lockie, with Foreword by A.G. Dickens, New York, 1974.

Thuau, Étienne, *Raison d'État et pensée politique à l'époque de Richelieu*, Paris, 1966.

Yates, Frances A., *The Enlightenment of the Rosecrucians*, London and Boston, 1972.

Zarka, Yves Charles, ed., *Raison et déraison d'État*, Paris, 1994.

1600–1620   Born in Paris on 2 February, one of the
             eight children of a bailiff at the Bureau of
             Finances and his illiterate wife. On 14 May
             1610, King Henry IV is assasinated by a
             fanatic. Between 1614 and 1618, Naudé at-
             tends various Paris colleges, acquiring a
             humanist education and a MA degree. In
             1617, assasination of the Marquis d'Ancre,
             the Queen Mother's favourite and councillor.
             Naudé spends a year at the College of Cler-
             mont. Back in Paris in 1620 to study medi-
             cine; in the same year publishes a 22-page
             8vo pamphlet LE MARPHORE OU DIS-
             COURS CONTRE LES LIBELLES [The Mar-
             phore or Discourse against Libels], assum-
             ing thus the position of champion of the
             calumniated, position he mantained for the
             rest of his life.

1621–1630   Probably because of financial difficulties,
             Naudé drops out, after two years of medical
             studies, and takes a job as librarian with
             the President of the Paris Parliament, Henri
             de Mesme. A year later, publishes a thicker
             pamphlet from a Catholic, conservative
             stance against the incursions of the Rosi-
             crucians into France, INSTRUCTION À LA
             FRANCE SUR LA VERITÉ DE L'HISTOIRE
             DES FRÈRES DE LA ROSE-CROIX. In
             1624, Richelieu is appointed chief of the
             Royal Council. Naudé publishes his longest
             book (616 pp.) in Paris, in 1625, a treatise
             on such works, literary or otherwise, and
             their authors, that were considered heretical
             along history, APOLOGIE POUR TOUS LES
             GRANDS PERSONNAGES QUI ONT ÉTÉ
             FAUSSEMENT SOUPÇONNÉS DE MAGIE.

At the end of 1626, travels to Padua to
continue medical studies, but is recalled
home on his father's death in June 1627 and
resumes his job with President de Mesme.
In the same year publishes his manual
ADVIS POUR DRESSER UNE BIBLIO-
THÈQUE [Advice on Establishing a Library]
On 2 July 1628, delivers the eulogy of Hippocrates' art at the reception of the new
graduates before the School of Medicine,
with special praises for the institution and
its traditions. It earns him a medical degree
in spite of his incomplete course of studies,
and besides, access to the cabinet of the
Dupuy brothers and their friends. In the
same year, the Huguenot stronghold of La
Rochelle is attacked by Richelieu's forces and
reduced a year later. France's clashes with
the Hapsburg monarchs over territory. In
1630, Naudé publishes his ADDITION À
L'HISTOIRE DE LOUYS XI, CONTENANT
PLUSIEURS RECHERCHES CURIEUSES
SUR DIVERSES MATIÈRES [Addition to
Louis XI's history, including several curious
inquiries into different matters].

1631–1642   Recommended to the outgoing Papal Nuncio,
Cardinal Bagni, for a post of librarian by a
Scottish freelance scholar and former Vatican librarian, John Seton. Is accepted after
the Dupuy brothers present the Cardinal
with a copy of the *Addition* to endorse the
recommendation. On Mayday 1631, Naudé
arrives in Rome where he meets Campanella.
In 1632, publishes DE STUDIO LIBERALI
SYNTAGMA, dedicated to Cardinal Bagni's
nephew, in Urbino, and in 1633, BIBLIO-
GRAPHIA POLITICA, in Venice. In the same
year, is granted the honorary title of Court
physician, allegedly at Bagni's intervention,
and travels to Padua to deliver a public address before the faculty there on 25 May

1633, which brings him the title of doctor
of philosophy and medicine. On 25 February
1634, Albrecht Wenzel von Wallenstein,
Emperor Ferdinand II's generalissimo is assassinated at Eger on the latter's orders.
Bagni moves to his seat at Rieti in 1635 and
there Naudé edits and compiles various texts
of local history, medicine, natural history,
etc.; in 1637, publishes SYNTAGMA DE
STUDIO MILITARI at Rome, and on returning to that city in 1639 allegedly prints his
POLITICAL CONSIDERATIONS ON COUPS
D'ÉTAT in French, privately, in twelve copies. Cardinal Bagni dies in 1641. Naudé
takes service with Cardinal Barberini,
nephew of the Pope, but in 1642 obtains the
latter's consent to return to France, following Mazarin's promise to take him on, as
part of his official family, at the intervention of Bagni's nephew. Richelieu dies on 4
December 1642, a few months after stifling
the Cinq-Mars conspiracy, one of the greatest against him. Louis XIII dies five months
later. Mazarin replaces Richelieu.

1643-1653   In Paris, with no official employment for
two years; edits and publishes texts and
manuscripts he has brought from Italy;
finally, in 1644, becomes Mazarin's librarian, and as such, starts on a campaign of
acquisitions in many parts of Europe, England included. In 1646 begins the revolt
against Mazarin, known as the Fronde. The
Peace of Westphalia in 1648, marking the
end of the Thirty-Year War, though war
between France and Spain goes on till 1659.
Naudé prints JUGEMENT DE TOUT CE QUI
A ÉTÉ IMPRIMÉ CONTRE LE CARDINAL
MAZARIN DEPUIS LE 6e JANVIER JUS-
QUE À LA DECLARATION DU 1er AVRIL
1649 [Judgement on all that was printed
against Cardinal Mazarin from 6 January

until the Declaration of 1 April 1649],
known for short as the MASCURAT, but
without any effect. The fate of the Cardinal's library is sealed: its books and assets
are sold by auction to satisfy creditors, in
keeping with a Parliament decree of 29 December 1651. Without a job, Naudé decides
to travel to the court of Queen Christina in
Sweden to take charge of the library there,
and keep his master informed of events at
the Swedish Court. Less than a year later,
and as soon as he is paid his gratuities,
Naudé leaves Sweden to return to France,
but on his way to Paris falls ill at Abbeville
where he dies on 29 July 1653.

POLITICAL
CONSIDERATIONS
ON
COUPS D'ÉTAT

This book has not been compiled to please everybody, had that been the author's intention, he would have abstained from writing it in the style of Montaigne and Charron, aware as he was of the fact that so many people are annoyed by the great number of quotations in Latin. However as he undertook the task by compliance, he was obliged to lay down on paper the same utterances, and refer to the same authorities which he mentions in his talks with His Eminence. Besides, it was not in order to make it public that this work saw the light of print; rather it went to press by the order, and to the satisfaction, of that great prelate who finds pleasure in reading only from printed books. For that very reason he wanted to have a dozen copies of this work printed, instead of copying it by hand as it should have been done. I know that this number is too small to enable the book to be seen by as many people as Balzac's PRINCE and Silhon's MINISTER. Nonetheless, as the things which it deals with are by far more important, it is also fit that they should not be within everybody's reach. In short, the author had only one aim: to please His Eminence both by compiling and seeing it in print.

TO THE AUTHOR

Some would wonder to see you as a youth
Already in full command of what Antiquity
Endlessly travailed in its infinity,
And with pains, uncovered gems of wisdom.

Others would admire the heroic hardiness
Intent on restoring here liberty,
So well you combat falsity
Even there where she is the mistress.

In short, each in your discourse will admire
A diversity of marvels that are there;
But here's bold the one I found among the others,

That knowing so well the nature of the Greats,
Their maxims and *their coups*, you've lived
So long a private life as modest and as innocent.

JAC. BOUCHARD at Rome
This 1st of the year 1639

To the Monsignor
The Most Eminent
CARDINAL DE BAGNI
My most kind and honoured
Master

Nay, indeed, it is no aim of mine that my page should swell with dark pretentious trifles, fit only to give solidity to smoke. To yourself alone, at the Muse's bidding, I shake out my heart to you.

Monsignor,

As You are in Rome now, enjoying the honours that are the reward of your merits, and the respite that the public offices, which so happily you filled during seven governments, a vice-legation and two nunciatures have earned You: I could not think of a better use of the free time, which your good will and extraordinary bounty made me also enjoy, than to entertain You with the most revealing maxims of politics and of those great affairs of state which Your Eminence has attended to with such remarkable prudence as has astonished the greatest men of genius who at present govern Europe and who have never succeeded better in their deliberations and most difficult enterprises than whenever they took the sound and generous advice that it pleased You in Your kindness to proffer. *No one should despair as long as Teucer leads, there is nothing to fear under his inspired command.*

5

Chapter I

Objections that might be adduced against this discourse and the necessary replies

Hardly had I gotten down the first lines of this discourse, Monsignor, that I found myself ensconced between two considerable difficulties, capable, in my opinion, of dissuading anybody else, with less courage and affection than I, from going on and from cooling the blood in the veins of the hottest heads in the quest of those solutions which are as extraordinary as they are dangerous. When such a thoughtful poet as Horace was in all honesty telling his friend Polio, intent on writing the history of the civil wars that occurred during his time: *the work to which you aspire is fraught with risks, drags you over treacherous cinders that hide the lurking fire*, what good result is to be expected from this undertaking of mine which is more risky and bold, to say nothing of the danger incurred when one wants to debunk the acts of princes and to unveil all that which they take pains to hide behind thousands of artifices, every single day? Besides, there are other two, of no less consequence, one of which I am in some way apprehensive as far as your person is concerned. Likewise, I have to confront the other, which regards myself.

About the former, I am ready to say with the poet, who has so well dealt with philosophy in his handsome verses that nowadays is the sole and unique support of his sect: *I fear that by taking this step, it might occur to you that you find yourself amidst the elements of impropriety and that you enter upon the path of impiety.*

At least should I not fear about hurting the ears of Your Eminence, frightening your sight, and troubling your sweet and easy-going nature, as well as the peace and the integrity of your conscience by the narration of so many ruses, deceptions, violent acts and other similar deeds, unjust (as they seem at first sight) and tyrannical, that I shall have to deduct, explain and defend further on?

Even Aeneas, one of the most resolute captains of Antiquity, was so much moved by sorrow as he had to give an account of the siege and the ruins of Troy to the Queen of Carthage that he could start only by saying: *though my heart shudders at the recollection and has recoiled in pain.*

And when a certain emperor, who had not been able to avoid the nickname of Cruel, although one day he told a magistrate as he was given to sign the sentence of two poor wretches: *would that I had not learnt to write,* might you not wish, with more reason, never to have seen this disquisition; because it would entertain you with what is least suitable to your great humaneness, sincerity and good will? And then, wouldn't I do better to follow Solomon's advice: *do not appear wise before your king,* and go on pursuing my studies which I have been nurtured on since my youth, rather than appear before You with extravagant notions, as Diognetus did in the presence of Alexander, in order to be thought of as a great engineer and architect; given mainly that I might aspire to obtain the same effect from my undertaking as the grammarian Phormio, with his military art, in the presence of Hannibal, held to have been the first and foremost military commander of his time; given that *we all think ourselves wise, full of spirit and beautiful, although we are nothing but buffoons.*

And truth to say, when I come to think of the dearth of means at my disposal to bring this undertaking to a satisfactory conclusion, and that is the second difficulty which I have to grapple with, I almost feel like giving up and getting away from it all, and that in order not to incur the rebuke, which in a similar situation Phoebus subjected his son to, in the works of the poet: *you ask for too great a thing, Phaeton, one which does not befit your strength.*

Thus he had the memorable fall because he had gone too near the sun; and many others, no less bold, confessed their failure, because of the insurmountable difficulty of their undertakings. And I who am a beginner in this kind of exercises, *with a bare sword and no tale of glory engraved on my round shield*, should I dare to mess about with these offerings, more mysterious than those of the goddess Eleusine, without having been initiated? With what certitude could I reach the core of these matters, enter the cabinets of the Great, penetrate sanctuaries where all these shrewd designs are hatched, without enjoying the confidence and proximity of their authors. Indeed, I would readily pardon whomever, seeing me persevere in this resolution, will judge me immoderate by violating nature, which never falls from one extreme onto the other so quickly; or to put it in more moderate words, it is more a matter of foolhardiness than of reason to want to sail on the high seas without a compass, and to negotiate a maze of ruses and infinite subtleties, without holding the net of this science, in order to develop the subject matter successfully. And that all the more willingly as he is none of those who can imagine the sun with less difficulty the farther they are from his face; or like those painters who are short-sighted, and usually because of it, make the finest paintings. Rather this political prudence resembles Proteus, of whom it is quite impossible to have any certain knowledge without descending *to the solitary place of the old man*, and scrutinizing with a steady and penetrating eye all his different movements, shapes and metamorphoses, by means of which *all of a sudden he will become a bristly boar, a deadly tiger, a scaly dragon or a lioness with tawny neck.*

Nevertheless, like the young Aristaeus, who was not discouraged from undertaking his voyage by the great difficulties which Arethusa mentioned, and as a result, won all sorts of satisfaction: so, too, the above objections have no more force in my case, and thousands other besides could not prevent me, although I do not entirely reveal the story of the design which I have in mind, having taken counsel with Pliny the Younger: *the right way is level, even if humble and lowly, those who run along stumble more often than those who creep; the latter win no praise, although they do not fall, whereas the former may win some praise even though they happen to stumble.*

That is the reason why, Monsignor, in order to overcome the two difficulties that I have got into above, and also the one that concerns Your Eminence in the first place, it should not be feared that this doctrine might affect your piety in any way, or trouble your peace of mind and the integrity of your conscience as it might appear at first sight, as these three lines from Lucretius would persuade You: the sun sheds its light over the vilest and basest things, without being for that matter darkened or blemished, *although with its rays it may touch the mire, it is not soiled by it; neither does light get dirty when it touches dirty things.* The theologians are not less religious while aware of the nature of heresies; nor are the physicians less prudent for knowing the composition and the strengths of all the venoms. The habits of understanding are distinct from those of the will-power, the former belong to science and are always praiseworthy, while the latter is concerned with moral actions, which may be either good or bad. Trithemius and Pererius have shown that it was expedient to have had magicians and to have truly known the means of conjuring the demons, so that by their sudden appearance convince the incredulous atheists. Ordinarily, the soldiers drill in order to learn how to handle the pike best and to fire shots from a musket, and so be able to kill people and destroy their fellow creatures more effectively and dilligently; but, still, they use those skills only against the enemies of their prince, or of their fatherland. The best surgeons go into training in order to acquire the skill of amputating arms and legs, and so save the sick: *limbs are amputated to assure the life of the rest of the body.* Why then should a great politician be forbidden from knowing how to exalt or abase, expand or tighten, condemn or absolve, spare the lives of or put to death whomever he would think expedient to treat one way or the other for the good and the peace of his state?

Many maintain that the wise and sensible prince ought not only to command according to the laws, but also to command the laws themselves when necessity demands it. In order to safeguard justice in great matters, Charron says, one needs at times to deny it in the small, and to do justice wholesale, one is allowed to cause harm retail.

To the objection that it is not proper to talk of these things nonetheless, and that by doing so, instead of instructing, one only puts *a two-edged sword into the hands of a fool*, I would answer that the wicked may abuse all that is best in this world and do as the bastard hornets which reduce the most beautiful flowers to bitterness: the heretics find the fundamentals of their impiety in the Holy Writ, Paracelsus' followers misuse Hippocrates' texts to validate their dreams, barristers quote the Code and the Pandects in their pleas on behalf of the most blameworthy, yet nobody ever dreamt of suppressing those books: the sword may equally attack and defend, the wine may intoxicate as much as it may nourish, remedies kill as much as they heal, and so far, however, nobody has said that their usage is not necessary. It is a law that all things have in common, namely that once instituted for a good purpose, they come to be abused oftentimes: nature does not produce venom to serve as poison and kill people, because if it were to do so, it would destroy itself; yet it is our own malice which puts it to such use; *the Earth has provided us indeed with remedies to relieve our ills; but we have turned them into poison in order to scorn life.*

Still one must carry on regardless and say that people's malice and depravity are so great and the means which they use to accomplish their designs so bold and dangerous that to wish to talk about politics as it is treated and practised today without any mention of these coups d'état, it is truly to ignore the *paideia* and the means which Aristotle mentions in his ANALYTICS so as to talk of all things to the point and following the principles and demonstrations which are proper and essential to them, because *not to know which things to seek and which not to is to ignore this knowledge*, as he says in his METAPHYSICS. That is why Lipsius and Charron, although they were not Timons and misanthropists, wanted to deal with this aspect, in order not to leave their works incomplete. And the same Aristotle, who had been accustomed not to undertake anything without being well informed, when he dealt with politics and the governments opposed to monarchy, aristocracy and democracy, and which are tyranny, oligarchy and ochlocracy, formulated the principles both of the vicious three and the legitimate three. In that he was followed by Saint Thomas in the latter's COMMENTARIES. After having blamed and discouraged by all possible arguments the tyrannical domination, Saint Thomas nevertheless gives an outline and the general rules for its establishment, in case someone might be so wicked as to want to enter upon it. And to see that it is so, here are his own words taken from chapter xi of the Commentary on the Fifth Book of POLITICS: *In order to maintain tyranny, the most powerful and the wealthiest have to be put to death, because such people might raise against the tyrant in virtue of the authority which they enjoy. Likewise it is necessary to get rid of the great minds and the scholars, because given their knowledge, they might find the means of destroying the tyranny; there should be no schools either, or other congregations by means of which one may become acquainted with the sciences, since scholars have a penchant for the great things, and as a result, are courageous and magnanimous, and such men easily rise against the tyrants. In order to maintain his tyranny, the tyrant must act in such a way as to make his subjects find fault with each other and trouble each other, induce friends to persecute one another and make dissension grow between the little man and the wealthy, and cause discord among the opulent. In that way, they would have fewer means of rebelling, because of their division. Likewise, the subjects must be impoverished, because in that situation, it would be hard for them to rise against the tyrant. Subsidies should be established, that is large exactions, and in a great number, because this is the means by which the subjects are fast rendered poor. Likewise the tyrant must stir up war between the subjects and even among foreigners, to render them incapable of negotiating anything against him. Kingdoms are maintained by means of friends, but the tyrant must not rely on anyone if he wants to preserve his tyranny.* And in chapter xii, which follows, it may be seen how he teaches hypocrisy and simulation: *In order to maintain himself in the tyranny, a tyrant must not appear to be cruel before his subjects, because to do so would render him odious, which would more easily make them rise against him: but he ought to render himself venerable by the excellency of a certain eminent virtue, since virtue is owed all kinds of respect; if he has not got that excellent quality, he has to feign it. The tyrant must conduct himself in such a way as to appear before his subjects as if he were endowed with some eminent virtue wanting in them, and for which they come to respect him. If he has got no virtue at all in fact, he should act in such a way as to make them believe that he has.* They are strange precepts, indeed, in the mouth of a saint, in no way different from those of Machiavelli and Cardan, but which nonetheless may be justified by two arguments as probable and legitimate. The first is that given that these maxims have been thus openly stated and aired, the subjects may more easily see when their prince's conduct tends to the establishment of a tyrannical domination, and as a result, call him to order: not unlike the sailors who do not hesitate to take precautions when they are able to foresee storms and gales by the warnings they get from pilotage and navigation charts. The second argument is that a tyrant that establishes his domination without advice and consultation *strikes everything for he fears everything; he vents his rage on all in order to make all believe that he has the power.* At times, he resembles a wolf that on entering a sheep pen cannot help slaughtering all, though one sheep alone may sate the wolf and appease its hunger; or, on the contrary, if he proceeds judiciously and follows the maxims of those better-advised and less passionate than he, perhaps he may be content to level the heads of the taller poppies only, as did Tarquin, or those minds who seem superior to the rest, as did Thrasybulus and Periander, and in that way the evil that could not be avoided would be by far milder and bearable.

Besides, one must not fear that the account of all these tragic accidents might offend the ears of Your Eminence or trouble your sweet and easy nature in the least. All the command of political affairs that You have gained, the long practice and experience that You have of the courts of the greatest monarchs, where these machiavellianisms are so frequent, do not allow that You may be taken for a novice in these matters. Moreover, it is not right for a great man to show the same disposition to compassion, although justice and clemency are two virtues fit for him. In his treatise ON MERCY, Seneca gives the reason why: *just as religion honours the gods and superstition offends them, all good people will embrace clemency and gentleness, but they would avoid pity, because it is the mark of a lowly and weak nature to allow itself to succumb to the misfortune that others are seen to suffer.* On the other hand, it would be a crime to think that there had been anything vile, obsequious and abject in Your Eminence, all the more so if it is true that *nothing befits a man more than a great soul*, as the same Seneca puts it. With what more reason this magnanimity is encountered in Your Eminence, accompanying in all honour and enhancing the great dignity which Your Eminence upholds not only as a Prince of the Church but also as principal counsellor of His Holiness and of almost all the most powerful princes of Europe; *for a great soul befits a great fortune, and whoever is not up to it and does not raise himself higher deserves to go to ground*, and so at least he knows that in that way the fortune is managed with less authority and fame. Thus, in the histories, we see that King Epiphanes was nicknamed the Insane because he despised his dignity as king and did not conduct himself accordingly, and that Ramiro of Aragon was greatly mocked and held in contempt by all his courtiers because he had not given up his monkish ways on quitting the monastery to succeed to the crown. Even our times provide us with such examples as that of a king of Great Britain who *was looked down upon and mocked for his desire to write books and for his pretence of man of letters*; and Henry III, so much praised and taken note of in our modern histories, and as he had lived among the monks, and from a maladjusted, excessive devotion, renounced sceptre and the government of his state, thus causing Pope Sixtus V to say: *this king does everything in his power to be a monk, and I have done everything I could not to be one.* And for what it is worth, one of the best pieces of advice ever given by Monsieur de Villeroy to Henry the Great, who led the life of a soldier and carabinier during the wars that had started on his accession to the crown, was to tell him that *a prince, who is not fiercely jealous of the respect due to his majesty, gives cause for offense and contempt. That even in the biggest confusions, the kings, his predecessors, had always conducted themselves as kings: that the time has come for him to talk, write and command as a king.* But why look for examples among foreign princes when the history of those who have governed the city in which Your Eminence finds Yourself at present gives special prominence to two sovereign pontiffs who still serve as fables and subjects of malicious gossip and mockery for posterity as they had not matched the greatness of their supreme dignity with that of the spirit; the great piety and religion marking their faces did not prevent Masson to say about the first, who happened to be Celestine V, that *he was a simple man, lacking in learning and incapable of understanding even human affairs.* About the second, Paolo Giovio, while talking about some fish that got up in price during his pontificate, says: *Adrian VI, who had an insipid taste for all kinds of meats as well as a dull wit and a depraved judgment as far as the administration of the Republic was concerned, had already raised the price of hake, which is rather an ordinary fish, a fact that brought him into the derision of the whole fish market.* Nevertheless, he showed more restraint and moderation than Peter Martyr, not the Florentine heretic, but the Protonotary Apostolic, hailing from a small town in the Duchy of Milan. About the election of the same pope he said the following: *at the assembly of the cardinals it happened to them what the fable recounts about the leopard and the lion over the kidnapping of a lamb, that while those two were tearing each other apart, valiantly disputing the prey, another four-legged beast of those most brutal and cowardly made it its own.* Thus one needs to avoid the great burdens, or else, handle them with a force and generosity of spirit so high above the ordinary that it may induce Fortune to back them up and favour him in all his enterprises: the maxim being quite definite, that whoever makes use of this principle and premise should have that character (*certainly, a sound mind cannot be bought nor can it be lent,* as Seneca says); in the conduct of his well-being, he cannot fail to be the exclusive worker and creator of his fortune; in reality, *the sage man makes his own fortune.* Although rather young of age and very poorly provided with money and soldiers, Alexander put his mind to subjugating the Persians and advancing as far as India, and he attained his aim; Caesar undertook to rule alone that great republic, which commanded the others, and he found the means. Two shepherds, Romulus and Tamerlane, had the will to found two powerful empires, and they carried it out; a merchant, Muhammad wanted to become a prophet, and from prophet, the sovereign of one third of the world, and he succeeded. And what do you think, Monsignor, was the main resort which brought about all these wonderful results? None other, truly, than the one which Juvenal teaches us always to set and place among the first of our wishes, *ask for a stout heart.* On the other hand, to wish now to specify the parts of which this forceful spirit is made and composed would mean to enchase one discourse in another, and do as Montaigne, who rather followed the whims of his fancy than the headings of his ESSAYS. Sufffices for the present to say that one of the first and most necessary elements is often to recall Seneca's saying: *Oh what a contemptible thing man is if he does not raise above human things*: that is to say, if he does not envisage with a firm and assured eye all the world like he were on top of some high tower, seeing it as a badly ordered theatre, full of confusion, where some play comedy, others tragedy, and in which he is allowed to intervene, *like some god coming from the machinery,* as long as he has the will, or the different occasions would persuade him to do it.

If by any chance, Monsignor, it may seem to you extraordinary and out of season for my age and perhaps also inappropriate for my condition that I appear so self-assured in these matters that are in themselves so delicate and ticklish, and even more so in the mouth of a young man whom Horace calls *slow to make needful provision*, and is not accustomed to devote himself to such serious and important studies *which befit the long boiled-away life of old men*, I may start by replying to Your Eminence that my present age is in no way disproportionate to the matter and the subject which I am dealing with. The poet who was the first to proffer these two verses: *the best of our days pass by and flee the first; the bad march in their wake and the sad old age*, may, if need be, stand guarantor and caution for my words, because he gives it such a fine epithet, on which Seneca would gloss as it was his fashion: *why the best, he asks, because we can learn a lot in our youth and turn our minds still nimble and amenable to improvement; because that time is the most appropriate to exert the mind by study and the body by laborious effort.* And as numerous people have engaged in many fine enterprises before the flower of their age, why should I be forbidden to follow them from afar and originate if not some generous and elevated acts, at least some strong and bold conceptions? Given mainly that I have always striven to acquire certain likings for things of the mind, which would not be useless to me now, as it is true that I have cultivated the Muses without, however, caressing them too much, and enjoyed studying, yet not getting deeply involved: I have gone through scholastic philosophy, without becoming eristic, and through the philosophy of the ancients and the moderns, without taking sides, *not having bound myself by oath to follow the opinions of any master.* Seneca was more useful to me than Aristotle, Plutarch than Plato, Juvenal and Horace more than Homer and Virgil, Montaigne and Charron more than all of them. I had not had the practice of the world to discover by their effects the ruses and the nasty things that are perpetrated in it, still

I have become aware of a great many in the histories, satires and the tragedies. During the seven or eight years that I spent in different colleges, pedantry may well have gained something over my body and my outer ways, but I can certainly pride myself on its not having encroached upon my mind at all. Nature, thank God, did not act as a cruel mother, but has given him a good groundwork, the reading of various authors has helped him greatly, but THE BOOK OF ST ANTHONY provided him with what is best. Moreover, I do not think that Your Eminence may find fault with my making use of these thoughts which are my own in order honestly to entertain You, being full of zeal and good affection in your service, without intent to meet some Agamemnon telling me as to the young man of Petronius who just finished a long declamation: *Young man, your talk has uncommon flavour, and what is most rare, the secret arts do not harm you.* Neither do I think of missing the occasion to turn to account my humble talent in the contemplative life to which I have devoted and dedicated all that rests of mine, not wishing to tarry and get bogged down in the active life, unless the service to Your Eminence, to whom I have first vowed obedience, may keep me engaged in it.

What is left now is to see whether I do not exceed the limits of my capacity by wanting to deal with these things apparently so remote from my understanding as the day from night; which is the last difficulty that I have set myself to overcome here. My answer could be brief, because the difficulty will soon disappear when one recalls this opinion of Seneca's, *a fine mind does not need too much learning.* But to be more specific, I admit honestly that I do not have that much presumption and good opinion of myself to think of winning the prize in this race, while I am still a novice. Nevertheless, heeding the Poet's saying: *it is worthwhile to advance to a certain point, though we may not go farther,* I shall exert myself a little and march on until I tire or stray from the right path, then shall rest and wait for some new knowledge or instruction to go on. The good man Aratus, who did not understand much about astrology, nonetheless, compiled a fine book on its phenomena; Celsus, who was a true grammarian, put together a very important book on medicine, notwithstanding; Dioscorides was a soldier, and Macer, a senator, yet both did write very well about plants; from a simple mason and architect, Hippodamus himself became a politician and the author of a REPUBLIC, mentioned by Aristotle. Besides, it has always been my opinion that whoever is the least gifted naturally and has studied some can infer and draw all kinds of conclusions from five or six good principles, as Pliny says about the ancient painters who were making the best pictures by mixing only four or five colours. One may add that the sciences seem to be chained and padlocked to one another, and to have such correspondence that whoever masters one also masters all those which are subordinate to it. Moreover, our century seems to favour this design greatly, because one can come to know and uncover all the biggest secrets of monarchies, the court intrigues, the cabals, the factions, pretexts and special motives, and in one word, *what the king whispered in the queen's ear and what tales Juno told Jupiter*, by means of so many connections, memorials, speeches, instructions, libels, manifestos, satires and similar secret items, which come to light every day and which in effect are capable of better and more easily shaping, loosening up the spirits, and making them more wordly-wise than any of the actions that are ordinarily practised at the courts of princes, of whose importance we can become aware only by taking great pains, unless we have penetrated their causes and diverse movements. Briefly, to conclude in a few words that which concerns the particulars of my person, *since Cato, since Curius, whose names are most revered, cared nothing about what the vulgar, the ignorant populace would say, I ponder and consider the example of respectable men.*

It is quite true that this design will be more difficult as it is one of the most refined which one may choose in politics, but also it makes me hope that the end will be more glorious; I for one have always liked to say together with Propertius: *I ascend the great road but the glory I expect to win gives me strength, I do not relish the crowns too easily gained,* and at the worst, daring when great things are at stake is honourable, when dangerous, the undertaking is hardy, when exalted and refined, the fall is glorious, on high seas, when the course taken is unfortunate, the shipwreck becomes famous; I sketch it out, another will complete it; I open the lists, another will attain the goal, I blow the trumpet, another will win the prize, there are so many people in this world travelling along roads traced by their predecessors; the number of minds that toil every day to imitate the others is quite large even without ensnaring mine in this slavery; and because all the authors who treat of politics have no intention to put an end to their customary disquisitions on the religion, justice, clemency, liberality and other similar virtues of the prince or the minister, it is better for me that I distance myself a little in order not to catch this contagion, or be enveloped by such a crowd. And in order not to arrive with the last, I take a new road that is not trodden by the *servile herd* of Horace, nor interrupted by those fetid mires and marshes where such a long time back, *the frogs used to sing their old plaintive songs in the mud.*

Among all the points of politics, though, I do not see any less troubled and less trodden, and better fit to be than that of secrets, or rather of coups d'état. What Clapmarius says of them in his treatise DE ARCANIS IMPERIORUM provides no valid exception, because having no idea of the meaning of the title of his book, he only talks about what the other writers have already said and repeated a thousand times concerning the general rules of the administration of states and empires. And to the extent this matter is so new and high above the common sentiments of the politicians, it has hardly been touched by any of them, as Bodin remarked in the sixth of his methods as follows: *Many have dealt widely and in depth with the institutions of mores, the recovery of peoples, the advent of princes, and the consolidation of the laws, but they passed very lightly over the affairs of state and said nothing about the revolutions of empires, and of what Aristotle calls sophisms or princes' secrets and Tacitus calls secrets of imperium.* I shall travel always keeping the reins tight, and taking all the precautions, and show all the possible modesty and reticence in order to season and moderate these discourses, of which one may say better than Plato did about those on theology, *these discourses are very difficult and dangerous.* Cardan and Campanella held it to be an important precept firstly to acquire a perfect idea of a subject-matter, if one wants to treat or present it well, and if possible, transmute all one's concetration and all one's imagination into it. Hence it often happens that those comedians who are best endowed with this imaginative faculty act their characters better. In France, it is said that before giving that fine description of the horse he came across, Du Bartas would at times shut himself in some chamber, and standing on all fours, would snort, neigh, gambol, buck, amble, trot, gallop, curvet, and try by all kinds of means to counterfeit the horse. Agrippa himself confesses that when he wanted to compile his harangue against the sciences, he imagined that he were a dog barking at all sorts of people; and when he wanted to write about pyrotechnics or about fireworks, he would convince himself that he had changed into a dragon that was blowing fire and sulphur through his muzzle, eyes, ears and nostrils. As far as I am concerned, were I to deal with or write about some subject matter absolutely good and profitable, I should be pleased to make use of that kind of imagination, but in this matter, which is so inclined to injustice, I shall never imagine myself a Nero or a Busiris, in order to more effectively find the means of undoing and exterminating humankind. It would be enough not to incur the blame and the censure which Nero inveighed against the politicians and counsellors of his time, saying that *they gave their advice and opined as if they were in Plato's republic and not amid the scum of Romulus.* Were I to know that the little I shall say may cause some abuse and disorder greater than that nowadays in practice among the princes, I would throw pen and paper instantly into the fire, and avow eternal silence, in order not to acquire the renown of a subtle and cunning man versed in political speculations while losing that of an honourable man, which alone I want to capitalize and take pride in, for the rest of my life.

Chapter II

What are properly speaking the coups d'état and of how many kinds

In order not to dwell on these prefaces for ever, and finally talk about the subject matter for which they have been written, that great man Justus Lipsius defined prudence in a few words, while dealing with it in his POLITICA: *a selection and a triage of things that are to be avoided or desired*; and after having amply discoursed upon it as it is usually treated by the schools, that is to say, as a moral virtue which has as its only object the respect for the good, he goes on to speak of another prudence, which he called mixed, because it is not as pure, sound, and whole as the former, since it involves a few frauds and stratagems which are ordinarily practised at princes' courts, as well as in the administration of the most important affairs of government. Likewise, he takes pains to show by his eloquence that prudence of this latter kind must be considered honest, and that practically it is legitimate and permissible. Afterwards he defines it quite judiciously: *sagacious planning which deviates from virtue and the laws for the good of kingdom and king.* And from there turning to its specimens and their differences, he establishes three main species: the first, which may be called fraud or minor deceit, very small and of no importance, has mistrust and dissimulation subordinated to it; the second, which still retains some virtue, though less than the first, has *bribery and deception* as its parts, that is the means of winning the friendship and the service of some, and of deluding, deceiving and misleading the others by false promises, lies, presents and other ways and means of contraband, if one may say so, and rather more necessary than permitted or honest. As for the third and last, he says that it detaches itself completely from virtue and the laws, plunging headlong into malice, having perfidy and injustice as its two bases and most secure foundations.

Nevertheless, it seems to me that to look for the nature of these state secrets in particular, and come to the point of our disquisition and see what is specific and and essential to them, we must consider prudence a moral and political virtue, which has no other objective but to look for the different ways and the best and easiest contrivances for successfully handling those affairs that man sets about. Because, as a result, the affairs and the different means cannot be but of two kinds, some easy and ordinary, and the others, extraordinary, distressing and difficult; so, too, one cannot set up but two kinds of prudence: the first, ordinary and easy, and the second, extraordinary, more rigorous, severe and difficult. The first category includes all those aspects of prudence that the philosophers customarily talk of in their moral treatises, in addition to the first three, mentioned above, and which Justus Lipsius attributes solely to the mixed fraudulent prudence. Because, truth to tell, if one takes a close look at their nature and the politicians' need to resort to them, it is impossible to be right about their being unjust, vicious or dishonest. In order to get a better understanding, one needs to be aware, as Charron says, that the sovereign's justice, virtue and probity plod along somewhat differently from the private person's: the scope is larger and freer, because of the great, weighty and perilous burden which he bears, and that is why he finds it convenient to walk with a step, which to others may seem unsettled and irregular, but which is necessary to him, loyal and legitimate. Sometimes the sovereign needs to sidestep and bend, mix prudence with justice, and as the saying goes, *make use of finesse as the fox does*: it is in this that the doctrine of good government consists. The agents, nuncios, ambassadors, legates are sent both to spy on the actions of the foreign princes and to dissimulate, cover and disguise those of their masters. Louis XI, the wisest and most sensible of our kings, held as main maxim of his governance that *whoever does not know how to dissimulate, does not know how to reign, either;* and Emperor Tiberius, *of all the virtues he had, there was none but dissimulation that he loved best.* Does one not see that the greatest virtue, which holds court nowadays, is to be distrustful of all the world and dissemble with everyone, because the simple and open virtues are in no way appropriate to the trade of governance and quite often betray themselves and the state? Not only these two aspects, to be distrustful and to dissemble, which consist in omissions, are necessary to princes, but also quite often it is requisite to pay no heed but take action by commission, in order, for instance, to gain some advantage or to reach one's goal by covered, equivocal means and subtleties; to finesse by fine words, letters and embassies, acting and obtaining by subtle means what the difficulty of times and of the issues at stake makes it impossible to attain otherwise. *If one cannot go straight into the harbour, one reaches it by manoeuvre.* Likewise, one needs to undertake and devise secret practices and intelligence to subtly win the hearts and affections of the officers, servants and confidants of other lords and princes, or of his own subjects, what Cicero calls in the First of his MORAL OBLIGATION, *to win the hearts of men and to attach them to one's own profit.* What is the point then of introducing a special, mixed prudence, on which these actions depend in particular, as Justus Lipsius shows, when they may rely on the ordinary, taught by the politicians every day, inserted in their reasoning, in the persuasions of ministers, and practised without the least suspicion of injustice, as if they were the main rules and maxims for the good policing and administration of states and empires? Moreover, they are not worthy of the name of governmental secrets, coups d'état, *secrets of imperium,* as those which in order to be placed under this latter kind of extraordinary prudence, set in motion the more difficult and unpalatable affairs, that above all others deserve to be called *secrets of imperium,* because it is the only name given not only by me but also by all the good authors who wrote before me.

And here, indeed, we may notice the mistake of

many politicians and of Clapmarius, in particular, who intent on compiling a thick book on *secrets of imperium*, reduces them to certain general principles, and says for a start that state secrets are but the various means, reasons and counsels of which the princes make use in order to maintain their authority and the public order, without however transgressing common law or raising any suspicion of fraud and injustice. And on that genuine and well-established premiss, he divides them into two kinds and says that the first should be called secrets of imperium or of public affairs, and which in keeping with the three forms of government, he further subdivides into other six. Thus, monarchy, for instance, ought to have certain means and particular reasons to allow it to be looked after and be commanded by several who would reduce it to an aristocracy; others change it into a democracy in order to guard it against the rule of the mob, while these latter two have to act in such ways as not to become monarchical or lapse into some other form of government, opposed to them. To the second kind belong those which he calls and qualifies by the name of secrets of domination, to which those in command must resort to in order to maintain their positions of author-ity, whether monarchical, popular or aristocratic. He goes on to confirm it by means of a strange enumeration of all those means, to the extent he has been able to find them in Livy, Sallust, Ammianus Marcellinus and many other authors, who all seem to agree on the meaning of those words in the way Clapmarius uses them throughout his book. And that does not make me in the least fear the indignation of all those great personalities for my taking the liberty, without asking their permission, to tell them that by usurping this expression of secrets of state, as it is used above, they seem to stray from its meaning and misunderstand the nature of the thing, being sure that the Latin phrase *secretum et arcanum*, which they use to convey it should not be attributed at all to the principles and maxims of a science that is common, understood and practised by each, but only to what for some reason must be neither known nor divulged because as Marbod the Poet notes: *what is communicated does not remain secret.* Likewise, we learn from the grammarians that the word *arcanum* (secret) might be derived from *ab arce* (from stronghold), or else, as is the opinion of Festus Pompeius, the Augurs had the habit of offering some sacrifice, which they wanted to prevent people from knowing, or because all the secret things and of consequence are better kept *in arce* (in the chest) than in any other place. Those who take them *ab arca* (from the chest) do not seem to be too far from that same opinion, and the good authors have never used the two words but to lend them a similar meaning. Virgil: *I will speak at length, and unrolling the scroll of fate, I will disclose its secrets,* and in another place: *to honour you by confiding my secrets and feelings to you.* Horace: *neither wine nor ire, though inciting, will make you reveal the secret entrusted to you.* And to end, here is Lucan, didn't he say, by talking of the sources of the Nile, that they were unknown even to the Egyptians themselves? *Nature has kept secret from anybody your fountainhead, oh Nile, and there is no people which could have seen you in your beginnings, she closed on it and let the nations admire them rather than know the place.* Nevertheless, I shall remark in passing that one may draw a fine parallel between the course of the Nile and the secrets of state. Because like the peoples who live nearer its fountainhead and draw thousands of advantages from it, unaware of the cause, so, too, peoples admire the happy effects of these master strokes without for that matter having the slightest knowledge of their causes and various motivations. Now, having shown that those writers corrupted the words, we may also state that they so perverted the nature of the thing that they offer us general precepts and universal maxims, founded on justice and the right of sovereignty, and as a result, permitted and practised openly and publicly every day, but which, nonetheless, they regard as secrets of state. Likewise, they pay no heed to the great difference between those mentioned above and those we are going to talk about. Anybody may become a savant and a practitioner of the former by as little study of the authors that have dwelt on them as they wish to devote,

while on the other hand, those which are now at issue
are born in the most private chambers of princes and are
neither deliberated in full senate nor inside the assembly
of a parliament, but rather among two or three of the
best-advised and trusted ministers that a prince may
have. And indeed, we see that after he had won the battle
of Actium and quelled the civil and foreign wars,
Augustus, intent on giving up the title of emperor and so
grant freedom to his fatherland, did not tell the Senate,
although he had augmented it by six hundred senators,
nor his Privy Council, made up of twenty people, the
most learned and judicious he could find, but he sug-
gested and submitted the whole of the matter to the
judgement of his two main friends, ministers and confidants, Maecenas and Agrippa, *to who he was in the habit
of imparting the secrets of the Empire,* as Dio says. And
if we wish to go back to that great man who had laid his
fortune in his hands, Julius Caesar, we find out in Suetonius' *Julio* that he had only Quintus Pædius and Cornelius
Balbus to communicate with, τὰ μυζιχώτατα, that is
to say, what was most secret and hidden in the soul. The
Lacedaemonians, who had greatly expanded their state
after Lysander's victory, set up a council of thirty people
to govern the affairs of their Republic, but not content
with them, they would choose twelve from their most
sensible and judicious citizens to act as oracles, and
which by their responses would decide on the coups
d'état. Nowadays, the Venetians do the same with the
help of the Six Procurators of Saint Mark; and there is
no sovereign so weak and unimportant, and who is so ill-
advised as to submit to the judgement of the public what
hardly is confined to the hearing of a minister or a
favourite. That is what made Cassiodorus say: *it is only
when the issue is too difficult that one learns the merit
of being made part of a prince's secret,* and somewhere
else, where he talks of a secret councillor of Theodoric,
*he would confer with you on the certainties of peace and
on the doubts of war, which was a singular favour on
the part of a wise and prudent king, and as he took care
of everything, he would confess to you the most secret
thoughts of his heart.* Would it not have been the last

straw, had Charles IX deliberated on St Bartholomew's Day massacre with all the counsellors of his Parliament, or had Henry III decided in his assembled council the death of the Seigneurs of Guise? I believe, indeed, that they would have succeeded as much as when one is trying to catch hares by the beat of a drum, or birds by the stroke of bells. Moreover, I would like to ask these gentlemen, given that they call the common rules for the administration and government of kingdoms *secrets of empire*, what name could they give to those secrets, mixed with little security and subject to extraordinary prudence, of which we are now talking? For to call them, as Clapmarius does, following Tacitus, *villanies of imperium*, is rather to take notice of those that are carried out with a particular good in mind, and by some tyrant, at the expense of many others that are performed in the interest of the public, and with all the equity which one may bring in these enterprises that, however, can never be so well detailed not to be always accompanied by some kind of injustice, and as a consequence, be liable to blame and calumny.

Having explained the words, we must now turn to the nature of the thing which they define. Now, to go in depth and grasp it well, one needs to proceed with the search from above and show how in the monastic rule, or the rule of one, and in economy, or the administration of the family, both of which are linchpins of politics, there are certain ruses, detours, stratagems, which many used and still use every day, in order to get through their pretences. Charron in his book OF WISDOM, Cardan in his works entitled THE MIDDLEMAN and ON THE PROFIT THAT CAN BE DRAWN FROM ADVERSITIES, as well as ON WISDOM, Machiavelli in his DISCOURSES ON TITUS LIVY and in his PRINCE have amply supplied the precepts thereof. It will be enough for me to give some examples but not before remarking what Justus Lipsius has said of the latter: *we easily realize about him that this paper smudger of Italy is not to be blamed so much (though nowadays the most wretched join in his condemnation) and there are some ruses, as the saintly man says, which are honest and praiseworthy, and that*

Gaspar Schioppius wrote a little book in his defence. Nevertheless, one may resent him for *letting the wretched south wind get to the flowers, and the wild boars to the crystal springs*, being the first to take the plunge, break the ice, and by his writings, sully, if one may say so, what the most judicious used as most hidden and strongest means to make their enterprises more successful. Thus I too would have made it my duty to add to what he has said, if the above-mentioned, as well as other politicians had not preceded me, and at one time or another, made it a subject of discussion, what Juvenal was saying of poetry: *it is foolish clemency to be sparing of paper that will be wasted anyhow when you run into so many poets everywhere.* As for the secrets of the monastic rule, I do not think that there are any more refined with regard to their ends than those practised by certain persons, who in order to distinguish themselves from the rest of their fellow-men would instil in the latter some idea of their divinity. Thus we see Salmoneus, who had a bridge of bronze built for him along which he drove his carriage with strong horses harnessed to it, brandishing a torch like fireworks all along, and so he thought he was imitating Jupiter's lightning and thunder, of which the Poet took occasion to say: *I saw Salmoneus paying cruel penalty for having imitated Jove's crashing flames from Olympus.* Psapho, who was no less ambitious than the above, would feed a great many magpies, blackbirds, jays, parrots and other similar birds, and after he had taught them to utter the words 'Psapho is God', he set them free so that those who would hear so many extraordinary witnesses of his divinity would be more readily inclined to believe it. Likewise, Heracleides Ponticus gave orders to one of his servants, a most loyal confederate, that at the time of his death, he should hide under his clothes a big grass snake that he had been long tending with a purpose, namely that the beast awoken by the commotion of the burial would dash forward among the mourners and so give the populace reason to believe that Heracleides had been deified. Empedocles, on the other hand, acted with more courage and generosity, as befitting a philosopher;

given that he was quite old and overwhelmed with glory and honours, he flung himself of his own accord into the volcanic craters of Mount Etna in Sicily to make people believe in his ascent to heaven, no more and no less than Romulus, who in order to instil the idea of his own ascent, had drowned himself in the Goat's Marsh. *Eager to be thought a god immortal, Empedocles calmly threw himself into the burning Aetna.*

The atheists, who seek to gloss every paragraph of the Holy Writ, maintain that the following line in the DEUTERONOMY: *No one to this day knows his burial place* — should be understood in the same way, and that Moses must have flung himself headlong into an abyss so as to be exalted to heaven by the Israelites, and that instead of believing as they should, and so remain in agreement with the Christians, that he had truly hidden his body in order to prevent the Jews from idolizing it after his death, knowing very well that they were inclined less by nature than by the obsession which they shared with the Egyptians to worship all those who had done them some good or whom they believed to be of a singular and extraordinary virtue. The same opinion may be gathered from what Diogenes Laërtius reports about the golden thigh of Pythagoras, as Plutarch in his life of Numa says openly that it was a feint and a stratagem of that philosopher, intent to establish the idea of his divinity as much as in the other cases. But what Hercules did was by far more ingenious; as he was very versed in astrology, proof are those fables about his life which make him hold up the pillars of the universe alongside Atlas, he chose just the time and the hour of the apparition of a great comet in order to place himself by the burning stake where he wanted to put an end to his days, in such a way as to make the new celestial fire seem to bear witness and make people believe about him what later the Romans let their emperors make them believe by means of an eagle which rose in flight from the flames as if carrying the soul of the deceased and place it between Jupiter's arms. Many others, who were more modest and more restrained in their designs, were content to make us aware of the care the gods were taking of them through the continuous attendance on them by some genius or particular divinity, as did Socrates, Plotinus, Porphyry, Brutus, Sulla and Apollonius among the Ancients, not to mention all the Legislators, and among the moderns, Pico della Mirandola, Cecco of Ascoli, Hermolao, Savonarola, Nifo, Postel, Cardan and Campanella, who all boasted of having had a genius that talked to them, without for that matter being possible to accuse them of having practised the theurgical rites from the book falsely attributed to Virgil, ON THE MEANS OF SEEING GENII, or mentioned by Arbatel in I don't know what jumble of similar books which is a great mistake to print under the name of Agrippa. Likewise, as far as I am concerned, I would like much better to establish the truth of these stories on the basis of that wonderful force of the contradictions of the mind, very well explained by Marsilio Ficino and Giordano Bruno and from which Palingenius, too, does not seem to distance himself too much in three or four places of his ZODIAC.

If we are reluctant to say rather that all those gentlemen had played the impostor, intent on emulating the stories of Numa, Zamolxis and Minos or more likely those which the rabbis and the cabbalists amusingly forged from the Patriarchs of the Old Testament, wanting us to believe in good faith that Adam had been governed by his angel Raziel, Shem by Jophiel, Abraham by Zadkiel, Isaac by Raphael, Jacob by Peliel and Moses by Metatron, *but let the Jew Appela believe it, I shan't.*

Whatever that may be, one can realize from the historians that these ruses have not always been useless, because Scipio, who had practised them judiciously, acquired the reputation of a great, respectable man among the Romans and was sent to conquer the Spains when he was not yet twenty-four; but see also how Livy talks about it: *Scipio was not admired solely for the genuine arts and sciences which he commanded, but also for a certain artifice which he had discovered and would use successfully to keep up appearances; and he would undertake several things in the presence of the people or by means of visions which he said he had had during the*

night, or as divine warnings, prompted by the heavens.
It was thus that many princes and private persons acted,
and whenever their minds were not capable of such art-
fulness and superior inventions, they would be content to
lend as much lustre and splendour to their actions as was
possible with the help of others. That is why Tacitus said
that Vespasian had *a special art to give lustre to
everything that he would do and to everything he was
saying,* and Corbulo is described by the same as *drawing
attention to himself by his wisdom and experience, but
also by the mere display of showy attributes,* and that
with great reason, because as he says in another place,
*princes must rule everything for the sake of their good
name,* or following what Cardan has to say, *esteem and
opinion are the queens of human matters.*

One may go on and make many other observations
about the private conduct of people, but since this matter
is as trivial as it is of little consequence, I shall go back
to what Cardan said about this subject in the book quoted
above, and turn to the secrets of the economy, or the
rules and administration of families, of which I shall be
content to mention by way of example only some that
were practised in order to suppress and parry the nasty
tricks played by women on their husbands, *when insatiable, they affect to fill the hole of their drain.* Apropos
of which I recall having read one in the facetious stories
by Bouchet or by Chaudière, which now would pass for
earnest, as if it were by far more appropriate to correct
such ribald dispositions than that of the mule which spent
eight days without drinking, mentioned by Cardan in his
book ON WISDOM. A certain physician, they say, as he
got wind of his wife easing her boredom from time to
time as she *entered a brothel reeking with long-used
coverlets,* and that she had made an appointment for the
very next day in order to play him false, was not moved
at all, nor did he pretend to be, but round midnight and
as his wife did not dream of it in the least, he woke up
with a start claiming that thieves were inside the room,
reached for his weapons, fired two or three shots from
the pistol, screamed blue murder, cried for help, struck
the tables and the wainscot with his sword, in short, he

did all he could to strike terror and horror inside his house. In the morning, as everything was peaceful once again, he did not fail to feel his wife's pulse, which he feigned to be highly altered and quite faint because of the fright she had gone through during the night, and for that he had some ten or twelve ounces of blood drawn from her, and as the purge caused a little reaction, he started to grow alarmed as if it were a great fever, redoubled the bleedings to seven or eight good ones, then he went on shaving, cupping and purging her magisterially, and he repeated it so often that he made her keep her bed for longer than six months without being sick, and in that interval he had plenty of time to break her habits and connections, diminish her rosy and attractive complexion, and above all, freeze, bring under control and weaken the fervour and heady and acrimonious humours of her temperament so much, that he subdued that fire in her, more unquenchable than that of asbestos, *which nothing could extinguish nor could it be quenched in any way.* But the secret which the peoples of China used to practise to remedy the same disorder that found a way into their families was by far gentler and more effective. Because they prescribed and established as one of the first laws of the kingdom that all the good graces of women would henceforth depend on the smallness of their feet, and those who had the smallest and cutest feet would be judged the most beautiful. No sooner had the law been made public that all the mothers, without any regard for the consequences, started to squeeze, tighten and wrap the feet of their daughters so well, that the latter could no longer leave home nor keep straight but on the arms of two or three women servants. Thus, as this artificial feature turned into a natural conformation not unlike that of the macrocephali mentioned by Hippocrates, the Chinese have insensibly stopped and stabilized the quick silver which their women had in their feet, making them resemble the tortoise which the Poets called *tardigrada, carrying its house upon its back, and which Appelles painted and placed under the feet of Venus in Kos.* By that means they were prevented from going for walks with other good men and from attending to their customary pastimes. Likewise, the Venetian ladies are forced to stay at home more often than they wish by the use of their big chastity belts of unmatched discomfort. The story recounted by Mocquet, though, is by far stranger and seems more like a coup d'état: he claims to have learnt of it and even witnessed the practice among the Caribs, fierce and barbarian peoples, that at the death of the husband from whatever causes, the wife is constrained, under the pain of infamy, derision and abandonment by all her friends and relations, to take her own life at the same time by leaping into a big fire set up by herself with so much pomp and rejoicing as if it were her wedding day. Greatly surprised, the aforementioned Mocquet asked the reason for all that and was answered that it had been wisely established to remedy the great malice and lubricity of the women of that country, who before the law was made public, used to poison their husbands when they got tired of them or when they felt like marrying someone more robust and strapping and *who would stretch the string of the bow better than Ulysses*. While that remedy well suited the nature of those who ordered it, the one practised by Denys, the tyrant of Syracuse, to stop the night gatherings and banquets, was not quite unlike it: while not showing that they displeased him or that he feared that they were carried on with the intention to conspire against his state, he was content little by little to introduce exemption from penalty for all the thefts and lacernies that were committed during the night, turning them rather into a laughing stock, and by that tolerance, emboldened all the bad boys of the city to treat those they met in the street at night so badly, that nobody could leave their houses after sunset without running the risk of being robbed or killed by that sort of thieves. Let us now arrive at some other examples, less serious, and consequently, less dangerous and nefarious as far as their practice was concerned. Wanting to make their subjects eat fresh fish at low price, the republics of Greece did not resort to any special tariff about which the ιξυοπωλαι or fishmongers (as we call them) would have had reason to complain. But taking the advice, which the comic poet Alexis claims Aristonicus gave them, they forbade the aforementioned fishmongers, upon grave pain, to sit while selling their merchandise in the market place, *so that tired and annoyed to have to stand, they would sell them all fresh.* Likewise, as Festus Pompeius says, the Romans forbade Jupiter's priests to mount for fear that they might *wander too far from the site of justice and so neglect the sacred rites,* while on my part, I dare say that if one wants to remedy the great confusion caused by the excessive number of coaches in the city of Paris, one need but confiscate all those found with less than five persons in them in the streets of the city, because by means of this order, those who drive alone every day will put on the cover, and the others, who could not afford to increase their families by three or four, would easily resolve to reduce them by three or four useless mouths, even if they were those of a driver and two horses.

It would be easy to increase the number of like examples and secrets of economy, if the above could not readily give us any idea of the others and pinpoint the way from this second to the third degree, which is that of politics and the government of peoples under the administration either of one or of several. We may mention three things that could serve its elucidation without leaving out anything in that way: first, to command the general science of the foundation and conservation of states and empires; and this science does not include only the traditions of Plato and Aristotle but also all that Cicero in his book ON LAWS, Xenophon in his PRINCE, Plutarch in his precepts, Isocrates, Synesius and other authors thought they had to be understood and practised by those who governed. It is also true that it includes certain rules universally agreed to and welcomed by everybody, as for example, that things do not happen either by accident or by necessity, that there is a God, primary author of all things, who is in charge and has set up the reward of Paradise for the good and the pains of Hell for the wicked; that some must command and others must obey; that it is the duty of a man of honour to defend the honour of his God, his king and his fatherland, in spite of everything; that the prince's main strength rests in his subjects' love and unity; that he has the right to raise money from them in order to meet the expenses of war and the upkeep of his house and others, explained very well by Marnix, Ammirato, Paruta, Remigio Fiorentino, Zinano, Malvezzi and Botero, in their political discourses and argumentations.

The second is truly what the French call *maximes d'état* and the Italians, *ragion di stato*, although Botero has included under this name all the three distinctions which we want to draw, saying that *the ragione di stato is the knowledge of the measures for founding, preserving and expanding a dominion*. In that way, he dealt only with those which, in my opinion, would define it as abuse of common law for the common good. To the extent this latter definition is more special, particular and precise, one may start from it when distinguishing between those primary rules for the foundation of empires, which are established on the basis of the laws and in conformity with reason, and the second category, which Clapmarius wrongly calls *arcana imperiorum* (secrets of imperium) and we, with reason, maxims of state, because they cannot be justified by public law, either civil or natural, but only by taking into consideration the public weal and utility, which often go beyond the private individual.

Thus we see Emperor Claudius, who could not take to wife Julia Agrippina, his niece by blood, his brother Germanicus' daughter, because of his homeland's laws, resort to state laws, on which he based his obvious infringement of ordinary laws, and married her, in order that *she, a woman in the freshness of her youth*, as Tacitus says, *and the mother of many children, should not carry off the grandeur of the Caesars to some other house*. In other words, out of fear that the woman might marry in some great house and so the blood of the Caesars would spread to other families and produce a multitude of princes and princesses, who in time, migtht have certain claims to the Empire, and as a result, become occasions for the disruption of public tranquillity. For the same reason, Tiberius would not get a husband for Agrippina, Germanicus' widow and the mother of the aforementioned, although in tears and with strong remonstrations she asked him for one, based on such firm and legitimate reasons that she could not be turned down without an injustice being committed, which nonetheless, was justified by the law of the state, because Tiberius did not overlook *how much it went against the republic*, that is to say, the serious consequences of such a marriage and the children that might issue from it, as great-great-nephews of Augustus, as the Roman Republic might some day fall on hard times and succumb to factionalism, because of the various pretenders to the succession of the empire. No law permits such things by which we may cause evil and disadvantage to the one who has done none to us; and yet, that maxim of state mentioned by Livy, namely, that *nobody should act in such a way as the whole authority of the law should fall into the hands of one people*, compels us to extend our help to our neighbours against those who have never offended us, out of fear that their ruin may serve as a step that would hasten ours and that as soon as our companions would be devoured by these new Cyclops, we may expect no other grace than that granted to Ulysses to be saved for the satisfaction of their last hunger. This is the pretext used by the Aetolians in order to obtain the help of King Antiochus, while Demetrius, the King of the Illyrians did the same to incite Philip, King of Macedonia and father of Perseus, to take up arms against the Romans. That is also the reason why that great statesman Cosimo de' Medici did not take anything more seriously than preventing Milan from falling under the authority of the Venetians, as the race of the viscounts and dukes of Milan was extinguished, and Henry the Great, aware that the Duke of Savoy had failed to take Geneva by surprise, said out loud that had the Duke made a success of his coup, he would have besieged him from within, the following day. Nonetheless, when the king of Spain wanted to invade the estates of the same duke, France, in keeping with the aforementioned maxim, forcefully rushed to his aid. The same maxim also served as a legitimate excuse for the alliances of Alexander VI and

Francis I with the Great Seigneur; it served as pretext for the secret treaties of the Spaniard with France's Huguenots, and as passport for so many troops, which from time to time we have slipped not only in Valtellina but also in the Netherlands, although apparently against the rules, if not of religion, at least of the common piety of our conscience. But without that maxim in mind, one would not have broken so many leagues in Guicciardini; Charles V would not have abandoned the Venetians to the Turk; Charles VIII would not have been so promptly chased out of Italy; Paul V would not have so easily enjoyed the benefit of the Duchy of Ferrara, nor the present Pope, the benefit of the Duchy of Urbino. So many princes would not have wished the restitution of the Palatinate, nor so much prosperity to the king of Sweden and that Casale should be left to the Duke of Mantua, were it not in virtue of that maxim to curb the measureless ambition of certain peoples that wanted to practise upon the neighbouring princes what the wealthy burghers practise upon the poor, *oh, if that corner could be added, which now spoils the shape of our little field.*

Moreover, the law of war does not allow that those, who lay down their arms in order to implore the mercy of the victor, be outraged in any way; yet, whenever the amount of prisoners is so large that they cannot be easily guarded, fed and kept in a sure place, or those of their party do not want to ransom them, it is allowed to finish them on principle, all the more so, as they could starve an army, resist it, favour their confederates' actions and cause thousand other difficulties. For that reason, Aldus Manutius thought himself able legitimately to excuse Hannibal for killing all the Roman prisoners, who had refused to follow him at the temple of the Goddess Juno, on his departure from Italy. Furthermore, concerning that action and others, Valerius Maximus said of him: *Hannibal whose prowess consisted mostly in ferocity.* One may refer the ways of acting or the particular customs of certain peoples, as far as their government is concerned, to similar maxims, as for instance, our Salic Law, so religiously observed, touching on the succession of males to the throne and the exclusion of women, by means of which the kingdom was preserved during the League against the Spanish invasion. Having protested as null and void all the foreign pursuits, the good and loyal French sent away those fine counter-claimants by means of the formal text of the law: *Francorum Regni succesor masculus esto* (The successor to the Kingdom of the Franks is to be a male). Of a similar nature is the law of the Chinese that forbids, under pain of death, the admittance of foreigners to their land, and in the case of the Great Turk, the custom is to put to death all the relatives, while the custom of the king of Ormuz is to blind them; the Ethiopians, on their part, confine them in the highest cleft of an inaccessible mountain; with the Athenians, it was ostracism; with the Valais people in Germany, the mazot; the Council of the Discoli at Lucca; the Canal Orfano at Venice; the Inquisition in Spain and Italy, and other such laws and ways of acting peculiar to each nation, and that all had as foundation no other law than that of the state, but which ways and laws, nonetheless, are very religiously observed as being wholly necessary for the running and the conservation of the states which practise them.

Finally, the last thing which we have mentioned above, that needs consideration in politics, is the coups d'état, to which the same definition may apply that has already be given with regard to the maxims and to the reason of state *ut sint excessus iuris communis propter bonum commune* (those that are an overstepping of common law for the sake of the common good), or to expand on it in our language, *daring and extraordinary actions, which princes are constrained to carry out against common law when faced with difficult and seemingly desperate situations, without regard for any order or form of justice, risking the interest of the private person for the sake of the public good.* But in order to better distinguish them from the maxims, we may add that what is done in the light of the latter — causes, reasons, manifestos, declarations, and every other way and form of legitimizing an action — precedes their operations and effects, whereas to the contrary, in the case of coups d'état, one sees the lighning without hearing the grumblings in the clouds, *it strikes before it lightens*. The matins are said before the bells start chiming; the execution precedes the sentence; all is done as in the Judaic way; one is caught unawares as Rome by the Gauls, and without thinking of it; one is struck by the blow which he had intended to deliver; another, who was thinking himself safe, dies of it; still another suffers from it without having given it a thought. Everything is done at night, in darkness, through fog and gloom. The Goddess Laverna presides over it and the first favour which one asks her for is: *grant me to escape detection, grant me to pass as just and upright, wrap my sins in night, my lies, in clouds*. Nevertheless, the good thing about them is that they contain the same justice and equity as that claimed for the maxims and the reasons of state. But for the latter, it is allowed to publicize them before the stroke, whereas the main rule of the coups d'état is to keep them hidden to the very end. Thus, the notorious executions of the Count of St Pol under Louis XI, of Marshal de Biron under Henry IV, of the Earl of Essex under Isabella, Queen of England, of the Marquis d'Ancre, under the present King, of the two brothers, under Henry III, of Maion under William, first king of Sicily, of David Riccio under Mary Stuart, Queen of Scotland, of Spurius Mellius, Roman knight, under Ahala Servilius, colonel of the Roman cavalry, and of Sejanus and Plautian under different emperors, were all as legitimate and necessary as the others, although the first three should be ascribed to the maxims and the reason of state, because the cases were prepared for judgement in advance of the execution, while all the others should be ascribed to state secrets and coups d'état, because the judgement took place only after the execution. Moreover, we may add the following difference to it, that is, religion might be greatly profaned, were the formalities to precede the execution, as when the Venetians say: *somo Venetiani dopo Chrestiani* (we are Venetians first, and Christians only afterwards), or when a Christian prince asked help from the Turk, or Henry VIII set his kingdom against the Holy See, the Duke of Saxony fomented Luther's heresy, Charles of Burbon sacked

Rome, and was the cause of the Pope's imprisonment and of the deaths of three cardinals, or when the issue is altogether extraordinary and of very great consequence by the good or evil that may come of it; on such occasions one may still use the terms coup d'état, as one may judge from the following count of some of those that were practised not by the infidel and cannibal Turks but by Christian princes. In order not to flatter or spare our nation, the kings of France should be counted among them: Clovis, the first Christian king, committed such strange acts, so remote from any kind of justice, that I do not know how the good man Savaron got the idea to compile a book about his sanctity; Charles VII was content to practise that of Joan the Maid of Orleans; Louis XI violated the trust placed in his constable, misled everybody under the cover of religion and made use of Provost l'Hermite to do away with many people, without any formal proceedings. Francis I was the cause of the Turk's descent into Italy and did not want to observe the treaty concluded at Madrid. Charles IX saw to that memorable execution on St Bartholomew's Day and the secret assassination of Lignerolles and Bussy. Henry III rid himself of the Messieurs of Guise; Henry IV joined the Dutch in an offensive and defensive league, to say nothing about his conversion to the Catholic faith; and Louis the Fair, whose every action is a miracle, and the coups d'état are the efects of his justice, did order two, which are worthy of note: the death of the Marquis d'Ancre and the intervention in the Valtellina. As for the Venetians, if it is true that they abide by the maxim mentioned above, one must also admit that they remain immersed in a continuous Machiavellianism, and so keep silent about many others, which they commit every day. By rejoicing in the captivity of St Louis in the Holy Land, the Florentines did not commit a state secret but a highly blamable and shameful act, and as Villani says: *it was remarkable that when the news reached Florence, where the Gibellins were ruling, they had a feast, but were greatly mistaken.* Regarding the popes, one may re- call Celestine's prison, the poison of Alexander VI, the assassination attempt on Fra Paolo as very sure evidence that they do not shed all their humanity, once they are elected. Charles of Anjou, king of Sicily, had Conradin and Frederic of Austria beheaded; Peter of Aragon authorized the Sicilian Vespers. Alfonso, king of Naples, and Alexander VI had recourse to Bayezid against the forces of our Charles VIII. Henry VIII raised England to rebellion against the Holy See. Charles V neglected to infeud the Milanese to the Duke of Orleans, as he had promised on his passage through France; while capable of destroying the Protestants, the same made use of them in order to wage war against us and called them his black bands. He diverted what Germany had contributed to the war against the Turk in order to ruin Francis I. His hatred of the king of England, because of his aunt, hardened Rome's stance against Henry VIII, and in that way, gave occasion to the schism which followed, and afterwards, joined with the latter in a league, and made him take arms against the kingdom of France. His lieutenant, Charles of Burbon, took Rome and instaured such a persecution against the ecclesiastics that *there was no man to be found, who would dare to walk in the street wearing the habit of friar or cleric.* Briefly, there was such a carnage in the Indies and the newly discovered lands as its match has never been seen. Philip II never wanted to allow the Pope. to interfere in the affair with Portugal, and hanged all the French soldiers, who had gone to the aid of Dom Antonio, and who knows by what means he coped with the return of Henry IV to the Church. He could learn about the latter's reconciliation with the Holy See from Cardinal d'Ossat, who in his letters, extremely well recorded all the artifices which were then practised against our monarchy. These examples, taken from the history of only ten or twelve princes, yet by their big number, may, I think, serve also as genuine evidence, to show that although Machiavelli's writings are banned, his doctrine is but practised by the very same who authorize the censorship and the prohibition.

After having spoken at length of the definition of the coups d'état, it is as much to the point to consider their possible classification. It seems that the first and most legitimate thing is to divide them into just and injust secrets of state, that is to say, into royal and tyrannical, and that one may ascribe Plautian's and Sejanus' deaths to the former while the deaths of Remus and Conradin to the latter category.

But beside this division, which I think should be considered the main division, one may go on separating those concerning the public good, from the others, which consider only the private interest of those who undertake them. Intent on practising the former, Hannibal ordered the Roman prisoner, who had fought and overcome an elephant in his presence, to be put to death, *saying that he is not fit to live who can be constrained to fight with beasts*, although it is more likely, as John of Salisbury has so judiciously remarked, that *he did not want a prisoner to be honoured with the glory of an unexpected triumph, and discredit the beasts which by their abilities had struck terror throughout the world*. And the Aelians, people of Greece, as they had invited the sculptor Phidias of Athens to come and make them a statue of the Olympian Jupiter, when they saw that the statue turned to be wonderfully done, thought that if they let Phidias return to Athens, where he had been recalled, he could make another, which might dim the glory of their statue, and so accused him of sacrilege and cut off his two hands, after which they dispatched him in such a state, *not ashamed of owing their Jove to sacrilege*, as Seneca says, and the poor Phidias *made such a Jove as the Aelians wanted to be his last work*. As for those of private individuals, they have been practised by all the legislators and new prophets, as we shall see later on.

Moreover, they may be divided into casual and fortuitous, such as when Columbus convinced some inhabitants of the New World that he would deprive them of the Moon (which was getting nearer an eclipse), if they were not willing to provide him with victuals in abundance, and on ther other hand, those which are undertaken after mature deliberation for the apparent good which one judges to be able to gain from them, as most of those we have mentioned here.

Likewise, there are simple ones, which end in a

single coup, such as Sejanus' death, and composite ones, which are either followed or preceded by certain others. Preceded: like St Bartholomew's Day, by the death of Lignerolles, the wedding of the king of Navarre, and the wounding of the Admiral. Followed: like the execution of the Marshal d'Ancre, by that of Travail, by that of his wife, the Marquise, and by the exile of the Queen Mother.

Furthermore, there are those carried out by the princes when the necessity and the conjuncture of events demand it, such as those we claim to deal with exclusively in this exposition, and others performed by their ministers, who quite often make use of the authority of their masters in order to conclude many affairs either for their private gain or for the public good, without for that matter, the prince being in the position to know the initial resorts or movements. Thus, we see that Postel's advancement under Francis I was a little coup d'état on the part of Chancellor Poyet, and that the bad report about the philosopher Bigot, submitted to the same king, had been drawn by Castellau, bishop of Mâcon, and in our times, Reboul's death, the imprisonment of the Abbot Du Bois, and the red hat of Monseigneur the Cardinal d'Ossat have all been attributed to Monsieur de Villeroy; no more and no less than that of Perron, to Monsieur de Sully, and the execution of Travail to Monsieur de Luynes. Yet, because it would be too long and perhaps tedious here to list all the possible divisions in this matter, and which are quite useless and superfluous, I shall be content with all those already mentioned and allow everyone the freedom to invent and introduce such other categories as one thinks fit.

Chapter III

With what precautions and on which occasions
should coups d'état be practised

I come now to what is most essential to this exposition, and because the good and wise physicians never prescribe violent and dangerous remedies without mentioning all the precautions needed for their legitimate use, I too must do the same on this occasion. I shall do it all the more willingly because these coups d'état are like double-edged swords that may be used and abused, like Telephus' spear, which may wound and heal, like the Diana of Ephesus, who had two faces, one sad and the other gay; in short, like the medals that are the inventions of heretics and show the face of a pope and of a devil under the same traits and contour, or like those pictures which represent death and life, depending on the angle from which one looks at them. In addition, this is peculiar to some Timon only, to errect gallows in order to cause people to hang themselves. As for myself, I defer too much to the nature and the rules of humanity, which it prescribes to us, to relate these stories in order to be practised the wrong way, *were I as lucky as my breast is clear, there is not yet any whom my mouth has hurt.*

Wishing to prescribe the rules which must be observed in order to use them with honour, justice, utility and propriety, I shall resort for that reason to those mentioned by Charron, and give as the first rule that they are meant for defence and not for attack, that they are meant to preserve and not to aggrandize oneself, to protect oneself from deceits, malicious acts and damaging enterprises or suprises and not to do them. The world is full of artifice and malice: *by frauds and tricks, kingdoms are subverted,* says Aristotle, and *do you want it to be forbidden to be saved by the same means?* adds Lipsius. For a purpose, it is permissible to play its counter-purpose, and when dealing with the fox, to counterfeit the fox. The law pardons the offences which force compels us to commit: *it is the characteristic of all beings to defend themselves and their lives as well*, says Sallust, and relatedly, Cicero: *it is against nature to disregard the common good*, and even for that it is necessary to hedge now and then, to adjust to the times and the persons, to mix venom with honey, to apply cauteries where corrosives don't work, the iron where the cautery has no effect, and quite often the fire where the iron is missing.

The second rule, whether out of necessity or for the obvious and important public utility of the state or of the prince, which he has to seek, it is a necessary and unavoidable obligation, because it is always his duty to secure the public good: *he is always doing his duty, whoever sees to the utility of men and society*, as Cicero says. This law, so common and which should have been the main rule of all princes' actions, *the salvation of the people is the supreme law*, absolves them of many small conditions and formalities, to which they are obliged by justice. Likewise, they have the command of the extension or reduction of laws, of confirming or abolishing them, not following only what seems good to them but acting in keeping with what reason and public good allow: the prince's honour, the love of the homeland, the safety of the people more than balance the small errors and injustices. Moreover, we shall apply the prophet's saying as long as it may be done without profaning anything: *it is expedient if one man should die for the people, in order that the whole nation does not perish.*

The third rule is that in all these matters one should advance by small steps rather than gallopping, because *no delay is too long whenever it is a matter of a man's death*, and that it be not turned into a trade and commerce for fear that the too frequent use leads to injustice. Experience teaches us that what is awe-inspiring and extraordinary does not become apparent every day, the comets only appear from century to century, the monsters, the floods, the conflagrations of Vesuvius, the earthquakes happen only very rarely, and the rarity lends lustre and colour to many things, which they lose suddenly, if too often used, *vile seems to us whatever we saw the previous year, and the contempt increases with its contemplation.* I add that if the prince keeps himself within the bounds of these practices he could not be easily blamed, nor would he pass for a perfidious or barbarian tyrant, as these qualities should not in fact be attributed but to those who have turned them into a habit, and those habits depend on a large number of often repeated actions, *habit is a many-time repeated act,* as much as a line is a sequence of dots, a surface a multiplication of lines, induction, an accumulation of proofs, and the syllogism, a tracery of various propositions.

The fourth rule is always to choose the most gentle and easiest means, and that attention should be paid to the precept addressed by Claudian to Emperor Honorius: *will you be content with the punishment of Mettius? Excessive severity is a sad thing.* Only a tyrant would say: *let him feel that he is dying,* and only the devils can take pleasure in the torments of men; in those actions, the horses of the Olympic races should not be imitated, because once led in the open arena, they could not be restrained. One should proceed as a judge and not as one of the parties, as a physician and not as an executioner; as a reserved, prudent, wise and discreet man and not as a madman, vindictive and abandoned to extraordinary and violent passions: this fine virtue of clemency, *which teaches to consider foul and cruel to revel in the pain and blood of man,* is always more highly regarded than ruthlessness and severity. Hercules' mace was given to him, the poets say, in order to defeat the giants, punish the tyrants and do away with the monsters, and yet, it was made out of the fork of an olive, a symbol of peace and tranquillity. Quite often, a dying big tree may recover after some of its branches are cut off, and as often, a simple bleeding done at the right time breaks the course of great maladies. In short, one should emulate the good surgeons who always start with the operations that are the easiest to bear, while the Jews used to give certain beverages to those sentenced to death, in order to blot out the feelings and the pain of torture. One head only, that of Sejanus, should have satisfied Tiberius; Hannibal could have rendered all his prisoners harmless without killing them; the sack of Rome would have been less odious had the temples and their ministrants been treated with consideration, and the Marquis d'Ancre would not have been less rightly punished, had he not been dragged along and torn to pieces, *I would call cruel,* Seneca says, *those who have reasons to punish but do not have the method.*

The fifth rule is to justify those actions and diminish the blame which they usually bring whenever the princes find themselves reduced to and in need of practising them, and do not do them but with regrets and sighing, as a father who lets a member of his child to be cauterized or cut off in order to save its life, or lets a tooth to be pulled out to give it rest. That is what the poet Claudian does not forget in his description of a good prince: *the prince be slow to punish, prompt with the rewards, and grieve when forced to be severe.* Therefore, those executions should be delayed or at least should not be hastened, be chewed over and ruminated often, all the possible means be considered which could alter and avoid their being carried out, or else, to soften them and make them easier. In one word, to decide only with as much difficulty as a man, caught by a storm at sea, has to surrender all his possessions to the fury of the elements, or as a sick man, when faced with the decision to have his leg cut off.

Likewise, it is not my intention here to put an end to the number of those precautions by mentioning one which may be thought to be the last of those that might be taken: let it be added to his writings by whomever wishes to do so, I on my part shall never add it to mine, not thinking it reasonable to prescribe ends and limits to clemency and humaneness. Let it widen its boundaries as far as it wishes, they will always seem to me but too short and narrow. Whenever one is not afraid that one's horse would stumble, one gives it free rein most certainly; whenever the wind is good, one may unfurl all the sails; the virtues should be limited but by the vices that are contrary to them, and as long as they distance themselves so far as one is not likely to give in to them, one has nothing else to do but to restrain them. It is true that their course is not so obvious with regard to the subject matter now under consideration here, as in many other cases, but it also happens that a prince, who cannot be entirely good, may be half good, and one, who by a superior reason cannot be entirely just, need not be in the least cruel, unjust and wicked. But while we have got these five rules and precautions, I find them sufficient to give those with a little wit and inclination to do good some idea of what is reasonable, and although I did not make them specific, the discretion and the judgement of wise men make it impossible to ignore them, given that *prudence shows man what to do and what not to do*. Moreover, it is my intention that of all stories which I have related above and which I shall recount further on, only those which comply with these five rules, or those of prudence in general, pass for legitimate and conform to what is appropriate and rational.

But all the above maxims and precautions serve only to render us better informed about and better disposed to the implementation of these coups d'état. Now we need to see in which circumstances and on what occasions one may practise them. Without revealing anything, Charron suggests four or five in his book ON WISDOM, but only fleetingly, and doing as the Scythians, who shoot their best arrows when they appear to flee at their fastest. I shall develop them by giving reasons and examples, and by adding many others which will serve as titles under which one may list those to be later · encountered in the works of various authors and historians.

Among the occasions, there is no doubt that the first [he mentions] are to be set in motion, although in my opinion they are the most unjust, namely those which one comes across during the establishment and the new erection or change of kingdoms and principalities. And to talk first of the erection, when we consider the beginnings of all the monarchies, we always find that they started by means of some of these inventions and deceptions, making religion and miracles head a long series of barbarities and cruelties. It was Livy who first remarked: *one must concede to antiquity that by combining human things with the divine, the beginnings of cities were rendered more august.* As we shall show further on, this is very true, but for the time being, we must stick to generalities, and begin our demonstration with the foundation of the first four and greatest monarchies in the world. That the much celebrated Queen Semiramis, who founded the Empire of the Assyrians, was so assiduous to persuade her subjects that having been exposed in her babyhood, the birds took care to feed her, bringing her beakfuls as they did by their chicks; and moreover, wishing to confirm that fable by the last acts of her life, she ordered that after her death, the rumour was to be spread that she had been changed into a dove and had flown off together with a great number of birds which had come to her very chamber to fetch her. Furthermore, she decided to feign and change her sex, and from the woman that she was, she wanted to become a man, acting the part of her son Ninus and counterfeiting him in every action; and in order to be more successful in that enterprise, she decided to intro- duce a new kind of dress for her people, which greatly helped to cover and hide what set women most easily apart from the rest: *her garment covered arms and legs and a tiara covered her head, and in order not to seem to hide anything under this new dress, she ordered that all her people dress alike, which fashion has persisted ever since among that people,* and by that means, *she was thought to be a boy when she first dissembled her sex.* Cyrus, who founded the monarchy of the Persians, also wanted to make it legitimate by the means of the vine which his grandfather Astyages had seen born *na- turally by his daughter, and whose tendrils over- shadowed all Asia,* and by the dream he himself had when he took up arms, and by choosing a slave for companion in all his enterprises; but he put to an even better use the idea that a bitch had fed and suckled him in the forest where he had been exposed by Harpagus, until a shepherd took him to his wife and fed him carefully in his house. As their designs were more refined, Alexander and Romulus thought it necessary to practise a greater number of more efficacious stratagems. Although, like the predecessors, they had started with that about their origin, they brought them, nonetheless, to the highest possible elevation, whence Sidonius had the opportunity to say: *the great Alexander, and no less the Roman, had been conceived by gods in serpent's shape.* Because, as far as he was concerned, Alexander made people believe that taking the shape of a serpent, Jupiter had been in the habit to call on and delight in his mother Olympias, and when he saw the light of day, the goddess Diana attended so closely Olympias' delivery that she failed to secure the temple she had at Ephesus, which in the interval, was entirely consumed by a fortuitous blaze. Moreover, in order to strengthen even more the idea of his divinity in his subjects' belief, he gave instructions that the priests of Jupiter Ammon in Egypt should *greet him as the son of Ammon whenever he entered the temple, and in order to play his part even better, he would ask them whether he had revenged himself on all his father's murderers, and they would answer that his father could not be murdered nor could he die.* Alexander even took such steps in that direction by ordering Parmenio to demolish all the temples and abolish all the honours which the peoples of the Orient paid to Jason, so that *no other name in the Orient be more venerable than that of Alexander.* We may add to it that after certain prisoners shared with him their knowledge of the remedy against the poisoned arrows of the Indians, he thought it better to spread the belief that God had revealed that cure to him in a dream, when he made it public. But if this insatiable greed led to his being worshipped, he finally recognized, following Callisthenes' remonstrances, the obstinacy shown by the Lacedaemonians and the wounds he received every day in combat, that all his forces would never be sufficient to establish that new apotheosis and that a far greater fortune was needed in order to gain a little spot in heaven than that needed to master down here, and dominate the whole earth. To these stories one may add that of the death of his father Philip, to which he consented together with his mother Olympias, and also of Cleitus, whom he killed with his own hands, because the latter had gained too much authority over the soldiers. One discovers that Alexander had practised secretly what afterwards Caesar did quite openly: *it is in order to rule that the law is violated.*

As for Romulus, he gave himself credibility by means of stories about the god Mars and his familiarities with his mother Rhea; of the she-wolf who had suckled him; by the deceit with the vultures, the death of his brother, the sanctuary which he had set up at Rome, the abduction of the Sabine women, the murder of Tatius, that he left unpunished, and finally by hiw own death, as he drowned in the marshes, in order to make people believe that his body had been carried off to heaven, because it could not be found on the ground. When one adds to these coups d'état of Romulus, those of Numa Pompilius, his successor, and practised with the help of his nymph Egeria, and the supersitions which he introduced during his reign, it would be easy afterwards to judge *by what fortune this famous Rome mastered the world and raised her aspiration to the heights of Olympus.* It is also to the point to remark that as this monarchical domination could not be established without many ruses and deceptions, no fewer were needed to destroy it, as the Tarquins were chased out of Rome because of the rape of Lucrece, and the state was changed from a republic into a kingdom. Thus, we may start with the simulated madness of Junius Brutus, his feigned fall, his elder staff presented to the oracle, and go on with the execution of his two sons, which he carried out because they were friends of the Tarquins' and because they were accused of wishing to bring them back into the city, and also because the education which they had received during the monarchical state had been contrary to that which he wanted to introduce. And in order to crown all those actions by some great coup d'état and by a genuine secret of imperium, he chased Tarquinius Colatinus out of Rome, although he was Lucrece's husband, had been his colleague during the consulate, and had contributed to the ruin of the Tarquins to no lesser extent. Although he used as pretext that the name of the Tarquins was so hateful to the Romans that they could not stand it even in the case of their friends, his main aim was not to leave behind any trace of those he had pushed to the last extremity; moreover, he did not want to share the glory of that action with a person whose merits he himself had avowed and made publicly known: *we remember, we admit, that you have evicted the kings, you did your service and ousted the very name of royalty.* Were we to examine all the other monarchies and all the states that are inferior to these four, we could fill a thick tome with similar stories. That is why it would suffice as the last illustration of our maxim to examine Muhammad's practice at the time of the foundation of his religion, as much as of the empire which nowadays is the most powerful in the world. Indeed, as all the great minds had always had the ingenuity to turn to their advantage the widest reported ignominies that had happened to them, he, too, apparently wanted to do the same; so seeing that he was very likely to fall from an epileptic fit, he decided to make his friends believe that the most violent paroxysms of his epilepsy were as many ecstasies and signs of God's spirit descending upon him; he also persuaded them that a white dove which would come and peck grains of corn from his ear was angel Gabriel coming to tell him on behalf of the same god what he had to do. Besides, he made use of monk Sergius to compile an Alcoran, which he feigned to have been dictated to him by the very mouth of God. Finally, he rallied a famous astrologer to prepare the peoples by his predictions about the state change which was to come and of the new law which a great prophet would establish, in order to make them accept his more willingly, when ready to be made public. But one time, noticing that his secretary Abdala Ben-Salon, at whom he had wrongly taken umbradge, started to uncover and make public such impostures, he cut his throat in his house one evening and set fire to each of the four corners of the house, with the intention to convince the people the following morning that it had been the fire coming from heaven to punish the said secretary who had tried hard to alter and corrupt some passages in the Alcoran. Nevertheless, it was not that finesse which capped all the others, as another was needed to complete the mystery: he persuaded his most faithful servant to descend to the bottom of a well situated next to a high road in order to shout from it when he passed by accompanied by a large crowd that usually followed him: *Muhammad is God's beloved, Muhammad is God's beloved,* and as it happened in the way he had wanted, he suddenly thanked the divine magnanimity for such a distinctive token, and entreated all those that were following him to fill the well without delay and erect on top of it a little mosque to mark that miracle. And by that contrivance, the poor servant was forthwith knocked senseless and buried under a hail of stones which deprived him of the means of ever revealing the falsity of the miracle: *but the earth caught the sound, and indeed the babbling reeds.*

A second opportunity that may be had to practise these covered coups is the conservation, or restoration and re-establishment of states and principalities, when by some misfortune or simply by the length of time that undermines and wears out everything, they start to lean towards ruin and threaten an imminent ruin, unless order is soon restored, and that more so as all things lose their own conservation, and are obliged as much as possible to preserve the principles of their being, if not of their well-being. I am convinced also that it is allowed, nay, necessary that whatever served to establish them serves to maintain them as well. Besides, if Ovid's opinion is true: *it is no lesser virtue to preserve than to gain, the latter is the work of chance, and of art in the other case,* one must reasonably conclude that these coups d'état are more necessary for the conservation and the administration of monarchies than for their foundation; at least, they will be more just, because before a state is formed and erected, the need to do so is missing; rather, most often it is a stroke of luck or the effect of the power and ambition of some private person. But when it is already established and civilized, one is under the obligation to maintain it. Now, as it would not be right to resemble those vagabonds and crackpots, *who take pleasure in living with strangers, finding it troublesome to live on their own*, and so after having taken so many proofs and examples from foreign histories, it would not be inappropriate, I think, to leaf through ours a little, because it may provide us with some as remarkable as those of the Greeks and the Romans. And truth to say, when I consider what Clovis, our first Christian king, did, I must admit that I have not yet seen anything like it in the whole Antiquity. As Gaul was divided into four different nations at the time he came to the crown, the Visigoths possessed Gascony, the Burgundian was master of Lyonnais, the Romans ruled Soissons and all its appurtenances, and the French, who at the time were almost all heathen, governed the rest, he was seized by the desire to gather together and reunite those four separate pieces under his imperium, as Aesculapius had done with Hippolytus' limbs. To that end, and considering that the pagan religion had began insensibly to grow old and shrunken, he took the decision to become a Christian, after he had won the battle against a German prince at Tolbiac. In that way, he reconciled himself with, and won the good will not only of his wife, Queen Clotilda, but also of many prelates and all the common people of France. On that, I must remark in passing that it would still seem to me more fitting to attribute the initial motives of such a remarkable change to some saintly inspiration, granted to King Clovis by the prayers of the good Queen Clotilda, and interpret all the doubtful things charitably. Nevertheless, I must here range myself with the politicians, who alone enjoy the privilege of interpreting them negatively, or at least of noticing some ruse and stratagem among them, in order always to remain on the side of the most perceptive and to sharpen the wits of those whom they instruct by the narration of these remarkable actions, sensible to, and discerning of the truth, but which more often than not are based on unsubstantial conjectures and on impressions which do not affect, and can in no way prejudice the truth of history. Thus, as we go on to talk of this conversion of Clovis in keeping with Pasquier's impressions, as well as

those of other politicians, we shall say that the crown
descended from the skies, the miracles of the coronation,
the oriflamme, of which Paolo Emilio doesn't say a word,
were little coups d'état, intended to sanction the change
of religion, of which he wanted to make use of as of a
powerful machine, in order to ruin all the small princes,
his neighbours. And as a matter of fact, he started with
the Roman, against whom the common hatred of the
foreign nations rallied, then the Visigoth and the
Burgundian, under the pretext that they were Arians, and
afterwards set upon the princes Ragnacarius, Chararic,
Sigibert and his son, descendants of Clodio, who were
still occupying some little strips of France, and had all of
them fraudulently assassinated, without any other pretext
than to avoid the resentment which they might have felt
one day, because of the wrong done to them by his
grandfather Merovech. And after this, I let it be judged,
as I have already done above, what reason might have
had Monsieur Savaron to compile a book by which to
prove and establish Clovis' sanctity. I for one think that
the best proof which he could have given us was to make
him say as a certain poet did make Scipio say: *if by
slaughter one may ascend into heaven, to me alone its
largest gate would open.* Nevertheless, as men's wisdom
is pure folly before God, it happened that his successors
allowed themselves to be led by their mayors of the
palace as buffaloes by the nose, and the kingdom, after
changing various hands, ultimately fell to Pepin,
offspring of Clodio's family, as it is very well explained
by Pasquier. And so, to tell the truth, Clovis expanded
and united the kingdom of France, but nonetheless, he
could not for long preserve it for his house, nor for its
descendants. Being in that way united by Clovis, and
shortly after, much enlarged by Charlemagne, France
maintained herself in quite a flourishing state a long time,
until the English got out of their nest, brought the war
and waged it so obstinately that they almost became her
masters. Under Charles VII, it was necessary to resort to
some coup d'état in order to chase them out of the
country: thus, resort was made to that of the Maid of
Orleans, which was admitted as such by Justus Lipsius

in his POLITICS and by some other foreign historians, but in particular by two of ours, that is, du Bellay Langey in his MILITARY ART and du Haillan in his HISTORY, not to name many other writers of lesser importance. Now, as this coup d'état was as successful as everybody knows and the Maid was burnt but in effigy, our affairs started to worsen a little later, both because of the previous wars and those which followed, and France became like those cachectic and unhealthy bodies whose breathing is laboured and are kept alive only on the strength of remedies: as she has since maintained herself by means of stratagems practised by Louis XI, Francis I, Charles IX and also by those who succeeded them and of whom at present I shall say nothing, because all our history books are full of them. What is needed further is to mention those coups d'état which seem most remarkable to me.

The third reason that may legitimize these coups d'état is when they are meant to weaken or abolish certain rights, privileges, franchises and exemptions, enjoyed by certain subjects to the detriment and the reduction of the prince's authority, as when Charles V, wishing to ruin the right to election and secure the Empire for his family, made use of Luther's sermons and allowed him the time to establish his doctrine, and while his preaching was getting a foothold in Germany, the Electors would be stealthily divided, as a result. Thus Charles V got the means to ruin them more easily when he wanted to set upon them. That is what Monsieur Duke of Nevers has so well remarked in a discourse, that he had printed in 1590, about the conditions of the affairs of state and dedicated to Pope Sixtus V, and nothing is left to me but to reproduce here the very words he used: *the pretext of religion*, he says, *is not a new thing and many great princes have made use of it in their belief of attaining their goals by it. I wish to mention the war waged by Charles V against the Protestant princes of Luther's sect, because he would have never undertaken it, had he not the intention to make the imperial crown hereditary in favour of the House of Austria. For a start, he attacked the Electors of the Empire in order to ruin them and abolish the election, otherwise he would not have postponed from 1519, the year of his election as emperor, to 1549 the decision to take up arms and extinguish the heresy, which Luther had began to set alight in Germany since 1526, as it would have been very easy to do, and not wait for it to set ablaze the largest region of Europe, had the zeal for the honour of God and the desire to support the saintly catholic religion dominated his mind. More likely, he reckoned that such a novelty might bring him advantages rather than losses both as regards the Pope and the princes of Germany, because of the division engendered by this heresy among them, particularly between the secular princes and the others, and also among the simple lay people, which he let grow until it had the effect which he had planned, and then incited Pope Paul III to make war on the Protestants, under the pretext of religion but with the intention to exterminate them and make the Empire hereditary in favour of his House.* That was also remarked by Francis I in his APOLOGY of the year 1537: *the Emperor, under the colour of the armed religion of the league of the Catholics, wants to oppress the other and gain ground for the monarchy.* That was, truth to tell, a great ruse pondered over a long time with much discernment and prudence. But Philip II practised another, the effect of which was much more prompt and assured, although a thing of lesser consequence, since its only aim was to abolish the privileges formerly bestowed on the Kingdom of Aragon, and which had been so advantageous in fact and so courageously defended by that people that the kings of Spain could not boast absolute authority over them. Thus, seeing that a fine occasion to ruin them was on hand, as his state secretary and their compatriot Antonio Perez had retired to Aragon to secure his livelihood under the privileges granted to that kingdom, after he had broken free from the prison of Castile, the king thought it a fine pretext to pull such a thorn from his foot. That is why, as he surreptitiously worked the Jesuits to incite the people to take up arms in order to defend the privileges and the liberties of their land, he, on his side, gathered a big army and feigned that he

wanted to combat that of the Aragonese. At that moment
the Jesuits began to play their game and chant their
palinode, showing again to the people that truly the king
had reason on his side, that his forces were too strong
and theirs too weak to run the risk of some encounter
after which there would be no pardon. Briefly, they did it
so well that fear and bewilderment gripped the hearts of
the Aragonese, their army dispersed, each one confound-
ed, ran away and hid himself, while the army of the king
of Spain paid no heed, entered Saragossa, erected a
citadel there, demolished the main houses, put some to
death and banished the others, and left out nothing that
could ruin and crush that province completely; and nowadays, it is more subdued and submissive to the king of
Spain than any other province.

On the other hand, when some significant law has
to be enacted, or some important regulation or ruling, it
is good to use the same means and to resort to these
maxims; even if it were not so, we have got so many
examples from the practice of the Romans and other
peoples considered among the wisest, that it would be
unseemly to doubt it. Is there anything more cruel than
to decimate a whole legion for the flight or the cowardice
of a few individual soldiers? Yet, that law was enacted
and closely complied to by the Romans, in order to bind
all the soldiers to their duty by the terror of the
executions. And the same Romans wanted to prevent the
household slaves' attempts on the lives of their masters,
and so, ordered that whenever such an offence was committed in some household, all the slaves who were found
in that place had their throats cut at the funeral of their
master; and that law was so religiously observed that
when Pedarius, the prefect of the town, was murdered by
one of his slaves, the number of those executed was four
hundred, despite the intercessions on their behalf made
by the whole people of Rome, and even despite the
opinions of some senators, which Cassius opposed openly
and with so many reasons that the contrary opinion,
although considered utterly inhuman, was enforced, as
reported by Tacitus. It is also Cicero's precept that
gentleness and clemency are to be proffered, qualified by

some severity for the sake of the public good, without which a state cannot be administered. In order to secure the life of their prince, the Persians had formerly enacted the law that whoever attempted his life was to be punished not only himself but also all his relatives, who were put to death by the same torture, as mentioned particularly in the case of Bessus. And Ferdinand Pinto claims to have been in a realm where he saw the same custom being put in practice against more than fifty or sixty people, all of whom were the relatives of a young page, who at the age of ten or twelve had been bold enough to kill his king. The great Tamerlane, when he learnt that a soldier from his army had drunk a pint of milk without paying for it, had him disembowelled in the presence of all his companions, in order to keep them obedient to his commands by that extraordinary example. The crimes of counterfeit money and of heresy were no more serious a hundred years ago than they are now, yet in those times, the counterfeiters were boiled alive in oil and the heretics burnt at the stake, with no other purpose than to impress the terror of those tortures on the minds of those for whom the simple protection by their prince was not enough to bind them to their duty, *and so provision should be made for the salvation of the multitude, rather than for the appetite of each in part.*

Another occasion to remain strict in the implementation of these maxims is when it becomes necessary to ruin some power, which because it is too great, numerous or extended over many different places, cannot be brought down by ordinary means, *as it is defended by numerous troops as well as by phalanges.* Although it was always greatly desirable to overcome it as easily as the kings of Spain did with the Moors and the Marranos, up to more than two hundred and forty thousand families, whom they chased from their kingdom twice, and that by virtue of a simple edict and command, yet, because not all the affairs are similar in their circumstances, nor are maladies always accompanied by the same symptoms or accidents, it is often necessary to change the remedies, and at times to practice some which are more violent than others: *ulcers that have sipped into the marrow are not healed by a soft hand, but with iron and fire, the flames penetrate to the quick, burst and empty the vein of tainted blood, drying up the fountainhead of the illness.* The pillage which Mithridates inflicted in a single day upon forty thousand Roman citizens scattered in various parts of Asia was one of the coups d'état of which I claim to speak. Like the Sicilian Vespers, authorized by Peter, king of Aragon, and subtly hatched by Prochytes, great seigneur of the land, who disguised as a Cordelier hatched up the plot so well, that on the day of Easter or Pentecost in 1282, at the first stroke of the bell for the vespers, the Sicilians massacred all the French to be found on their island, sparing neither women nor little children. Something similar happened less than twenty years ago, on the Isle of Magna, when the inhabitants of the city of Corme delivered themselves in one night from an army of thirty thousand men that had been sent by Arcomat, lieutenant of the king of Persia. But as in the history of France we have got the example of the Massacre of St Bartholomew's Day, which is one of the most remarkable that may be found anywhere, we must tarry and consider it under all its main circumstances. Thus it was undertaken by Queen Catherine de Medicis, offended by Captain Charry's death; by Monsieur de Guise, who wanted to avenge his father's assassination by Poltrot at the request of the Admiral and the Protestants, and by King Charles and the Duke of Anjou, the former wishing to revenge himself on the Protestants for having made him withdraw from Meaux to Paris sooner than he would have wanted, and both of them, thinking to ruin the Huguenots who had been the cause of all the troubles and massacres which occurred in the kingdom in an interval of thirty to forty years. The affair was in the works a long time and planned with such a determination to keep it secret, as Lignerolles, a gentleman of the Duke of Anjou, as soon as he gave the king, though indirectly, the impression that he knew something, was dispatched in a duel, secretly provoked by the king himself. The place chosen to attract all the wealthiest and most influential among the Huguenots was Paris. The occasion, decided on, was the wedding of the king of Navarre, who was of that religion, and of Queen Margaret. The wound inflicted on the Admiral by the Duke of Guise, his old enemy, marked the beginning of the tragedy: the means of execution, the arrival of twelve hundred harquebusiers and of the Swiss companies into Paris, had even been approved by the Admiral, in his belief that they were there to defend him against the house of Lorraine; in short, everything was so well prepared, that if it failed in anything, it was in execution. For were it to have been carried out rigorously, one must admit that it would have been the boldest coup d'état, and the most shrewdly carried out that has ever been practised in France or elsewhere. That, of course, is my opinion, although the Day of St Bartholomew is at this hour condemned by Protestants and Catholics alike, and Monsieur de Thou has conveyed to us the opinion which he shared with his father by these verses of Statius: *time has wiped out that day and the coming centuries may not believe that it happened while we keep silent and cover our people's crimes by burying them in the depths of the night.* I am not afraid, though, to say that it was a very just action and very remarkable, the cause of which was more than legitimate, although the effects were quite risky and extraordinary. It seems to me that it was great cowardice on the part of so many French historians to have foresaken the cause of King Charles IX and not to have shown the right reason which he had to break up with the Admiral and his accomplices: the latter had been tried several years before, which ended in that famous ruling that was translated into eight languages, made known to and served on all his troops, if one may say so; a second ruling, explaining the first, was given, and all the Protestants had so often been declared criminals of lese-majesty that there had been much reason to praise that action as the only remedy against the wars which have been fought since, and may continue till the end of our monarchy if one fails to heed Cardan's axiom which says: *don't attempt anything unless you intend to carry it through.* One should have emulated the expert surgeon, who as long as the vein is open, draws blood until he causes complete loss of consciousness, so as to clean the cachectic bodies of their bad humours. To start well does not mean anything unless one stays the course: the price is at the bottom of the bill, and the end always adjusts the beginning. Although one may object to my stance by saying that there are three circumstances of that action, which rendered it extremely odious to posterity: the first, that the procedure was not legitimate; the second, that the bloodshed was too great, and the third, that many innocent people were hedged in with the guilty. But to satisfy, I shall answer to the first objection that on that matter one should listen to our theologians when they treat of *the faith which is kept with the heretics*, and yet, I would say off my bat that the Huguenots have broken faith many times, and as they tried hard to take King Charles by surprise at Meaux and in other places, one could pay them in the same coin; and then, don't we read in Plato that those who command, that is, the sovereigns may at time deceive and lie when a noteworthy good for their subjects is expected from it? Well, could there happen anything better to France than the total ruin of the Protestants? By their little judgement they pulled our leg in such a way as almost to make us fail to see through it, as the Admiral who had come to shut himself and the flower of his party in the biggest and most hostile city which he ever had come across, without distrusting the Queen Mother, whose servant Charry he had killed, the Lorraine scions, whose father had been assassinated on his orders, and the King, whom he had made return at great speed from Meaux to Paris. Didn't he know that his religion was so hateful even to the most gentle and tractable that it could be abominated and detested in his person and in that of so many cut-throats who ordinarily accompanied him? Besides, the rumour which was spread at the same time that they had set about treating us as they were treated forthwith, the moment their plot was uncovered, could that rumour not be true? Many hold it for certain, and I, for one, think that each and every one, save the politicians, may regard it as consistent. As for the bloodshed, of which it is said to have been enormous, it was not equal to those of

Coutras, Saint-Denis, Moncontour, nor to so many other slaughters of which they had been the cause. And whoever would read in the histories that the inhabitants of Caesarea killed twenty-five thousand Jews in one day; that a million two hundred and forty thousand died in Judea in seven years' time, that in Pliny, Caesar boasted to have sent to their death a million one hundred and ninety-two thousand people during his foreign wars, and Pompey even more; that Quintus Fabius dispatched to the other world one hundred thousand Gauls from the colonies; Gaius Marius, two thousand Cimbrians; Charles Martel, three hundred thousand Teutons; two thousand Roman knights and three hundred senators were sacrificed to the passions of the Triumvirate; four whole legions to that of Sulla; forty thousand Romans, to that of Mithridates; Sempronius Gracchus ruined three hundred cities in Spain, and the Spaniards all those of the New World, with more than seven or eight million inhabitants. Whoever will consider all these bloody tragedies, a large number of which have been recorded in the treatise ON CONSTANCY by Justus Lipsius, will have reason enough to be astonished by so much barbarity and also to believe that the massacre on St Bartholomew's Day was not among the biggest, though it was one of the most just and necessary. As for the third difficulty, it seems to be quite considerable, given that many Catholics were caught in the same storm and served as quarry in their enemy's race for revenge. Yet Crassus' maxim in Tacitus suffices as a short answer: *every great example has something unjust about it that is made up for, as regards private individuals, by the public utility which it provides.* Whence that action, so legitimate and reasonable, was and still is so much decried and criticized; I for one attribute the first cause to the fact that it was done by halves, that the surviving Huguenots were reluctant to approve of it, and many Catholics, who see clearly that it did not serve its purpose, cannot help saying that one could have done without it because there had been no wish to carry it through, or contrariwise, had all the heretics been dispossessed, none would have been left in France, at least, to blame it, and the Catholics would have had no reason to do it either, seeing the great tranquillity and well-being that would have been brought to them. The second reason, to follow the poet's saying, is: *the mind is less irritated by what is whispered in one's ear than by what the steadfast eye sees.* Furthermore, we see that this execution is not talked about in bad terms in Italy and other foreign kingdoms as it is in France, where it took place in the middle of Paris and in the presence of a million people, and likewise, it was not the Poles who received the story and the particular narrative from the most seditious and resentul ministers while the Bishop of Valence was trying hard to keep an eye on their votes for the election of Henry III, and they did not make it too hard for him, because they knew that a prince's character should not be judged only on the basis of some violent and extraordinary action forced upon him by very strong and fair reasons of state. Besides, that action is not yet so remote in our memory, while most of our histories have since been written by Huguenots, and finally, we have also got the ample and special description in the MEMOIRS of Charles IX, Beza's HISTORY, the MARTYROLOGIES, and many other books compiled by design by the Protestants to condemn that action, while nothing in them has been forgotten that might render it odious and blameworthy, and induce those who hear the deposition of those corrupted witnesses to share their opinion, although all those who strip it of those small incidents and want to judge it without passion get a contrary impression. In rest, nobody can deny that on St Bartholomew's Day so many factionists and commanding persons died that ever since the Huguenots have not been able to put together armies on their own and that the coup has not put an end to all the cabals and plotting going on both inside the kingdom and outside, and finally, that it was no little thing that the Catholics' quarrels, squabbles and seditions were of no profit to them, in spite of their greatest efforts. It is also true, as some politicians have remarked, that the same Day was the cause of an evil which could never be in doubt, since all the cities that did the St Bartholomew and killed the Huguenots to obey the king and seek the means of restoring peace within the realm, were the first to start the League, because they feared, and not without reason, that the king of Navarre, who was a Huguenot, on ascending to the crown, might be intent on reprisals. Thus, one may say that by not having been carried out as it ought to have been, the St Bartholomew's Day did not abate the war, as intended, but stirred another, even more dangerous.

Moreover, when it is a matter of authorizing a man and the affair in which he is involved to give credit to some prince, to win over someone or lead and coax him to some important decision, I think that it is easier to come to the desired result by combining those acts with stratagems and ruses of state. Thus, we see that all the ancient legislators, intent on authorizing, strengthening and placing the laws which they gave to their peoples on solid bases, had no better way of doing it than making publicly known and and persuading the people with all the assiduousness of which they were capable that they had received those laws from some deity: Zoroaster from Oromasis, the Trismegistos from Mercury, Zamolxis from Vesta, Charondas from Saturn, Minos from Jupiter, Lycurgus from Apollo, Draco and Solon from Minerva, Numa from the nymph Egeria, Muhammad from angel Gabriel, and Moses, the wisest of them all, describes for us in the EXODUS, how he received his law directly from God. Despite the fact that the reign of the Jews has been entirely ruined and abolished, *the Mosaic religion has remained as a supersition among the Hebrews and the Muhammadans,* says Campanella, *and in a most limpid reformulation among the Christians.* It may have given to Cardan the idea, I believe, to advise those princes, who without the advantage of birth, or short of money, supporters, military forces and soldiers, cannot rule their states with splendour and authority, to rely on religion as in the old days David, Numa and Vespasian did so felicitously. Philip II, king of Spain and one of the wisest princes of his time, resorted to a very fine ruse in order to earn early authority for his son among the peoples which one day he would command. To that end, he gave an order highly detrimental to his subjects, spreading the rumour that he wanted to make it public and confirm it any day, at which the people began to murmur and complain. Nonetheless, he persisted in his resolve, which was followed by redoubled complaints from his people. Finally, the rumour reached the child's ears and he promised to help the people and prevent by all possible means the publication of the edict, and in that sense, threatened those anxious to implement it, overlooking nothing of what might have revealed his keenness to deliver the people from that oppression in such a way, as King Philip came to rescind his game and stopped talking about the edict. Whence each and every one imagined that the young prince's opposition was the only cause for its suppression. By that device, his father enabled him to win an empire in the hearts and the affection of the Spaniards more certain than what he, the king, commanded in the Spanish lands, because *love is by far more persuasive than fear to obtain what one desires*, says Pliny the Younger. Briefly, when we take a closer look at the means used to convert Henry IV to the Catholic religion and confirm him in it, we discover that it was an action carried out with much spirit and industry. Although we ought to consider it genuine and certain, as indeed he evinced for the rest of his life, nevertheless, nobody is allowed to think of it otherwise. But if we want to take the liberty to examine it in the light of politics, we may easily notice three things, namely that the motives of his conversion were none other than the obstinate resistance of Monsieur du Maine, who on this occasion is described in Tavannes' MEMOIRS as *the only author, after God, of the conversion of Henry IV*, while the truth is that he was thinking only of himself while he was negotiating very advantageous terms at a time when His Majesty was not yet converted. But whether God fortified his zeal or whether mundane hopes spellbound ᵕhim, he neglected himself, or as the Italians say, he went broke, and did nothing for himself but did a lot for France. Among the motives of this conversion, one counts the advice given to the king by Monsieur Sully, one of the main and most sensible Huguenots in his army, *that France's crown was worth the pain of attending a Mass*. As far as the circumstances of the conversion are concerned, two most remarkable things happened: the first, that the king was instructed and catechized not by some bigoted or supersitious theologian who might have presented the entrance to our churches as similar to the porches and vestibules of which the Poet has said: *Centaurs stabled in the market place as Scyllas of double form*, but by René Benoit, doctor of theology and curate of the St Eustace parish, who if one believes the common rumour and recalls what happened when he was at death's door, was neither too zealous a Catholic nor an obstinate Huguenot. Whence by skilfully handling the king's conscience as he had that of his parishioners for twenty-five or thirty years, he only made him understand the main mysteries, without exaggerating many of the lesser ceremonies and traditions, and conducted the conversion rather as a sensible man and a politician than as a scrupulous and supersititous theologian. The second remarkable thing was the story of the possessed Marthe Brossier, which truth to say, was only a hoax, staged by some zealous Catholics and supported by a good cardinal, so that the devil, of which she was allegedly possessed, was exorcised through the inherent power of the Holy Sacrament, in order to give the king the opportunity to believe in the real presence in the Eucharist, of which presence, or rather transubstantiation, he was thought not to be entirely convinced. But not one to be easily astonished, he wanted the physicians and the surgeons to be called to give their opinion before resorting to exorcisms. It was formulated in the terms reported by Monsieur Marescot in his booklet about that story: *many natural causes, numerous fictions and none due to the devil*. When that poor possessed woman realized the ignorance and the stupidity of all the bigots of Paris, she was threatened with the whip unless she came through the ordeal without delay. That is why a certain abbot led her to Rome from where Monsieur Cardinal d'Ossat chased her so speedily that she had no respite to astonish anybody. The last thing which we may notice about that conversion is what happened afterwards. The politician who must profit by and draw a lesson from the slightest syllable and remark of the historians might ponder over the reply given by a peasant to the same King Henry IV, who travelling incognito, asked the peasant what was being said among the people about his conversion: one always smells the herring in the bag. Likewise, Marshal Biron, as he was upset for having been denied the governorship of Bourg-en-Bresse, told one of his friends that had he been a Huguenot, he would not have been turned down. It is from Cayet that I have got these two observations, which nobody but the politician needs to consider probable, because they are denied by many other people directly opposed to them.

Finally the law of the opposites, which must be dealt with in the same category, compels us already here to range the occasions that may present themselves so as to limit or undermine the too great power of the one who would like to abuse of it to the detriment of the state, or who by the large number of his supporters and the cabal of his connections, has rendered himself redoubtable to the sovereign, and even to see whether he should be dispatched secretly, without getting through all the formalities of a well-ordered justice. It may be done, provided he is guilty and would have deserved a public death anyhow, had it been possible to punish him in that way. The reason on which Charron launched into circulation this maxim is that only the form is violated in such a case, and that the prince, being the master of formalities, may also dispense with them whenever he judges it to be right. Among the Romans, whenever someone tried hard to obtain an office without the consent of the people, or if he raised the slightest suspicion that he aspired to royalty, he would be sentenced to death in virtue of the Valerian Law, that is as soon as possible and without any form of justice, of which one thought only after the execution. Moreover, the famous jurist Ulpian went even farther regardless, when he said: *if a manifest thief or sedition breaks forth, or a bloody faction, or any other just cause, do not admit of any delay; it is permitted to punish not in order to hasten the punishment but to prevent the cause of the danger, and only afterwards to frame the indictment that made possible the punishment.* The execution of Parmenio and of Philotas by Alexander were like that, as were those of Plautian and of Sejanus, among the Romans, of William Maion in Sicily, of the Messieurs of Guise and Marshal d'Ancre, under the reign of two of our kings, and of the Colonel of Lancers at Padua, to whom Antonio de Leve gave some spoilt broth, because he had been stirring up trouble and sedition. Although those actions could not be legitimated but by an extraordinary and absolute necessity, and that it is injustice and barbarity to practise them too often, the Spaniards nonetheless found the means to reconcile them with their conscience and to overcome many difficulties by the practice. To that end, they appointed secret and hidden judges for whomever was considered a state criminal, who investigated and decided his case, sentenced him and then sought to carry out the sentence by all possible means. Antonio Rincon, a Spaniard, and as a result, a subject of Charles V, who could not remain safely in his country, took refuge with Francis I who sent him to Constantinople to negotiate an alliance with Soliman. Foreseeing the damage which that embassy could cause him, the emperor had Rincon and his colleague Cesare Fregoso killed, as they were travelling down the Po on their way to Venice, by the intervention of Alfonso d'Avalos, his lieutenant with the Milanese. So much was made of it, that the said emperor thought himself guilty and even one of our bishops was willing to plead the emperor's innocence: *Rincon, a Spanish exile and Francis' envoy to Soliman, was not unjustly killed, though the death of Fregoso might have been beyond the bounds of justice.* Having left the party of the king of France, Andrea Doria joined that of the emperor, under whose favour he held the city of Genoa as in slavery. Gian Luigi Fieschi, citizen of the same city, undertook to liberate it with the help of Henry II and of Pier Luigi Farnese, Duke of Parma and Piacenza. First, he killed Giannettino Doria, but accidentally he drowned himself when the scheme was hardly begun. What did Emperor Charles V do? On the basis of that incident, he decided in his secret council that Pier Luigi was guilty of lese-majesty and at the same time sent Doria the order to

assassinate him and to the Gonzaga governor of Milan to
seize the city of Piacenza, which orders were punctiliously executed according to his plan; and though he did
whatever was possible to prove that he had no part in
that execution, nevertheless, all the historians wrote the
opposite, and the distich reported by Noel Conti tells us
enough about what was thought of that at the time:
*Farnese the Hero was killed without the Emperor's
order, but the murderers were rewarded by his order.*

Moreover, Cardinal George of Hungary, wasn't he
sentenced in the same way and executed with even more
inhumanity by Ferdiand of Austria who had feared that
the said cardinal had been seeking the aid of the Turk to
rule Transylvania for ever? And haven't we seen in the
last four years alone that Wallenstein was assassinated at
Eger by the secret plotting of Count Oñate, who at the
time was the king of Spain's ambassador to the emperor?
That Burgomaster La Ruelle received the same treatment
at the hands of Count Warfuzée, following the orders
given to him by the Marquis d'Aytone, military governor
of the Low Countries, with such precise formalities, like
having him *make his confession and be resigned to God's
will* before his death, which formalities were not overlooked so as to add to the validity of the action and make
it resemble a criminal sentence declared and executed
legitimately? In short, this kind of justice is so much in
use in the houses of Austria and Spain that the father
himself did not want to except his own son from it when
he judged it less expedient for the welfare of his kingdom
to spare his life than to put him to death. *You may
indeed prosecute crimes after they are perpetrated, but
unless you prevent them, once committed, it would be in
vain to seek judgement,* as said very well by Cato when
talking about Catiline's conjuration in Sallust. And it
pleased God that this great emperor, Charles V, who had
undertaken so many other coups d'état, be short of those
to be practised upon the person of Luther, when he
appeared before the Conference at Augsburg; otherwise
we would not be constrained to say with the poet Lucan:
*Alas, how many streches of land might have been
acquired by the blood which the civil wars have shed!*

Nor would we have proven how true these lines by Lucretius are: *religion has perpetrated wicked and impious acts.* While setting Germany and other foreign countries aside, it has been established that from the first tumults aroused by the Calvinists until the reign of Henry IV, the so-called Reformed fought five very cruel and gory battles against us and were the cause of the death of over a million persons, of the taking by surprise of three hundred towns, and of the expenditure of one hundred and fifty million for the pay of the gendarmerie alone, while nine towns, four hundred villages, twenty thousand churches, two thousand monasteries and ten thousand houses were burnt or demolished to the ground. If one adds what happened during the latest war against the present king, I am certain that a sight of horror can be put together, capable of moving to compassion the most inhuman hearts and make even the most reticent exclaim: *religion can persuade to such evils that serve as horrible instances to the mortals.* Since nobody has yet reflected upon this story of Luther, I shall say in passing that three great mistakes were made while he began publishing the heresies: the first, his being allowed to proceed from the correction of mores to that of doctrine, because the commonest is always the best, that it is very dangerous to change anything in it, and also of little use; that it is not up to one private individual to do it, and lastly, that a highly civilized Christian kingdom ought never to accept other novelties in matters of religion than those which the popes and the councils are accustomed to introduce from time to time to accommodate the needs the Church may have, which Church should be the only rule of the Holy Writ and of our faith, as the councils are of the Church, and among the councils, the latest ought to be preferred to all those that preceded it. The second mistake was made when Luther had come to Augsburg in all good faith to confer, and if possible, to come to an understanding with the Catholics, Cardinal Cajetan ought instead to have accepted his offer to say and write no more on the issue in question, provided that in return, silence were imposed on his adversaries, Ecchius, Cochlaeus, Sylvester Prierias and others and he were not pressed to retract in public and recite the palinode of all that he had said and preached with so much ardour and vehemence. Then, the third mistake was not to have resorted to a coup d'état when he was seen taking the bit between his teeth and deliberately balking at the legate's ill-judged zeal. Because some bone should have been thrown into his mouth or his tongue padlocked by bringing an eagle into play, because the bulls and the sirens are no longer in use, in other words, he should have been won over by some good benefice or pension, as has been done since by many more learned and authoritative ministers. It's not thirty years since Ferrier took it upon himself to go to Rome and maintain that the pope was Antichrist, yet the Queen Mother did not need to take a lot of trouble to make him quit his party and join ours, and Monsieur Cardinal Richelieu, would he ever have concluded so many glorious enterprises against the Huguenots, had he not made clever use of the king's finances in order to win over all their captains? Horace's words are true, indeed: *gold passes between the guards and likes to break stone walls with more force than lightning.* If Luther could not be tamed in that way, one should have used another means, making sure to take him to a safe place as one has done more recently with Abbot Du Bois and the Benedictine Barnes, or paid no heed but dispatched him without a sound by some magic sign made, as it is said, by Catherine de Medicis, or publicly and by the form of justice, as the fathers of the council did with Jan Huss and Jerome of Prague, although truth to tell, the former means were more appropriate, because they were the most gentle, easy to carry out and covert, and also more certain to produce the hoped-for result, which was not the case with the latter, as it might have embittered the duke of Saxony and even more confirm Luther's audience in their false opinions. The saying of an ancient of the Christians that *the martyrs' blood is the seed of the Christians* may also be said of all those who started by upholding ideas which they persuaded themselves to be true. And, in fact, Henry II, intent on choking by this kind of torture not the heresy but the opportunities which the foreign princes might have had some day to cross him by means of the Calvinists as they had turned against and frustrated the emperor by aiding the Lutherans in Germany, he got it so wrong that the number of heretics was increasing with each day, and under Charles IX, France was finally thrown into confusion in a manner known to everybody. And Henry III, who could do no better but rely on their forces, which thing heated so the melancholy and the injudicious zeal of the Dominican friar who was not afraid to lose his life to take the king's. Having been called to Rome from Germany to serve on the reformation of the calendar, the learned mathematician Regiomontanus died there at the height of his work, and if his friends are to be believed, and most of the heretics as well, the incident was a coup d'état on the part of Gregory XIII, who preferred to play with the goblet than to see his plan and the work of Italy's ablest astronomers not just delayed but turned upside down by the opposition of such a learned personage. But it is quite certain that Regiomontanus' death should not blacken the innocence of such a good and generous pope, because it was more the crime of George Trabzon's children, who upset by their father's death and thinking Regiomontanus to have been the cause by his too unsparing criticism of his Latin translation of Ptolemy's ALMAGESTA, finding numberless faults in it, decided to pay him back and treat him more the Greek way than the Roman. On the other hand, if the Venetians had been as innocent of the death of their fellow citizen Loredan as the pope of that of Regiomontanus, Bodin would not have remarked in his METHOD that he did not survive a furious mutiny of the mariners against the populace, which he appeased single-handedly, after all the magistrates and the assembled forces of the city had failed to keep in check. Perhaps they feared that once he became aware of his power and his authority over the subjects of the republic, it might have occurred to him to become absolute master of their state. It is also possible that they did it from jealousy and a spirit of competition, as Aristotle recounts about the Argonauts who did not want Hercules' company for fear that all the glory of such a fine enterprise as theirs might be attributed to his value and virtue alone: *for a man scorches with his brilliance which outweighs skills lowlier than his own.* And the same adds that the Ephesians banished their prince Hermodorus because he was too much of a philanthropist. That was the reason for the introduction of ostracism at Athens, and what forced Scipio and Hannibal to put to death two brave soldiers who were their prisoners. But if the stratagem allegedly used by the Venetians not long ago is true, when they spread the rumour that the Duke of Ossuna wanted to seize their city, I think that it was one of the most judicious of which we have ever talked; for them it was very important to do it, in order to make the ambassador of one of Europe's greatest princes to give up his practices, which only led to the ruin of their state, and to force him, as a result, to be honourably recalled. That is the way one should reserve these great remedies for the dangerous maladies, and use them as Horace says that one should do with the gods that are introduced into the tragedies to achieve and finish what the humans cannot accomplish: *let no god intervene, unless a worthy deliverer, to cut through the knot.* Or as the mariners make a double anchor, which they cast only after they have lost any other hope. And as a matter of fact, if a councillor or a minister would propose to overcome all the difficulties, that present themselves, by the means of one of these expedients, he should not be held for less stupid and wicked than a surgeon who wants to heal each wound by cauterizing or cutting off the limb which has received it: *because extreme remedies are to be applied to extreme maladies.* Moreover, when the same councillor abuses these remedies in order to back his interests or to give freer rein to his passions, he not only betrays his master's trust but also renders himself guilty before God and before men by the evil he undertakes to carry out; and so is even the sovereign, when he employs it otherwise than when the public good or his welfare, which is not separate, demands it, acts prompted by passion and the ambition of a tyrant, rather than as required by the office of a king. Thus we see that Queen Catherine de

Medicis, *of whom the mathematicians said that she had been born to ruin the homeland,* could not bear to be married to the son of a king and not become queen, and so resorted to the artifice of a Montecuculi to get rid of the only obstacle, in the person of her husband's elder brother. *It was found afterwads that the affinity contracted with Clement was the cause of all that madness, though without the husband's knowledge; but as soon as he was dead and the brother was next to succeed him in the paternal realm, no care was taken to look into the matter and the truth was suppressed,* as Monsieur de Thou has so well remarked in the original of his story. Afterwards, she took to protecting the Huguenots by means of letters and secret counsel, in order to thwart the power of the supreme commander and of Monsieur of Guise, in whose assassination at his arrival before Orleans she is said, in Tavannes's MEMOIRS, to have boasted of having been involved, as since then, she was involved in that of the Admiral, without however having other motives for playing all her bloody tragedies but the desire to satisfy her ambition to reign under the name of her children and maintain the enmity between those whose authority gave too much umbrage to hers.

Chapter IV

Of what beliefs one must be persuaded
in order to undertake coups d'état

It is not enough to have shown the occasions appropriate for carrying out these stratagems, unless we also state the ideas and beliefs one must be persuaded of, in order to execute them without wavering and succeed. And although the title of this chapter seems to be about the qualities and circumstances of a minister who may advise them, I shall not abstain from laying down the main, because they are very sure maxims, universal and infallible, which not only councillors but also princes and all persons of good sense and judgement should follow and adhere to, in all the matters that they may encounter, and without which the arguments applied in state affairs are often grotesque, mangled and resembling the tales of old wives and of coarse and unimaginative men rather than the words of wise persons, versed in wordly affairs.

Boethius, that great state councillor of King Theodoric, will provide us with the first maxim, which he expresses in the following terms in his book ON CONSOLATION: *it has been established upon an eternal law that nothing born into the world is unchanging.* And St Jerome agrees when he says in his EPISTLES: *all things die that are born, and those, that grow, age.* The poets also share the feeling: *there is nothing immortal that accompanies the world: neither cities nor the possessions of men, nor golden Rome.*

And generally, they do not stray from it, all those who closely observe how this great circle of the universe, once it started on its course, has never ceased to sweep away and wheel about monarchies, religions, sects, cities, people, beasts, trees, rocks, and on the whole, everything that finds itself included and enclosed in this great machine. The skies are not exempt, either, from change and decay. The first empire of the Assyrians and that of the Persians, who came after, were also the first to come to an end. Nor did the Greek and the Roman last much longer. Those powerful families of Ptolemy, Attalus, Seleucus now only serve for stories: *are we suprised by the demise of men, that monuments crumble, is it really death which has come to axe names and stones?* That island of Crete where there were a hundred cities; that city of Thebes which had a hundred gates; that Troy built by the hands of gods; that Rome which triumphed over all the world, where are they nowadays? *Now a cornfield is where Troy was once.* Thus one should not be taken in as those halfwits who imagine that Rome will always be the see of the Holy Fathers, and Paris, that of the kings of France. *Do you see that Byzantium, proud to be the seat of a twofold empire? This Venice that glories in a thousand years of firmness? Her turn will come, and you too, Antwerp, the dazzler among the cities, the time will come when you are no longer*, Lipsius would judiciously say. Although this maxim is very true, a good mind will never despair of being able to overcome all the difficulties which may prevent others to carry out or undertake these important affairs. For example, in the case of a minister, who contemplates the means by which to ruin some republic or empire, either for God's sake or to serve his master, this general maxim will induce him from the outset to believe that such an enterprise is not impossible because there is none that enjoys the privilege of being able to last and subsist for ever. On the other hand, if the issue is to establish some other, he would refer to the same axiom to decide its undertaking, and convince himself of its easy success, as did the Swiss, the inhabitants of Lucca, the Dutch and the Genevans, not in those centuries of which we have no recollection any longer, but in the last two, and somewhat of a recent date. The same is with the states as it is with men: they die and are born quite often; some are suffocated by their principles, others carry on regardless and gain strength and weight at the expense of their neighbours; many even reach old age, but ultimately strength forsakes them, they make room for others and give up their place, incapable of defending it any further. *As we discern everything changing, some nations are destroyed, others gain weight.* And then, the first illnesses have them worry, the second illnesses weaken them, and the third carry them away. Gracchus, Sertorious and Spartacus gave the first blow to the Roman state; Sulla, Marius, Pompey and Julius Caesar carried it to the incline, two fingers' breadth from ruin, and after the furies of the Triumvirate, Augustus buried it: *the fate of the Roman Empire was obviously hard pressed*, and from the most celebrated republic of the world he made the greatest empire, and likewise, from the greatest empires, at present in existence, famous republics may one day emerge. But it must be noticed also that these changes, these revolutions of the states, the deaths of empires do not happen without dragging laws, religions and the sects down with them, or perhaps it is more accurate to say that these three internal principles, as they grow old and decay: religion, through heresies or atheisms; justice, by the venality of offices, the partiality of the great and the authority of the sovereigns and the sects, by the liberties which every Tom, Dick and Harry take with the dogmas by introducing a new one or re-establishing the old, they tumble down and destroy everything built on top and push matters towards some revolt or memorable change. Indeed, if one takes a closer look at the present situation of Europe, it would not be too hard to conclude that pretty soon she might serve as the theatre in which many similar tragedies will be acted, because most of her countries are not too far from the age which has made all others perish, and that such long and distressful wars have given rise to and intensified the aforementioned causes that may ruin justice, as the too big number of colleges, seminaries, students, alongside the ease with which books are printed and circulated, have already seriously undermined the sects and religion. And in fact it is beyond any doubt that more new systems are devised in astronomy, that more novelties have been introduced into philosophy, medicine and theology, that the number of atheists has increased since 1452, and after the fall of Constantinople, all the Greeks, and with them the sciences, took refuge in Europe, and particularly in France and Italy, more than in a thousand years before. I, for one, challenge the most versed in our French history to show me anyone accused of atheism before the reign of Francis I, known as the restorer of letters, and besides, one might be hard put to show me the like in Italy's history before Cosimo and Lorenzo de' Medici indulged the literati. The same happened during Augustus' century, when the poet Horace was saying of himself: *the study of the insentient science has made me swerve from the cult of the gods whom I consult but seldom.* Lucretius sought to win the good will of his readers by telling them that he wanted to deliver them from the discomfort and the pains that religion was giving them: *until I go on loosening your minds from the bonds of religion.* While St Paul would say to the Romans: *I have come to you when God was not in you.* It was under the kings Almansur and Miramolin, more studious and lettered than all their predecessors, that the Aladdinists or libertines enjoyed a great vogue among the Arabs. Furthermore, we may say together with Seneca: *as in all things, we are tried by the intemperance of letters.*

The second opinion of which one should be persuaded in order to be successul in coups d'état is that not all the world needs to be stirred in order to incur changes in the greatest empires. They often happen when no thought is given to them, or at least without too great preparations. And as Archimedes would move the heaviest loads by means of three or four sticks ingeniously assembled, so, too, at times, one may shake, even ruin them, or give rise to great crises by means hardly worthy of any consideration. It was of that that Cicero warned us when he said: *who is he that can afford to ignore that the shortest instant may work the greatest transformation in the course of time.* According to Moses' doctrine, the world was made from nothing; to that of Epicurus, it was composed only by the cooperation of various atoms. And these big rivers, which roll along impetuously almost from one end of the earth to the other, are usually so small towards their fountainheads that a child may easily ford them: *see what big rivers stream from such little fountainheads?*

The same is true of political affairs: an overlooked spark may as often as not ignite a big fire: *it is by neglect that conflagrations increase their strength.* And as only a small stone loosened from the mountain was enough to destroy the great statue, nay, the great colossus of Nebuchadnezzar, so, too, a trifle may easily overturn great monarchies. Who had ever thought that the abduction of Helen, the rape of Lucrece by Tarquin, and that of Count Julian's daughter by King Roderick would have such noteworthy effects in Greece as much as in Italy and Spain? On the other hand, who would have ever thought that the Aetolians and the Arcadians would doggedly go to war for the head of a wild boar; the people of Carthage and of Byzacium would fight over a scooner's cask; the Duke of Burgundy and the Swiss over a cartful of sheepskins; the Frisians and the Romans, in

Drusus' time, over some oxhides, and the Picts and Scots over some strayed dogs? Or that in Justinian's time, all the cities of the empire were able to split and breed a mutual deadly hatred because of the disagreement over the colours worn at public games and entertainments. Nature herself seems to favour this procedure when she brings forth the great and stately cedars from a little seed, and elephants and whales from an atom seed, if one may say so. It is thus that she tries hard to imitate her Creator who has the habit of drawing the greatness of his actions from the feebleness of their principles, and of leading them from an anaemic beginning forward to an accomplished perfection. And, as a matter of fact, when he wanted to deliver his people from the Pharaoh's captivity, he did not send some king or some prince accompanied by a strong army, but made use of a simple man, *slow and hesitant of speech, who minded his father-in-law Jethro's sheep.* When he wanted to punish and to terrify the Egyptians, he made use neither of thunder nor of lightning, *but sent them so many frogs and fleas, locusts and all kinds of flies.* When the time came to deliver the Philistines, he did it with the hands of Saul, whom he crowned king of his people, while he, Saul, only thought of *looking for the asses of Kish, his father.* Likewise, to combat Goliath, he chose David who *tended the sheep in his father's fields,* and in order to deliver Bethulia from Holophernes' persecution, he did not make use of strong and courageous soldiers, *but struck him down by the hand of a woman.* Nevertheless, because these actions are as many miracles, and as a consequence, we cannot draw our conclusions from them, let us briefly consider the greatness of the empire of the Turk and the wonderful progress which the Lutherans and the Calvinists make every day, and I am confident that one will be compelled to admire how the bitter disappointment of two monks, who had no other weapons but pen and speech, could be the cause of such great revolutions and of such extraordinary changes in policy and religion. After which it must be admitted that the Scythian envoys had good reason to show to Alexander once more that *at times the strong lions are pasturage for the smallest birds, iron is consumed by rust and there is nothing that is not under imminent danger from the feeblest thing.* Whence the duty of the good politician is to take into consideration all the minutest circumstances of serious and difficult affairs, in order to put them to good use by amplifying them, sometimes making an elephant out of a fly, a big sore out of a little scratch and a big conflagration out of a spark, or the other way round, by belittling all those things to the extent they may profit his intentions. Relatedly, I remember a little-noticed accident that occurred during the States General, held in Paris in 1615, and which nonetheless, might have ruined France and made her change her manner of government, had it not been promptly redressed. The Nobility had inserted in their book of remonstrances an article arguing in favour of the benefit which the cancellation of the annual fee would bring France, as she would be better served through the paulette. The Third Estate thought the proposal greatly harmful to them, and so, laid down another in their book, by which the king was supplicated to take away the pensions he had granted to many gentlemen who rendered no service to him. Each party began disputing the issue, and each side sent deputies to have its reasons heard. They met and began to heap abuse on each other, the deputies of the Nobility calling those of the Third Estate louts, and threatening to set their spurs on them; the latter reposted that they did not dare to do it and even if they only dreamt of it, there were one hundred thousand men in Paris who would draw the right conclusion on the spot. Meanwhile, several magistrates and ecclesiastics, who were present at those disputes, considering the danger which they might lead to, dashed to the Louvre Palace to warn the king of what was going on, prayed and conjured him to put things right without delay, and acted in such a way that His Majesty, the queens and all the princes brought their authority to bear, and it was forbidden on the pain of death to mention those articles any longer or to talk about all that had happened relative to them. And it did us good to find such prompt remedy: because had the deputies of the Nobility proceeded from words to acts, those of the

Third Estate might have grown so violent, stubborn and vindictive, and the people of Paris so excited and disposed, that all the Nobility present there would have run the great risk of being attacked, and perhaps afterwards, the same might have happened in all the other cities of the realm, that usually followed the capital's example.

Had that happened, it would have been with the help of the populace, which without discernment and knowledge of what was sensible, would have unexpectedly and unthinkingly fallen upon the first who had come into the path of their rage. It is not inappropriate to warn and state as a third opinion and rule of conduct that for the best coups d'état carried out with the participation of the populace, one must also have a close knowledge of its nature and of the extent to which its intrepidity and reliance may be used for one's designs, and dispose it to them. Those who have given the most complete and specific description rightly represent the populace as a beast with several heads, vagabond, errant, mad, scatter-brained, badly behaved, humourless and unreasonable. Palingenius says that *the judgement of the common people is poor and its intellect weak*. About its passions, the same adds that *enraged, the mob turns most violent*. When its ways and mores, *here the mores of the mob, it hates the present, desires the future and celebrates the past*, when alongside all the other qualities, Sallust describes the crowd to us as *shifty of temper, seditious, querulous, covetous of novelties and hostile to repose and tranquillity*, I pay no heed, but say that it is inferior to the animals, worse than the animals and a hundredfold more stupid than the animals themselves, because not used to reason, the animals allow themselves to be led by instinct, which nature endows them with, to regulate their lives, actions, passions and habits, from which they never stray, unless human wickedness forces them to. There, where the people (by this word I mean the coarse plebs, the morass and the dregs of the people, people under some guise whether of low, servile or mechanical condition), being endowed with reason, abuses it in a thousand ways and by its means becomes the stage on which the orators, the preachers, the false prophets, the impostors, the political tricksters, the mutinous, the seditious, the disappointed, the superstitious, the ambitious, in short, all those who have got some new design, act their bloodiest and most rabid tragedies. Moreover, we know that this populace is compared to a sea exposed to all sorts of winds and storms, to the chameleon that may display all the colours save white, and to the sternhold and the cesspool or the sewer into which all the household waste is poured. Its finest traits are to be inconsistent and shifty, approving and disapproving a thing in the same breath, rushing from one contradiction to another, gullible, rebelling promptly, always grumbling and growling: briefly, all that it thinks is only vanity; all that it says is false and absurd; what it disapproves of is good, and what it approves is bad; it sings the praises of the infamous and everything it does or undertakes is but sheer folly. That is also what made Seneca say: *human affairs do not fare so well that the greatest number prefer the better things; proof of the worst is the crowd.* And the same gives no other advice about how we come upon sound ideas, and what the satirical poet calls *that which is solid*, but to abstain from following those of the people: *we are saved if we part company with the mob.* When Postel tries to persuade the crowd that Jesus Christ saved only men and that Jeanne, his mother, should save women, it will believe him on the spot. When David George claims to be the son of God, it will worship him. When an enthusiastic and fanatical taylor plays the king at Münster and says that God has destined him to punish all the powers in this world, it will obey him and respect him as the greatest monarch on earth. When Father Domptius announces the advent of Antichrist, ten years of age and with horns, it will prove to be horrified. When impostors and charlatans claim to be Rosicrucian brothers, it will run after them. Were the crowd to be told that Paris was on the point of destruction, it would run away; that the whole world was to be flooded, it would build arks and ships without delay, in order not to be caught unprepared. Were it to be told that the sea is to dry up and one would be able to travel from Genoa to Jerusalem by waggon, it would make ready for the journey. It would be enchanted when told stories about Melusine, the witches' sabbaths, werewolves, goblins, fairies and apparitions. When some poor girl's womb troubles her, it would say that she is possessed, and believe some ignorant or wicked priest who makes her pass for one. When some alchemist, magician, astrologer, Lullist or cabbalist begins to cajole the crowd a little, it will take him for the most learned and honest man in the world. When a Peter the Hermit comes to preach the crusade, it will make relics from his mule's hairs. When told jokingly that a stick or a gosling are inspired by the Holy Ghost, it will believe it in earnest. When the pest or the tempest ruin a province, it would presently blame some greaser or magician for it. In short, if today someone tricks and baffles the crowd, it would allow itself to be awestruck tomorrow, never learning from past encounters how to conduct itself in those on hand, or in the future. And it is in these things that lie the main signs of the crowd's great weakness and imbecility. About its inconsistency, we have a fine example in the acts of the apostles: having hardly cast their eyes upon St Paul and St Barnabas, the inhabitants of Lystra and Derbe *raised their voices, saying in Lycaonian 'The gods have come to us in human form', and called Barnabas Jupiter, and Paul they called Mercury*, yet soon after, uncontrollable, *they stoned Paul and dragged him out of the city, thinking him dead.* The Romans worship Sejanus in the morning, and in the evening Sejanus *is being dragged along by a hook, as a show.* The Parisians have done the same with the Marquis d'Ancre, and after they tore to pieces the robe of the father Jesus Maria to save them as relics, two days later, they mocked him and made him their butt. When enraged, the crowd will behave as Horace's young man who *is incensed and as lightly pacified, changes every hour.* When at the boiling point of its sedition and mutiny, it meets with some man of authority, it will run away and abandon everything. When some reckless or brazen rogue shows up and makes it take heart, as the common saying goes, and blows the coals, the crowd will grow more irate than before. In short, we may attribute to the crowd particularly what Seneca said about all men: *always wavering, seizing one direction than another, gives up a claim, requests again what it has renounced, alternates between greed and the repentance of its vices.* As long as force acts on its side and it is the crowd that sets in motion every extraordinary event in the state, the princes or their ministers must learn to handle it and persuade it by means of fine words, seduce it and deceive it by appearances, win over and swerve it to their designs with the help of preachers and miracles, under the pretext of sanctity, or by means of nimble pens, making them put together clandestine booklets, leaflets, skilfully written apologies and declarations to lead it by the nose, and make it approve or condemn according to the label whatever is inside the sack.

But as there are always only two means capable of making men stick to their duty, namely the rigour of the forms of torture established by the ancient legislators to repress crimes, with which judges might be acquainted, and the fear of the gods and their wrath, in order to prevent those about whom they cannot obtain sufficient evidence in the absence of witnesses, as the poet Palingenius' saying goes: *religion is what freins the half-wild crowd, its other crimes are curbed by punishments applied from the outside, because its mind is always inclined to deviousness.* Likewise, the same legislators acknowledged that there was nothing to bear more forcefully upon the minds of people than the latter, as when the crowd comes up against some easy target, suddenly it takes its pursuit to the extreme; prudence changes into passion, whatever anger there is turns into rage, all conduct gives way to confusion; even possessions and life are cast off if by their loss, the divinity of some monkey's tooth, of an ox, a cat, an onion, or of some other idol even more ridiculous is to be defended, *nothing moves the multitude more efficaciously than supersition.* And, in fact, it has always been the first garb which has been lent to all the ruses and deceptions practised by the three different ways of life that bear a relation, as already said, to the coups d'état. As concerns the monastic way, in St Jerome, we have the example of those old monks of Thebaid who *feign their fighting the devils in order to convince the simple-minded and the common people of the miracles they perform and so increase their gain.* To that we may add the deception carried out by the priests of the god Canopus to render him superior to the fire which was the Persians' god. The invention of the Roman knight Mondus in the guise of Aesculapius to enjoy the beautiful Paulina, the alleged visions of the Jacobins of Berne and the false apparitions visible to the Cordeliers of Orleans, all of them are too common and trivial to go on talking about them. If in doubt about the practice of similar abuse in the economy, one need only read what Rabbi Moses writes about the priests of the idol Tammuz or Adonis, who in order to increase offerings, would often make it shed tears for the inquities of the people, but with tears of molten lead, which they fabricated by means of a fire kept burning behind his image, and indeed, there will be no room left for doubt after reading in the last chapter of Daniel that as he was spreading ashes over the floor in the chapel of the idol Bel, he discovered that during the night, by underground passages, the priests together with their wives and children would come to take away all that the poor and exploited people used to think that it had been consumed by that god which they were worshipping in the guise of a dragon. Finally, with respect to politics, one must dwell on them more, because it is our main objective, and show the ways in which princes or their ministers *who draw their profit from minds entrapped by superstition,* have known to handle religion carefully and make use of it as the easiest and surest means available to them to carry out their most subtle enterprises. Thus I find that they have used it in five main ways, under which afterwards, one may enter many smaller ones. The first, which is the commonest and most ordinary, is that shared by all the legislators and politicians who have convinced their peoples that they have the gods' ear, in order to carry out more easily what they wanted to accomplish, as we see Scipio, in addition to those ancients already meantioned, make people believe that he undertook nothing without the advice of the Capitoline Jupiter,

Sulla, in turn, thtat all his actions were favoured by Apollo of Delphi, whose miniature image he always carried with him, and Sertorius, that his bitch brought him news about all that was concluded in the council of the gods. But to come to the histories nearer to us, it is certain that by similar means Giacomo Bussolari was for a time most influential at Pavia, Giovanni of Vicenza at Bologna, and Girolamo Savonarola at Florence. About the last, Machiavelli left us this remark: *the people of Florence are not stupid, yet Girolamo Savonarola managed to convince them that he conversed with God.* About sixty years ago, William Postel wanted to do the same in France, and even more recently, Campanella, in Upper Calabria, but they could not succeed any better than their predecessors, because they did not have the power in their hands, and that, as Machiavelli says, is a condition necessary to all those who want to establish some new religion. And in fact, it was by its means that the Sufi Ismail, as he introduced a new sect in the religion of Muhammad with the help of Treschel Cuselbas, eventually usurped the Persian empire. He arrived almost simultaneously with the hermit Schacoculis, after having successfully acted his character in a desert for seven years. Finally, he removed his mask and declaring himself the author of a new sect, seized several cities, defied the Pasha of Anatolia, together with Corcut, son of Bayezid, and would have carried on regardless, had he not annoyed the Sufi of Persia by his attack against a caravan. The latter had him cut to pieces by his soldiers. Lipsius ranges with him a certain Calender, who by a simulated devotion, undermined the whole Anatolia and had a hold on the Turks' minds until he was defeated in a pitched battle. Likewise, he mentions an African Ismaili who took that path in order to snatch the sceptre of his master, the king of Maroc.

The second invention, by which the politicians have made use of religion as grounds for their designs among the peoples, was to feign miracles, fabricate dreams, invent visions, and produce monsters and prodigies: *that can reverse the way of life and trouble the state of things through great fear.* Thus we see that having been told by some physician about a sovereign remedy against his enemies' poisoned arrows, Alexander had people believe that Jupiter had revealed it to him in a dream, and Vespasian gathered people who feigned blindness and lameness so as to heel them by his touch; and it is for this reason that Clovis accompanied his conversion with so many miracles, Charles VII enhanced the credit of the Maid of Orleans, and the present emperor , that of father Jesus Maria, perhaps in the hope of gaining some battle no less important than that of Prague.

The third [scheme] has for its basis the false rumours, revelations and prophecies which are circulated with the intention to frighten, astonish, sway or else confirm, embolden and encourage, as the one or the other situation presents itself. And in this connection, Postel remarks that Muhammad kept a famous astrologer who did nothing else but preach a great revolution and an imminent great change both in religion and in the empire with a long succession of all kinds of prosperities, in order to clear the way for the same Muhammad by that invention and dispose the peoples to accept more willingly the religion which he wanted to introduce, and by the same means intimidate those who did not approve of it, with the insinuation that they might have to fight the course of fate by resisting this new favourite of heaven, the one greatly advantaged, *for whom Heaven combats and the bands rally at the sound of the trumpet.* It was by the means of such foolish convictions that Hernando Cortes occupied the kingdom of Mexico where he was received as if he were Topilzin, whose imminent coming had been predicted by all the diviners; and Francisco Pizarro, too, in the kingdom of Peru, where he was greeted with general applause by all the peoples, who took him for the one expected to be sent by Viracocha to deliver their king from captivity. Charlemagne himself advanced deep into Spain with the help of an old idol, which as had been predicted by the diviners, let go of a big key it was holding in its hand. And when the Arabs or Saracens came, led by Count Julian, to flood the same realm of Spain, there was hardly any move to repel them, because some time before, their faces had been seen painted on a canvas that had been found in an old castle near the city of Toledo, where it was believed that it had been stowed away by some great prophet. And I dare say along with many historians that without these fine predictions, Mehmet II would not have so easily seized the city of Constantinople. But what more remarkable example may be wished than that which happened in 1613, in connection with Acosta, the main city of the isle of Magna, in revolt against the sufi, that was taken with no difficulty by Arcomat, his lieutenant, in virtue of a certain prophecy that tradition bestowed upon its citizens and which was saying that unless the city surrendered to Arcomat, it would be arcomatized, in other words, if it did not surrender to Dissipus, it would be dissipated, even though it might not have been seized, given that its enclosing boundary was five leagues' long, had fifty thousand homesteads, and each year paid the sufi fifteen million and six hundred thousand crowns as firm revenue, according to the report of Garçia ab Horto who had been there thirty or forty years before. Thus it is a great path open to politicians to deceive and seduce the stupid populace, that is, to resort to predictions in order to frighten or arouse hope, accept or reject and do whatever might be in their favour.

But the use of preachers and of men who can turn a sentence is an even shorter and surer way, as there is nothing which cannot be easily overcome by this stratagem. The power of eloquence and of a coloured and assiduous address flows so delightfully in the ears, that one needs to be deaf or smarter than Ulysses not to be spellbound. It is also true that everything that the poets have written about the twelve labours of Hercules finds its mythology in the different effects of eloquence by which that great man overcame all kinds of difficulties. That is why the ancient Gauls had good reason to represent him with many little golden chains coming out of his mouth and attaching and sticking them into the ears of a large crowd of people which he trailed thus chained to him. It was by the same means that *Orpheus, holy messenger of the gods, made the woodsmen shrink from bloodshed and brutal living, whence the fable that he tamed tigers and voracious lions.* In the same way, Philip, king of Macedonia, one of the greatest politicians that has ever been, who knew quite well that *fortune follows everything one does with great cogency,* did not bother in the least to combat openly and use strong-arm tactics against the Athenians, as he saw that it would be easier to overwhelm them by Demosthenes' eloquence and the detrimental resolutions which the latter made the senate pass. Pericles, too, took advantage of Ephialtes' fine way of talking in order to make the same state of the Athenians wholly popular, and for the same reason, one used to say in Antiquity that the orators had as much power over the populace as the winds have over the seas. Afterwards, if we have to speak of our France, isn't it common knowledge that the famous crusade undertaken with such zeal by Godfrey of Bouillon was determined and concluded by the harangues and sermons preached by a simple man, nicknamed Peter the Hermit, as was the Second, by the preaching of St Bernard? Was there ever a murder more wicked and abominable than that of Louis, Duke of Orleans, perpetrated by the Duke of Burgundy in 1407? Nonetheless, Master John Petit, theologian and great preacher, came forward and knew so well how to attenuate, cover and disguise it by the sermons which he preached in the cathedral square in Paris, that all those who afterwards wanted to support the party of the house of Orleans were held by the people to be rebels and mutineers. That forced them to use the same artifice as their enemy, and place themselves under the protection of that great and charitable man, John Gerson, who came to their defence, and at the Council of Constance declared erroneous and heretical Petit's assertions. As John Petit had been the cause of a great evil under Charles VI, so there was a Cordelier brother Richard, under Charles VII, who was the cause of a great good, because in ten sermons that he preached in Paris, lasting six hours each, he made the people throw into the fires, lit easpecially at crossroads, all that they had in the way of tables, draughtboards, cards, marbles, billiard balls, dice and other games of chance which drive and push people to curse and blaspheme. But the good man hardly out of Paris, one started to despise and mock him openly, and people returned with even more application than before to their ordinary diversions. No more and no less than the strange metamorphoses and so-called miraculous conversions performed by the Capuchin father Giacinto da Casale in all the towns of Italy where he went preaching less than twenty years ago. They lasted as long as the said father remained in place to carry on the functions of his charge. As we descend to the reign of Francis I, we see the great and furious battle of Marignano, given with so much stubbornness and animosity by the Swiss without respite for two days running, until ultimately almost all of them dropped dead on the spot, for no more pressing reason than the harangue of the Cardinal of Sion, called by Paolo Giovio *the presiding priest of Sion.* After they heard him harangue, they decided to combat, engaged in battle and contested the victory to the last drop of their blood. We shall also see how Montluc, bishop of Valence, was dispatched to the Venetians so that by his fine words he should legitimize the aid which his master had secured from Turkey, in his defence against Emperor Charles V. After St Bartholomew's Day, the same Montluc, together with Pibrac, worked so well with pen and tongue that the Poles' determination to elect Henry III their king at the expense of other princes who did everything to assert their claims, could not be swayed by that great massacre, as already noted, despite the fact that they, the Poles, had been especially informed by the Calvinists of everything that had happened. Was it not also a remarkable thing that the first siege of La Rochelle was better resisted by the continuous preaching of forty ministers, who had taken refuge there, than by all the captains and soldiers with which the city was well provided? And at the time when the Parisians were eating dogs and rats, in order not to pay obeisance to a heretic king, were there not Boucher, Rose, Wincestre and many other curates who sustained them in their determination? Indeed, it is quite consistent to say that Montauban might not have been easier to seize than La Rochelle, had not minister Chamier been swept away from the bastions of that city by canon fire.

Likewise, when Campanella intended to become king of Upper Calabria, he appropriately chose as his associate in the enterprise Dionisio Ponzio, who had earned for himself the reputation of the most eloquent and persuasive man of his time. Furthermore, in the Old Testament we see that as God wanted to deliver His people through Moses, who was good only at commanding because he was stuttering and was a man of very few words, He enjoined Moses to use the eloquence of his brother Aaron: *your brother Aaron the Levite, I know that he is eloquent, speak to him and put my words in his ears,* after which God reiterates: *behold I have appointed you god of the Pharaoh and Aaron your brother shall be your prophet, you shall speak to him all that I command you and he shall speak it to the Pharaoh.* That is what since then the pagans, true apes of our mysteries, would convey by their Pallas, goddess of eloquence and the sciences, who nevertheless, was armed with lance, shield and helmet to show that arms alone would not make much of a foray without the eloquence, nor eloquence without the arms. And because the link and combination of these two very different qualities can hardly be found in one and the same person, as Virgil has shown so well in the example of Drances, *whose tongue is quicker than his right arm, frigid in combat,* it has been the reason why in order to supplement this shortcoming the greatest captains have always seen to it that they have in their retinue, or that they befriend, someone as forceful, who by the effort of his tongue backs up their swords. Ninus, for instance, made use of Zoroaster, Agamemnon of Nestor, Diomedes of Ulysses, Pyrrhus of Cyneus, Trajan of Pliny the Younger, Theodoric of Cassiodorus, and the same may also be said of all the great warriors who had flattered the *Venus that changes the hearts* no less, and besides, had not ignored that *a speech that is wise and well built has a miraculous force that rules over various feelings and ever governs judgement.* I, for one, consider eloquence so influential that until this hour I haven't found anything that is unaffected by its imperium. It is speech that persuades and gives credence to the most fabulous creeds, stirs up the most iniquitous wars, lends colour and concealment to the blackest actions, calms and appeases the most violent seditions, excites rage and fury in the most peaceful souls, in short, it's speech that plants and brings down heresies, makes England revolt and converts Japan: *it is one and the same fire that hardens the clay and melts the wax.* And were a prince to have a dozen men of that calibre devoted to him, I would consider him stronger, and believe that he would be better obeyed in his realm than by the means of two strong armies. But as much as eloquence may be used in two ways, by speech and by pen, one may add that the latter is of no less consequence than the former, and I may even say it surpasses it somewhat, because a man who speaks can be heard but in one place and by no more than three to four thousand people at best: *rejoice as a thousand eyes see you speaking.* He, who writes, may declare his conceptions everywhere and to everybody, and to that I may add that many good arguments often elude one's hearing by the rush of the words which cannot so easily mislead the eyes whenever they look over one and the same thing several times. And quite often, when the arms cannot prevail upon the people, the latter are won over by a simple declaration or manifesto. Thus Francis I and Charles V were no less waging war against one another by their letters and apologies than by means of swords and lances. And in our times, we have seen that the quarrel of the Pope with the Venetians, the debate about the oath of loyalty in England, the favours bestowed on the Marquis d'Ancre and the Messieurs de Luynes in France, the Count Palatine's war in Germany and of the Valtelinians in Switzerland have produced countless lampoons as harmful to some as they are favourable to others. Those who have seen the miraculous effects wrought by Cassandra and the ghost of Henry the Great against the Marquis d'Ancre, the Count of Provence and the Hermit of Mount St Valerian against the Messieurs de Luynes, the word whispered in one's ear and the public voice against the Marquis of Vieuville, even the ADMONITION and the POLITICAL MYSTERIES of Jansen against the good designs of our king, all those, I say, are no doubt the effect of such writings. And it is

God's will that those sent daily from Brussels are not so much against the present state of France, and that quite capable and attached people may be found energetically defending the king's interests against the mutineers, as Father Paul the Hermit courageously defended the Venetians' cause, and Pibrac and Montluc that of Charles IX and Henry III against the furious, malicious gossip of all the Calvinists.

But having amply discussed all these means of accommodating religion to political matters, we need not overlook the one which has always been mostly in use and most subtly practised, to undertake under the pretext of religion whatever could not be rendered valid and legitimate by other means. And in fact, the proverb commonly appropriated by the Jews, *all evils are committed in God's name*, is no less true than the rebukes which Pope Leo heaped on Emperor Theodosius: *private affairs are transacted under the shelter of piety and everyone holds religion for the handmaid of his greed*. As examples are so common, and books are full of them, and after having spoken so much of our French, I shall be content to dwell on the Spaniards and follow closely what Mariana, their most faithful historian, had to say in the matter. Thus, when talking of the first Goths who occupied Spain and the wars which they waged to chase each other away, he says that they made use of religion as a pretext to reign, and while talking of King Josenand, who obtained the aid of the Arrian Burgundians to chase away King Swinthila, his ordinary refrain is *he will show religion as the best pretext*. Then, referring to the kings of Chinchilla, *they put on the pretext of religion*. Likewise, describing the manner in which Ervigius had chased away King Wamba, he says: *the best is to conceal it under the appearance of religion*; and about two brothers of the house of Aragon, who armed themselves against one another *at the violent command of an imperious pontiff*, it was Boniface VIII, the good father remarks quite to the point that there was nothing more inhuman than to violate the law of nature in that way, *but there was so much religious faith*. Furthermore, the same speaks of Navarre, which *by his immense ambition to rule*, Ferdinand took away from his niece, and adds as an excuse: *but it was done under the pretext of religion and of the Pope's commands.* As we shall never come to an end by pointing to all the passages in which the brave author makes similar remarks, I shall attest to the fact that all his book is full of no other things. When it comes to Charles V, I shall produce as evidence against him what Francis I was saying in his apology of 1537: *Charles wants to encroach upon the states under the colour of religion.* And while speaking of the war in Germany: *the Emperor, under the colour of the armed religion of the league of the Catholics, wants to oppress the others and cut his path to the monarchy,* which was as well remarked by Monsieur de Nevers, as mentioned above. Finally, when the late King James was called to the throne of England, the king of Spain made haste to conclude a close alliance with him. The constable of Castile was sent there, the arrangement was published and Rovida, senator of Milan, calls this alliance a very saintly work, acknowledges the king of England as a very powerful Christian prince, offers him on behalf of the king, his master, all his forces on land and at sea and insists that the king of Spain has been acting *by a divine admonition, by divine will, divine assistance and no less by God's great grace.* Thus, if it is the nature of most princes to treat religion as charlatans do, and make use of it as a drug in order to uphold the credit and the reputation of their theatre, it seems to me that one mustn't blame a politician when he resorts to the same industry in order to succeed in an important affair, although it would be more honest to say the opposite and to speak sanely about it: *such things should not be revealed to the common people, given that among men there are so many villains and so many criminals.*

Nonetheless, all these maxims would remain lustreless and tarnished, were they not enhanced and like animated by another, which teaches us to seize them by their good bias and choose the favourable time and hour for their execution: *things timely done yield profit, whereas untimely things do much harm.* Besides, is it not enough to have acquired this ordinary prudence, common to many politicians, unless we refer to another, more refined, and which is appropriate only to the most crafty and experienced ministers, namely, to take advantage of fortuitous occasions and gain profit and benefit from what otherwise would be overlooked by another or might have caused him harm. One such occasion was that great eclipse which occurred under Emperor Tiberius, while all the legions of Hungary were so fiercely engaged in mutiny that it seemed quite impossible to appease them. Someone less perceptible than Drusus would have paid no attention to that event and would have never thought of drawing any profit from it. But seeing that the mutineers were mightily frightened by the darkness, because they ignored its cause, he took the bull by the horns and intimidated them in such a way as to overcome by that accident what all the others, and he himself beforehand, despaired of being able to do, that is, to restore order. The stratagem by which King Tullus ingeniously covered the withdrawal of Mettius Fufetius was of the same kind. He drew a matchless advantage by spreading the rumour and passing the word from squadron to squadron that he had sent the latter to take his enemies by surprise and cut off all their retreat. Livy and Tacitus, who relate these stories, were content to draw just particular conclusions, as the former only says: *it is a stratagem to say that what our deserters perfidiously do in combat is done by our order*, and the other: *in appeasing the commotions of a crowd, one must convert into wisdom and opportunity and mitigate what the fortuitous event presents and terrifies the crowd or is seen with superstitious eyes*. It is obvious that the following general rule should have been drawn instantly: *what chance presents should be converted into wisdom*, not only in the case of treason and mutiny, but in all other kinds of affairs and encounters: *men have been accustomed to put to work unforeseen occasions*, as Cassiodorus says. Thus we read that after having calculated the time of a great eclipse, Christopher Columbus threatened certain inhabitants of the New World by telling them that he would turn the moon to blood and deprive them of it altogether, unless they provide him with fresh supplies which he badly needed. As soon as the eclipse began, they sent him the provisions forthwith. I have already meantioned that Fernando Cortes made the inhabitants of Mexico believe that he was the god Topilzin, in order to penetrate their realm more easily, and that Francisco Pizarro made use of the same stratagem in his conquest of Peru, calling himself Viracocha. It was also by such means that Muhammad changed his epilepsy into ecstasy and Charles V made use of Luther's heresy in order to divide and weaken the princes of Germany, who if remained united, would have been in control of the authority which they wanted within the empire and staved off his plan of universal monarchy. Moreover, the same emperor, no longer fit to govern a state as large as his, and also seeing Henry II's rising fortune set boundaries to his empire, poked fun at his *farther still*, and made it to be said in satirical comedies: *Do stop at Metz where the boundary stone meant for you lies.* He covered all those disgraces with the veil of piety and religion, and shut himself in a cloister where he had also the facility to atone for the secret sin which he had committed by begetting a bastard son that happened to be his nephew as well. That way, Philip II got the idea to annul all the extraordinary privileges enjoyed by the Aragonese because of the protection they wanted to grant to Antonio Perez. Furthermore, among our kings of France, I have found that Philip I expanded his realm greatly and delivered it, if one may say so, from the mayors of the palace, while all the princes of France and even his brother were busy fighting the Saracens under the leadership of Godfrey of Bouillon, and during the Third Crusade, it may be said, Philip Augustus abandoned King Richard of England in order to return to France and muddle the affairs of the English, because in matters of state, *it does not attain its object unless it borrows strength from deceit and seeks acclaim by hidden track rather than open highway.*

Chapter V and the last

What conditions are required of the minister
with whom the coups d'état may be planned

Here I may be objected that I should not have dwelt
on the minister's conditions before talking about those of
the prince, because the latter is the first to set in motion
everything that goes on in his council, as the first motive
that drives all the heavens and as the sun that transmits
his light to all the stars and planets. To that, however, I
may reply that the sovereigns are given to us either by
succession or by election. Of these two ways, the former
follows nature, which we obey punctiliously, without re-
striction or consideration of any circumstances, even
when *God covers the sheep with gold and dresses the ass
in purple.* The latter way is dependent on intrigues, mon-
opolies, and the cabals of those who happen to be the
wealthiest and the most powerful friends, keen on favours and money to satisfy their ambitions. It would be
truly pedantic to suggest or think that only considerations of virtue and merit are taken into account in such
circumstances. But as regards the ministers, one may
philosophise differently, because they depend absolutely
on the selection which the prince may make. He is
allowed to, and even it is seemly honourable on his part
to hand-pick from among all his friends or servants the
one whom he would judge the best conditioned for the
serious employ which he wants to entrust him with: *he is
said to be the wisest who can think of those things which
he needs and enters public life alongside him who can
heed his good intentions.* Besides the honour which the
prince garners from such an election, he also gets a great
and considerable advantage, and unless he wishes to be
himself neglected and deserted, it is quite necessary to
proceed to this selection. Velleius Paterculus has remarked to the point that *great tasks require great assist-
ants,* and Tacitus, that *the prince who assumes extremely*

serious endeavours to extend the boundaries of his land needs help. Furthermore, as Euripides says it very well, σοφος τυραννος τζς σοφων συνψσια, *a prince grows wise by conversing with wise men.* And in fact, the histories teach us that those princes who had done nothing out of their heads, nor without the advice of some loyal and confident minister, have always been regarded as the wisest. Whence Alexander had Cleitus and Hephaestion always with him, and Augustus did not undertake anything without the advice of Maecenas and Agrippa, and Nero was the best emperor as long as he followed the advice of Burrus and Seneca, and to come to what we are more acquainted with, Charles V and Philip II had the Sieur de Chièvre and Ruiz de Gomez as confidants; as intimate counsellors of Charles VII, at various times, were Count Dunois, Louvet, President of Provence, Tanneguy du Chastel and a Count Dammartin. As for his son, Louis XI, who was defiant in spirit, swinging and always flustered, and would change his secret and conspiratorial servants many times, yet he had always someone with whom he was more open, witness Cardinal Balue, Philip de Commynes and his physician Jack Coictier; Charles VIII did the same with Cardinal Briçonnet and his succesor Louis XII, with Cardinal d'Amboise, who dominated him entirely. King Francis I was more intimate with Admiral d'Annebaut than with anybody else and Henry II with Constable Montmorency. In short, we see in the sequence of our annals that the two Lorraine brothers were the support of Francis II, Cardinal Birague, of Charles IX, Monsieur d'Épernon, of Henry III, Messieurs Sully, Villeroy and Sillery, of Henry IV, and Monsieur Cardinal Richelieu, of our King Louis the Fair and Triumphant.

Despite the fact that this maxim, that the princes need to have some secret and conspiratorial advisers, has been established as certain and genuine, the politicians have a hard time to decide whether they should be content with one or with several councillors enjoying the same degree of confidence. When one wishes to act with reason and by example, Xenophon would warn us in one respect that πολλου βασιλεως οφθαλμοι ε πολλα

ὦτα: *the king must have many eyes and many ears*, and
the triumvirate, which so felicitously governed France
under Henry IV, validates the truth of his say, even
without the examples of Augustus and the ancients. Besides, we know that in the case of several councillors,
there cannot be a unity of opinion and that with regard
to such affars, there is nothing more detrimental nor
more unfortunate than a diversity of opinion. That
hatred, ambition, vainglory or other similar passions
often suggest and authorize what is directly contrary to
reason, and in this regard, Tacitus observes to the point
that *Messalina's death convulsed the prince's household,
for a strife arose among the freedmen.* Not unlike the
physicians, who when in great number, often kill the
sick, the too great number of councillors almost always
ruins the affairs. In order to bring together these two
positions, which are so different, it seems to me pertinent to make certain distinctions and say that whenever
the prince considers himself as strong, judicious, authoritative and capable as to be above his councillors and
confidants, nonetheless, it is good to have three or four
of these, because after they give their opinions on some
incident, he will be able to derive several alternatives
regarding the means of action and choose that which he
will judge most expedient. But if he is feeble in spirit,
with little knowledge, and incapable to choose the best
advice and see to it that it is followed through, it is
undoubtedly more practical that he confide in one only,
whom he would select as the most judicious and dependable of all. Otherwise, if he commits himself to many, it
may happen that each has his particular interests, different from those of the others, and also his intentions
and his designs, which the prince is unable to sort out
and as leader decide upon, and so, intrigues and cabals
would form within his council and ambition and jealousy,
which follows ambition as closely as does love, would
ruin it; reason will be helpless while passion will prevail,
secrecy would be banned, yet the poor prince will be
disturbed in a strange manner: he would not know what
to decide to do nor which way to turn, he would become
the laughing stock of his people and the toy of his

ministers' passion. That is what was so judiciously remarked about Emperor Galba by Tacitus: *Galba's easiness of temper whetted the greed for more in his friends, who had tasted great fortune, because with one so weak and credulous, wrong might be done with less risk and greater gain.* As much happened to Emperor Claudius, and in our times, to Charles VIII, with regard to the affairs of Pisa and Sienna. Guicciardini makes a similar observation about Clement VII, and on its basis, the Italian politicians eventually established the following axiom: *every time a prince is in the hands of many, when he cannot keep his own counsel and show prudence, he becomes a prey to all.* On the other hand, if he relies on one minister only, entirely dependable, informed, observing the mutual obligations of master and servant, everything will turn out much better for the prince, his credit will be saved, his authority maintained, his person loved, his commands carried out, and all his state will receive such fruits as those received by France at present, under the wise government of Monseigneur Cardinal Richelieu.

Thus, once it is decided that a prince must have some minister or secret councillor, faithful and trustworthy, one must have a closer look at the way he may be chosen and the qualities to be looked for in his person. In other words, what his physical condition should be like at the time of hire, as well as other sequalae that he might carry in body and in mind. Afterwards, we shall add what the prince may contribute to the satisfaction of his minister, and with that bring to an end the present discourse.

As for the first item, regarding the quality, office or sort of person of a future minister, I find myself in the same quandary as Vegetius, when it came to decide the place and condition of those from among whom a good soldier might be chosen. Because not all the affairs are alike, so too all kinds of persons are not always good at all kinds of negotations, no more than in ancient times any wood was suitable for carving the statue of Mercury out of it. Nevertheless, in order to do away with the dilemma, a distinction needs to be made between the counselling minister and the executive minister, although both may benefit by the warning given by Livy: *it is more to you than to anybody else, Titus Otacilius, not to assume a charge that might overwhelm you*; yet they may be considered each in part and the conditions differentiated accordingly. Of the latter one may say that unfailingly he must be recruited from among the most noble and illustrious families so that he may carry out the task and the command given to him with more brilliance, greatness and authority. One must also consider carefully that his inclination and capacity be proportional to the job assigned to him, for *Thersites cannot claim Achilles' breastplate as his.* Likewise, an Appius was in no way accustomed to the people's affairs; Cleon had no understanding of the conduct of an army; Philopoemen had no idea how to command at sea; Pericles was good only to govern; Diomedes was good only for combat and Ulysses only to counsel. Similarly, one must take advantage of these various inclinations in order to call to each vacancy the one who may perform the job satisfactorily and with honour, being naturally endowed for it. Otherwise, it means to treat unjustly those who are born to command and subject them to others who are fit only to obey, to do wrong to those who are not bold and warlike by entrusting them with the command of an army, and to those who cannot speak nor harangue by employing them on embassies. It would be much more sensible, as an ancient cautions us: *to appoint to each function the one best suited for it.* On the other hand, as far as the secret minister is concerned, I think one may talk differently and do away with the dilemma mentioned above, whether to recruit him from the illustrous families of the state or from among the persons of modest condition. It seems to me that one may choose him from either, regardless, because *the Roman empire expanded as long as it did not disdain those in which virtue was manifest.* As regards nobles and great lords, however, the difficulty arises from the fact that they are envied by the others, that quite often, instead of obeying they want to command, that they are more likely to advise the prince according to their own private interests rather than the welfare of the state, that they want to promote their creatures and ruin those who oppose their cabals. Quite often they want to act by assuming the authority of their master, as the mayors of the palace used to do in France; they spread confusion within the realm, in order to render themselves necessary, are never content with what they are given, considering it always inferior to what they thought they deserved either for their services or in respect of the eminence of their house. In short, it seems to me that in this case, when it is not the nobility and dignity of persons that counts but rather the advice, counsel and judgement, one does not find it in a marquis, a duke, a prince any more than in the men of middling condition. The former may cause a lot more damage, whereas the latter may do as much good, are not as costly, are more submissive, easier to handle and deal with, and are by far less to be feared. And truth to tell, Seneca was right when saying: *virtue is not denied to anybody, it admits all, irrespective of status and sex.* Relatedly, Tacitus notes that the Germans even took their women's advice: *they do not despise their counsels, nor make light of their answers.* Plutarch confirms the same in the case of the Lacedaemonians, and many historians do it with respect to the Emperors Augustus and Justinian; and in Cicero's TUSCULANES: *wisdom often hides under a mean, tattered cloak.* It is the circum-stances and the affairs that uncover wisdom and make it shine and sparkle. Had not Matteo Palmieri, Florentine, been employed on the embassy to King Alfonso, of which he acquitted himself with dignity, one would always have believed that he was good only at pounding the mortar to make medicines and clysters. Likewise, had Cardinal d'Ossat not been involved in the affairs of the Roman court, one would have been convinced for ever that he was capable only of parading his learning in the colleges of Paris and of defending Ramus against Charpentier. The same may be said of Cardinals Balue and Ximenes, and of du Perron, *whose noble birth was their only and unique virtue.* It is said that good greyhounds are of all sizes, and why not then, that good minds are of all sorts and conditions? Cardan was a physician, Bodin was an advocate, Charron a theologian, Montaigne a gentleman, La Noue a soldier, Father Paul a monk, and finally: *even a kitchen gardener may often speak in season*. That is why I do not exclude anybody from this task, nor foreigners, because *Tiberius entrusted his own property to persons known only by their general reputation*; Charles V made use of Granvelle, Francis I, of Trivulce, Henry II, of Strozzi, and Charles IX, of Cardinal Birague. Nor the young, because *grey hairs are sign of old age and not of wisdom*, and because Cicero warns us that *an extraordinary virtue does not always wait for the advance of age*; witness the examples of Joseph, David, Hephaestus and Papirius. Nor the aged, because it was on the advice of his father-in-law Jethro that Moses chose seventy of them to rule the people of Israel together with him, and Louis XI thought that he had been overwhelmed by the War of Public Weal because he had refused to listen to the old councillors whom he inherited from his father. Nor the ignorant, because as Seneca says, *to a good mind the letters are of little use*, and following Thucydides' opinion, the rugged minds are more suitable to rule the peoples than those which are more subtle and refined. The characteristic trait of the great minds is that they are more inclined to innovation than to negotiation, *capable of innovating than of managing business*, to spending than to saving, to pursuing their point stubbornly than giving in or adjusting to the needs of the affairs, and finally dealing with the angels or occult messengers rather than with people: *they are dismayed to see go slowly what they have engaged in with speed*. Nor the learned, given that *Emperor Alexander made use of togas in council and literati in the army, and mostly of those who had a command of history*, to which it may be added that Cardinal Richelieu has been taken out of the depths of his library in order to govern France. Nor the philosophers, witness the examples given by Xenophon, Seneca and Plutarch. Nor the physicians, because by his good advice, Oribasis elevated Julian to the empire, Apollophanes was head of Antiochus' council, Stephanus was sent by Justinian to Chosroes, Jack Coictier and Olivier le Dain were Louis XI's councillors,

Chancellor L'Hospital's father was the adviser of Charles of Bourbon and Monsieur Miron of Henry III. Nor the monks, witness Father Paul of Venice, nor in conclusion, any other kind of people, provided they meet the conditions which we shall expound further on: *the great talent often lies hidden*, as Plautus used to say, while prudence and wisdom have no preference over any person: they inhabit Diogenes' barrel, as well as the schools, they lie under the habit and under nasty rags as amid the delights and the sumptuosity of the palace. It is a wild guess, *I do not know how it happens, but a good mind is always the sib of poverty.*

And yet the conditions which the minister must bring and contribute on his part in the service of his prince cannot be explained but with difficulty. It is what has made so many writers sweat, what has made the career of so many discourses, and produced so many books on the idea, the example and the perfect description of the good councillor, the loyal minister, the prudent politician, and of the statesman, although all these authors resembled more Diogenes' archers who seemed to take the longest shot at the target than Cicero in his book THE ORATOR, or Xenophon in his PRINCE. For my part, I who have not undertaken to publish a thick book of all the virtues as they have done, when only three or four are necessary to a minister, would say first of all that I want him to be such in fact as to be practically known to the prince and selected by the prince himself on the sole consideration of his merits, without any other recommendation than his own virtue: *to carry the prize thanks to his virtue and not to favours.* Many who climb on the stage of the world to gain access to honours and confidences make their appearance covered by borrowed ornaments, favours, friends, money, solicitations and ambitious pursuits, they present themselves as Aesop's crow, dressed in someone else's feathers and make a parade of what does not belong to them in order to obtain what they do not deserve. But their nakedness can always be distinctly seen through those garments which they have only borrowed, and which as soon, expose them to shame on the very stage of glory.

Whence a man who wants to preserve his credit and reputation up to the end, enters and partakes of the credit and the good opinion of his master, dressed as Hippias of Elis in garments of his own making, with science, prudence, virtue, merit, courage, in short, things which are of his own coinage. Like the sun, he must produce in his inner self the light which it radiates to the outside, for fear that otherwise he might resemble the moon, the brightness of which, acquired only as a loan, gives way as soon to a blackout. But as it is idle to talk of merits in general, unless one determines the virtues they are made of in particular, I think that they may be reduced to three major ones, namely, staying power, fairness and prudence. I want to dwell on them a little, in order to examine them in a way less common and trivial than that of the schools.

By staying power, I mean a certain temper and disposition of equanimity, firmness, heroism, ability of seeing, hearing and doing everything without becoming flustered, panic-stricken or disconcerted. This virtue may be easily acquired by continuous reflection on our nature, weak, anaemic and prone to all kinds of diseases and infirmities, on the vanity of pomps and honours of this world, on the feebleness and imbecility of our minds, on the changes and the revolutions in the affairs, on the various faces and metasimplifications of heaven and earth, on the diversity of opinions, sects and religions, on the short duration of all things, briefly, on the great advantages that lie in fleeing vice and attending to virtue. It is somewhat like Juvenal's description in the handsome lines of his Tenth Satire: *Ask for a stout heart that has overcome the fear of death, that deems the end of the span of life among the last gifts of nature, that can withstand all kinds of pains, that knows no ire, craves nothing, prefers Hercules' labours to love's delights and the feasts and downy cushions of Sardanapalus.* Chancellor L'Hospital, who was endowed with that strength of character unlike any of his predecessors or successors, defined it sill more succinctly, although in bolder terms, which he even used to compose his motto: *I should not be terrified if the fabric of the globe breaks and its ruins knock me down.* Behind this minister lagged so many feeble and effeminate characters, so many cowardly and pussilanimous souls that are terrified by the first difficulties, that flee when faced with the least resistance and lose their heads when told of some great decision. I want a character like that of Epictetus, Socrates, Epicurus, Seneca, Brutus, Cato, or to use more familiar examples, Father Paul, Cardinal d'Ossat, President Jeannin, Your Eminence, Ferrier and some other of the same mark. I want them to carry the good maxims of philosophy in their heads and not merely on their lips, to have an integral knowledge of nature and not just of some part; to live in the world as if they were outside it, and under the skies as if they were above them, in order not only to dread the ruin of this great machine as the Gauls had done, but also to realize early on that the court is that spot of the world where most of the silly things are said and done, where friendships are more capricious and interested, people more disguised, the masters less fond of their servants, and Fortune more blind and foolish; and also to learn early not to be scandalized by all those extravagances. Finally, I want the minister to be able to look straight in the eyes those wealthier and less deserving than he, be proud of a generous poverty, firmly adhere to what is good, to a philosophical but also civic freedom, be on earth as by accident, at court on loan, and at a master's service only to discharge his duty honestly. Thus, whoever is possessed of this first general and universal disposition, conducive to composure, frankness and natural kindness, by the same will also acquire the sense of loyalty: *I consider the best whoever is the most loyal,* Pliny would say to Emperor Trajan; and that loyalty will not be ordinary, curbed by certain circumstances, and subject to the various considerations of our private interests, persons, the outcome of affairs and a thousand others, but a loyalty proper to a brave man, meant to serve the one to whom he will promise it, in spite of everything in the world, without exception of place, time or person. It was thus that Cassius Blosius served his friend Tiberius Gracchus and Chancellor L'Hospital's father, his master Charels of Bourbon, whose physician and confidant he was even during his master's downfall and persecution and never deserted him but followed him in disguise, sharing in all his misfortunes, assisting him in all his designs against the king, the emperor and Rome, against the cardinals and the pope himself. It was a conduct which his son, that great chancellor of France, appreciated so much that he was quite willing to place him at the head of his testament as the most remarkable member of his family. As a consequence, a minister with such a disposition must first and foremost be endowed with loyalty, and whenever he needs to prove it, be able to say freely: *here I do not set bounds to things nor limits to time, I am devoted to endless submission.*

Moreover, he must be free of ambition, avarice, greed and any other desire but that of serving his master well, from a position of modest fortune, honest and capable of saving himself and his closest relatives from envy and necessity. Because once he starts aiming at more, seeking advancement in duties and dignities, he will not be able to hide that he prefers his own profit to that of his master and that he helps himself first. That means to open the door to disloyalty, perfidy and treason. There would be no more secret which he does not reveal, no advice which he does not give away, no more resolution which he does not announce openly, no more enemy whom he does not woo, in short, *public good is considered of less account than private advantage.* If he desires the greatness of his master it is only in order to promote his own; if he does not succeed by serving him loyally, he would not hesitate to disserve his master, to sell him and deliver him to his enemies, in order to satisfy his own ambition or his inordinate greed: *for there where there is cupidity, almost all the other vices find a place: crime, impiety, perjury, thievery, rapine, fraud, alongside other troubles, deceptions and betrayals.* It is what Stilicho practised long ago, in order to win the friendship of Alaric, king of the Goths, and rely on his help to conquer the Eastern Empire; he concluded a shameful peace with Alaric and forced the emperor to pay Alaric tribute under the name of pension. Likewise,

Pietro della Vigna, chancellor of Frederick II, was rightly deprived of sight for having concluded too secret an understanding with Pope Alexander III, his master's capital enemy. It was also for the same reason that Cardinal Balue remained twelve years squeezed in a cage in the tower at Loches, under the reign of Louis XI, and Cardinal Duprat fell out of favour and was a long time imprisoned under Francis I. This very same staying power and disposition forbids the minister to be too credulous or superstitious and bigot, because *credulity is more an error than an offence and easily steals even into the best minds.* Nonetheless, it is characteristic of a judicious and sensible man to believe *nothing that does not meet the eye.* Palingenius at least agrees, otherwise one might be duped, because *whoever readily believes is readily deceived.*

And as we have already said, there are four or five ways of ensnaring or duping the gullible and the superstitious. Likewise, whoever busies himself with their practice should not be so foolish to let himself be outwitted by others, intent on using them against him. Besides, a minister, whose mind is so base as to demean it and lay it open to the belief in so many fables, impostures, false miracles, deceptions and charlatanries that are devised ordinarily, cannot raise great hopes of being successful in many affairs that require him to take in his stride all these follies. The subtleties of the state, the courtiers' artifices, the plotting and the practices of certain wary politicians easily deceive a man plunged into excessive and superstitious devotions. A diviner's prediction, the cawing of a rook, stumbling on a Moor, a false rumour, some farce, deceit or superstition may make him lose his head, confound him and reduce him to taking some shameful and dishonest decision. Even if he is not inclined to it by nature, the superstition, twin sister of this great credulity, will take possession of him all the same, and make him lose the little, if any, of his mind left to him. *The squeaking of a mouse made Fabius Maximus give up his dictatorship, and Caius Flaminius, his command of the cavalry.* It will rob his body of rest and his mind of firmness, consistency and resolution: *whoever is imbued with superstition cannot find peace.* It will expose him to thousand panics and terrors and make him fearful and apprehensive of *nothing more than what children fear in the dark and which they fancy it will happen in the future.* It will make him commit more sins than those forbidden by the ten commandments, and rubbing his eyes with holy water and touching a priest's cope, he would think that he has wiped out all the evil deeds in his life: *by error of judgement one becomes the servant of impiety.* Superstition will make him find scruples where there aren't any, and before concluding an affair, he would want to talk about it a hundred times to a confessor. He would reveal to the latter the counsel given to his prince, submit it to his censorship, examine it closely according to all the rules of the casuists, and at the end, *audaciously exclude that which is given by God in order to admit that which is his own.* In short, it will make him silly, impertinent, stupid, wicked, incapable of seeing anything appropriately but only capable of causing the total loss and ruin of whomever employs him, as well as his own, because *whoever is entangled in superstition cannot avoid the miseries that follow; to him superstition is his torment; he thinks bad those things which are not, and those which are of little harm he amplifies and makes them lethal.* Such mysteries and ceremonies are not needed at all to make a moral man: Lycurgus was held in esteem, although he cut off many superfluous things, useless to religion. Cato the Elder passed for the most virtuous man in Rome, although he laughed at the man who took for a bad omen the fact that mice had gnawed at his boots, telling him that *it is not such a terrible thing when the mice gnaw at the boots as it would have been truly monstrous had the mice been gnawed at by the boots.* Lucullus was not considered impious for having fought Tigranes on a day marked as nefarious in the Roman calendar, nor Claudius for having despised the auspices of the hens, and no more than Lucius Aemilius Paulus for being the first to wreck and demolish the temples of Isis and Serapis. Whence one may conjecture that superstition is the true character of a feeble spirit, grovelling, effeminate, popular, of which every strong person, every resolute man, every good minister must say *let such insanity be directly driven from our house,* as did Varro, talking of something else which did not deserve better.

The second virtue, which should serve as basis for the merits and the good name of our councillor is fairness. When one wishes to explain all its components, one should compare it to a thick trunk from which grow three branches: one of them reaches up to God, another stretches out to oneself and the third to one's neighbour. And in turn each of the said branches grows various twigs on whose particulars I shall not dwell, as it suffices to consider things in general and not in detail. That is why I lay the main foundation of this fairness in the moral man, in a way of life that conforms to the laws of God and of nature nobly, philosophically, with an integrity free of make-up, a virtue without art, a religion without fear and without doubt and hesitation, and a firm stance to do good without any other respect and consideration than what is needed to lead such a life, to live as a man of honour and righteousness, *disliking to go wrong, the good love virtue.* But since this natural, universal, noble and philosophical justice is at times unavailing and inconvenient in the practice of the world where *we have no solid and express models of true law and natural justice but use their shadows and images,* quite often it may be necessary to resort to the artificial, particular, political justice, built to relate to the want and necessity of polities and of states, because it is as soft and coward in order to accommodate to human and popular weakness different times, persons, affairs and accidents, as the Lesbian law used to do. All these considerations force us quite often to resort to many things which natural law would reject and condemn absolutely. Well now, one must live as the others do, and amid so many corruptions, the one with the fewest must pass for the best, *happy he who is beset by the smallest.* Amid so many vices, one may at times legitimize one of them, and amid so many good actions, one may put it across. As among pikes, the most resilient are the best, the same saying applies to ministers: one should value especially those among them who can stoop and adjust to diverse events in order to carry their designs through and so imitate the god Vertumnus, who was saying in Propertius: *my nature may readily assume all sorts of forms, whichever you want me to take I shall look as handsome.* What he should remember always though is to observe these two precepts: one, to bring together and join utility and honesty as much as possible, without losing it from sight and staying in the closest possible contact with it, and two, never to serve as instrument of his master's passion and never to suggest or settle anything which he himself does not judge necessary for the conservation of the state, the people's welfare or the salvation of the prince, remaining under cover for the rest, in keeping with Plutarch's good piece of advice: *that often in order to do justice one need not do all that is just.*

The third and last virtue, which our minister must possess and perfect is prudence, so necessary to a man in that position that he cannot do without it, given as Aristotle teaches us that *prudence and civil science are the same mental disposition,* and in rest, it is so powerful that it alone dominates and rules the three times of our lives, *as it orders the present, foresees the future and records the past;* it is so universal that it covers all the other virtues, circumstances and observations which we can make here of science, modesty, experience, conduct, restraint, discretion and particularly what the Italians call *segretezza,* using a word peculiar to them. Juvenal has well said that *had we but wisdom, the numen would not go away.*

Nevertheless, as several things are needed to obtain gold, which is the king of metals: the preparation of the matter, the disposition of the Earth, the warmth of the Sun, the length of time, so too, in order to acquire this prudence, the queen of political virtues, the gold of kingdoms, the treasure of states, one needs great aids and very favourable circumstances, fortitude, sound judgement, nimble wit, the ability to learn from the lessons imparted by great personalities, the study of sciences, familiarity with history, the happy memory of things past, all are dispositions favouring success. Sound consultation, knowledge and the consideration of circumstances, the foresight of effects, precaution against unforeseen difficulties, and prompt dispatch are the fine results it produces, and finally, the peace of peoples, the salvation of states, the commonweal of men are the divine fruits that one harvests. But still that is to say nothing unless we also mention the signs by which the progress one makes in the acquisition of this treasure may be appraised, and whether one is genuinely as wise and prudent as to assist a prince in the administration of his state. From among the many which may be mentioned, I would suggest the following as the most common and ordinary: to know how to keep secret whatever is not appropriate to divulge, and to talk from necessity rather than goaded by ambition, not to believe too readily what he hears and all sorts of people, be more willing to give away what is his own than to claim what belongs to another, closely examine the things before judging them, not to speak ill of anybody, excuse faults and defend the reputation of every one, despise nobody, not even the most undistinguished, honour men according to their merits and qualities, praise his companions more than himself, serve and look after his friends, remain firm and steadfast through their adversities, change no plans and decisions without some great reason, deliberate unhurriedly and execute cheerfully and diligently; he is not to be flabbergasted by what is extraordinary, make no fun of anybody, and above all, spare the poor and his friends; he is not to be envious of the praise given to those worthy of it, even if they were his enemies; never speak unknowingly, give advice only to those asking for it, nor pretend to be knowledgeable in matters outside his profession, and talk with modesty and not with haughtiness and affectation of matters with which he is familiar, as Piso used to do, and of whom Velleius Paterculus has said: *he does what is to be done, without any ostentation*, to do more and talk less, be more patient than violent, wishing his enemies well rather than ill, lose rather than entreat, be no cause of any trouble or upheaval, and finally, love God and serve his neighbour, and neither seek death nor fear it. What has induced me to gather all these signs in particular is the importance of the selection of a minister, which is so great that princes are very much interested in avoiding any mistake, and moreover, as one shouldn't hope to find them all in one man, one could not help preferring the one who has the most. And when the prince finds him, it is because born without a crown, the crowns cannot do without him: if fortune has not made him king, his self-confidence renders him the oracle of kings and every-thing that he will utter is an order, everything he will say is law, his simple words will pass for reasons, his actions for examples, and all his life for a miracle.

After having explained the minister's obligations towards the prince, we are left to consider, however briefly, the prince's contribution to a good relationship with his minister. And because I have always thought with Horace that in matters of rules and precepts, the shortest are the best: *be concise in what you convey*, I shall reduce those which seem to me most necessary in this case to three major ones: the first would be to treat him as a friend and not as a servant, to talk and confer with him frankly, to conceal from him nothing of what he might know, to show him complete confidence and to deal with his minister as if he were dealing with himself. Without being ashamed to admit his weakness, ignorance, imbecility or any other fault which he might have, nor his resentment, his quarrels, his anger, displeasures and similar passions that might torment him. And if I have not so much authority to establish this maxim, one may at least defer somewhat to Seneca's opinion: *think*, he says, *whether someone is worthy of your friendship, and if it pleases you to accept him, do it with an open heart and talk to him as freely as to yourself*. That is also what he said earlier in far fewer words: *discuss all things with your friend, but first of all, your friend himself*. In case the authority of such a great man needs to be supported and sustained by more arguments, Livy offers us one very strong and valid: *every one wishes to be confided in, and confidence when won obliges to the same confidence*. The most experienced chemists maintain that in order to make gold one needs to use only gold itself: *do not seek anywhere else the origin of gold, gold contains the seed of gold, although withdrawn and concealed from sight, it forces us to labour long and hard to uncover it.* The lapidaries confirm every day that one needs to use a diamond to cut and polish a diamond. The birders need to use birds in order to get a good catch and Varro used to call them *fraudsters and traitors of their kind.* The moral philosophers too maintain that love cannot be won but by mutual friendship and affection: *Do you wish, my son, to learn in a short time the fine secret of the potion of love: love yours, you will be loved by them, there is no better recipe.* How otherwise would a prince find confidence in a friend, unless he on his part conveys his first, shows him his duty by doing his own: *if you wish to see me shedding tears you must be in pain first,* Horace would say. Another would retort: *why should I treat you as a consul if you don't treat me as a senator?* All or nothing: either enjoy the full confidence or have none of it. Declare an affair today, be silent about another tomorrow, start one and never finish it, always holding back something and not saying all are all signs of defiance, inquietude and irresolution that make the minister forfeit his opportunity to counsel and the good will concerning his office.

The second thing which the prince needs to observe regarding his minister is to keep him as a friend and not as a flatterer, allow him to speak and give his opinion freely, explain and back up his opinion without contradicting him or resenting him whenever he does not condescend to his own, because *the wounds inflicted by a friend are better than the kisses of a flatterer,* and furthermore, as a brave councillor was telling his master, *you cannot use me as a friend and as a flatterer at one and the same time.* When a prince wants to be flattered, he has enough gentlemen and courtiers who are only looking for the opportunity without needing to use for that purpose the one who ought to be his well of truth, and who will never succeed with *the one whose ears are so formed as to find offensive those counsels that are profitable and listen to nothing but what would please and lead to ruin.*

Finally, like those who stand in the sun for a while and grow hot from its rays, so too, whomever a prince or sovereign brings close to his person, feels the effects of his power and friendship in the reward due for his services. The most honourable and glorious which he may be granted is their recognition and his master's satisfaction, *it is a favour to repay with kind words the services received,* and even according to the common opinion, *to please the princes is not man's least commendation.* Nevertheless, one must go beyond that, and in turn practise that fine virtue of liberality by providing him with those things that are necessary to lead an honest life in a middling status, and as remote from ambition as from necessity. Philip II used to say to Ruiz de Gomez, his servant and confidant: *take care of my affairs and I shall see to yours.* All the princes ought to say that to their ministers if they want to be served faithfully and affectionately: *liberality is a sort of common bond that binds together the benefactor and the beneficiary.* And I presume it would be even better to set their minds at rest in that respect, so they cease being obssessed by poverty, that horrible monster, and bring a completely free mind, unencumbered by passions, to the handling of affairs, the first fruit of that liberality. Whereas the second is that it brings honour and repute to whomever practises it, all the more so, as according to Aristotle, among all the virtuous princes, *the most highly esteemed are those who have the fame and reputation of liberality.* It is the ultimate virtue that binds people entirely to the service of those who do them good. According to an ancient saying, he who was the first to invent the benefices intended to forge stocks and handcuffs, in order to chain the men, make them captive and drag them after him.

That is, Monseigneur, all that I have to say in this matter which I should have never taken upon me to dwell on, if Your Eminence had not ordered me to, and your generosity and easy disposition would not have allowed me to hope a favourable forgiveness for all the errors which I might have committed. I am aware that Your

Eminence had preferred other forces to mine, a more fluent and effective pen, greater erudition, a sounder judgement and a more universal spirit. But we should have had but few statues of Jupiter, had only Phidias been allowed to carve them and nowadays Rome would be without paintings and pictures, had none but Michael Angelo and Raphael of Urbino been active in it: the good workers are not so often come across as to afford to dispense with the bad, nor are the great politicians, so as to dissuade one from amusing oneself by dipping at times in the writings of lesser men, among which Your Eminence may please to count this book, and in this way, oblige me to dream of another, ampler in scope. Under your continued favour and benevolence, I dare to promise myself that:

The day will come (provided Lachesis spins out the thread of our life) when you and your deeds will be made more widely known, your name will resound in the Gangetic land and on the shores of the Spanish sea. Your fame will travel over the Hyperborean cities, and by me will be made known to the very ends of Lybia. Then my inspiration lent loftier wings by the Muses, I will show to all how dear to you justice is, how great is your piety and faith, how good you are in council and courageous in action, how munificent and merciful; your genius and your mores will be made by me the wonder of the Earth, but until then accept with good grace what I am offering you now, which is the reward for my present toil.

The End

NOTES

[Advertisment]

Page 3

Montaigne and Charron. Michel de Montaigne (1533–1592), French author, councillor, member of the Bordeaux Parliament, and later, mayor of that town, a sceptical moralist who is also the initiator of a new literary genre, the modern essay, copiously displayed in his three volumes of *Essays* (including an increasing number of quotations from the second edition on), and in his *Journal de Voyage*. Pierre Charron (1541–1603), French theologian and moralist, who in the first two books of his *Of Wisdom* [De la Sagesse], published in 1601, undertook a systematic transposition of Montaigne's ideas from the *Essays*, and in the third, a rehashing of Justus Lipsius's *Politica*. Montaigne's influence on Naudé is quite negligible: his name is used mainly as an excuse for his own numerous quotations and digressions, which are mostly anecdotal, betraying a pretentious display of what might have been mistaken for erudition. On the other hand, he made extensive use of Book III of Charron's *Of Wisdom* in the organization of his own material. What he shared with the two, however, was their scepticism.

Balzac's PRINCE and Silhon's MINISTER. Jean-Louis Guez de Balzac (1597–1654), French man of letters, who like Naudé later, hoped for a political career in the government of Cardinal Richelieu, and to that end, wrote among others a political treatise *Le Prince* (1631), yet failed dismally to win Richelieu's benevolence. Although elected to the Academie Française in 1634, he rarely attended its sessions, preferring his place of retirement in the countryside to it. Jean de Silhon (1596–1667) was one of Richelieu's secretaries and state counsellors, and subsequently director of the Academie Française. He was the author of *Le Ministre d'État ou le Veritable Usage de la Politique Moderne* (1631–1634).

'To the Author'

Page 4

Jac. Bouchard at Rome. Jean-Jacques Bouchard (d.1641), Naudé's fellow Frenchman in Rome, was Cardinal Barberini's Latin secretary, and led the double life of a scholar and a libertine, but eventually lost his life by his practice of political intrigue as a means of gaining all sorts of advantages. Author of *Confessions* which were printed for the first time in 1881. The 1667 edition of Naudé's *Considerations* omits the date of Bouchard's panegyric, while Dr King leaves it out altogether from his 1711 English translation.

[Dedication]

Page 5

Cardinal de Bagni. Giovanni-Francesco Guido del Bagno, known as de Bagni (1578–1641), son of an Italian noble family, gifted diplomat of the Papal court, was Nuncio in France between 1627 and

119

1630. Bagni had been promoted bishop of Cervia and then of Rieti, and later, Cardinal. He became Richelieu's candidate to the Holy See, but ill health obliged him to retire in 1639, first to Rome, and shortly after, to Southern Italy where he preceded Pope Urban VIII in death by three years. It was on the eve of his departure from France that Bagni hired Naudé as his librarian and took him to Italy.

Nay, indeed..., Persius, *Satires*, V, 19–22. Marginal note: 'Pers. Sat.5'.

No one should..., Horace, *Odes*, I.vii.27 (to Plancus). The 1667 edition adds: 'Horat.II Carm.Ode 7'.

Chapter I

Page 7

Horace was...telling his friend Polio. Quintus Horatius Flaccus (65-8 BC), Latin lyric and satiric poet under Emperor Augustus, concerned himself with literary criticism and literature in general. At the age of 27, he won the protection of Mæcenas, himself a man of letters and one of Augustus's closest political advisers, ultimately to enjoy the virtual position of poet laureate. Gaius Asinius Polio (74 BC - 4 AD), Roman orator, poet, statesman and historian, turned from poetry to history shortly after 35 BC, writing a *History of the Civil Wars* (that covers the interval between c60 to 42 BC).

the work to which..., Horace, *Odes*, II.i.6-8. Marginal note:'Ode I.lib.2'.

I fear that..., Lucretius, *On the Nature of Things*, I.80-82. Marginal note: 'Lucret.lib.I.'

Page 8

though my heart..., Virgil, *Æneid*, II.12. The 1667 edition adds: 'Virgil Aen.2.'

would that I..., Seneca, *On Mercy*, II.2. There, it is related as Nero's exclamation when Burrus presented him with the paperwork for the execution of two brigands. Marginal note: 'Senec.lib.2 de clem.'

Solomon's advice. Solomon (mid-10th c. BC), third king of Israel, son of David, is traditionally regarded as the author of the *Book of Proverbs*. *do not appear...,* Proverbs, 25.6.

as Diognetus did. According to Pliny the Elder, he was a man who measured for Alexander the Great (356-323 BC) the distances covered in the latter's marches and wrote a book on the subject. See *Natural History*, VI.17.

the grammarian Phormio. He was a philosopher who allegedly delivered a lecture on the art of war in the presence of Hannibal (247-182 BC), commander-in-chief of the Carthaginian army and one of the great military leaders of Antiquity. Phormio is referred to by Bodin in his *Method*, ch.IV: 'The Choice of Historians', ET p.52.

we all think..., source not identified. According to F. C.-D., it is from Varro, *Mennippean Satires*, 312. Marginal note: 'Varro'.

Phoebus subjected his son. Attribute given to Apollo, the sun god in classical mythology. His son Phaeton asked to be allowed to drive the chariot of the sun through the heavens for a single day.

you ask for..., Ovid, *Metamorphoses*, II, 54-55. Marginal note: 'Ouid. in Met.'

120

Page 9

with a bare sword...,paraphrase of Virgil, *Æneid*, IX, 549. Marginal note: 'Virgil.Æneid.I'. The 1667 editions adds: '9'.

the goddess Eleusine. Here Naudé alludes to the Eleusinian Mysteries, the most secret religious rites of Ancient Greece, yet it is impossible to ascertain whether he himself got it wrong or his source was erroneous. The goddess honoured on those occasions was actually Demeter, and the location of the ritual was Eleusis, the ancient Greek city west of Athens, whence the name of the ritual but not of any goddess.

to the solitary..., allusion to Proteus, the Greek mythological old man of the sea and shepherd of the flocks, said to have had knowledge of all things past, present and future, but to have been reluctant to tell what he knew and always trying to evade those who wanted to consult him by assuming all kinds of shapes. See Homer, *Odyssey* IV, 383–424.

all of a sudden he will..., Virgil, *Georgics*, IV. 407–408. Marginal note: 'Virgil in Georg.' to which 1667 edition adds: 'iv'.

the young Aristaeus. Aristaeus, ancient Greek divinity, son of Apollo and the nymph Cyrene, was born in Lybia but moved to Thebes where the Muses taught him the arts of healing and prophecy. He was said to have introduced the cultivation of the vine, olive and the bees, and to have been the protector of huntsmen and shepherds. He travelled widely, and ultimately disappeared in Thrace.

which Arethusa. A nymph in Greek mythology, Arethusa was part of the retinue of Artemis, goddess of the hunt, vegetation and wild animals, who according to one version, changed her into a spring to escape the advances of the river god Alpheus.

with Pliny the Younger. Gaius Plinius Cæcilius Secundus (c61–c113 AD), Roman barrister, administrator and author, adopted son of Pliny the Elder (23–79 AD), published nine books of private letters and a tenth book of official addresses to Emperor Trajan with the latter's replies.

the right way..., paraphrase of Pliny the Younger, *Letters*, IX. 26, to Lupercus.

Page 10

three lines from Lucretius. Titus Lucretius Carus (1st c. BC), Latin poet and philosopher, who in his long poem *On the Nature of Things*, propounded the atomic theory of Epicurus about the materiality of things, including the human soul that dies with the body. The lines in question are a prose paraphrase in French and not in Latin. In *On the Nature of Things*, I, 44–49 and II, 646–651, Lucretius talks about divinity and its immortality that is removed from human affairs. What Naudé does is to replace divinity by the Sun and lend it the qualities which Lucretius attributes to divinity, while in fact Lucretius considers the Sun as perishable as any other material thing, the Earth included.

although with its rays..., Palingenius (Pier Angelo Manzoli), *The Zodiac of Human Life*, Book VIII 'Scorpio', 160–161. It is interesting to note that Naudé quotes correctly from this book throughout, so he must have had access to a copy of the *Zodiacus*, written in Latin and first published at Basel in 1537, a forbidden book in Catholic lands from 1558 on, but very popular in the Protestant countries, with over sixty editions, translations and imitations. In England, for instance, it was used as a school textbook. It is a long poem of unequal literary quality, which deals with the stages of human life and is divided into twelve cantos. It is not an astrological almanac, but the epic of an age, in which fundamental questions about existence, morality, metaphysics, the daily life are discussed not without glee and satire. A post-morten trial of heresy was instituted against its author by Pope Paul III, his bones were unburied and burnt at the stake. Marginal note: 'Paling. in Scorp.'

Trithemius and Pererius. Johannes Tritheim of Heidenberg (1462 -1516), German Benedictine monk, bibliograph and author of an introduction to Claudius Ptolemy's work on the effects of stars. Naudé mentions him alongside Pererius and with St Thomas Aquinas, Roger Bacon, Pico della Mirandola and others in Chapter XVII of his *Apology*. On the other hand, I do not know who hides behind the Latinized name of Pererius. It might be Georg von Peuerbach (1423-1461), an Austrian mathematician and astronomer, whose pupil was Johann Müller, better known as Regiomontanus, or it could be Isaac de la Peyrère, a disciple of Giordano Bruno, or Bonaventure de Périers, author of *Cymbalum Mundi*. F. C.-D. identifies him with Benito Pereyra (c1537-1610), a Spanish Jesuit philosopher and theologian, but I do not know on what grounds.

limbs are..., Claudian, *Against Eutropius*, II, 18-19. Marginal note: 'Claud. 2. in Eutrop.'

Many maintain. See Lipsius, *Politica*, IV.xiv.8, and Plutarch, 'Comparison between Philopoem and Titus Flaminius' in *Lives*, III, 3.

Page 11

Charron says. See Charron, *Of Wisdom*, Book III, ch. 2, p. 1036 of 1729 ET. He in turn attributes it to Plutarch. See the latter's *Moralia: Precepts of Statecraft* 818a (24).

and do as the bastards...to bitterness. All this segment has been edited out in Dr King's ET of 1711.

Paracelsus' followers. Philippus Aureolus Theophraster Bombast von Hohenheim, better known as Paracelsus (1493-1541), physician, chemist and army surgeon, established the role of chemistry in medicine, gave the first clinical description of syphilis and authored the *Great Book of Surgery*. Highly controversial and argumentative, he was forced into the position of vagrant scholar, and died in mysterious circumstances at Salzburg, while in the service of the prince-archbishop of Bavaria.

Hippocrates' texts. Hippocrates (c460-c377 BC), Greek physician who is regarded as the father of medicine in Europe. Not all the works known as the *Hippocratic Collection*, were written by him, but were part of the library of the medical school of Cos where he had taught.

the earth has..., paraphrase of Pliny the Elder, *Natural History*, XVIII.i.2-5. Marginal note: 'Plin.lib.18.cap.1.' This whole paragraph contains different ideas, precariously gathered together by Naudé: one is about the versatility of things, another about polysemy, and still another, about people's need to legitimize their acts by looking for precedents in various sources that are considered authorities.

to wish to talk about politics. In 1622/3, Gaspar Schioppius [Sciopius] published a slim book entitled *Pædia politices*, in which he reproduced parts of his *Apologia Machiavelli*, that had been circulating in MS and it seems that Naudé drew on it too, for the discussion on coups d'état and stratagems.

which Aristotle mentions. Aristotle the Stagirite (384–322 BC), Greek philosopher, logician and scientist, born at Stagira in Macedonia, preceptor of Alexander the Great, founder of the Lyceum at Athens to rival Plato's Academy, after a life dedicated to knowledge and inquiry in every field, was forced to seek refuge in Chalcis, when on the death of Alexander, the Athenians began an anti-Macedonian rebellion, and it was there that he died a year later. Aristotle is the thinker that has contributed the most to the shaping of what may be termed the Western civilization. During the Renaissance, the interest in his thinking was renewed as it was dissociated from the scholasticism of the Church, and it was also then that his *Politics*, and particularly its Book V, began to serve as the basis of the political theorizing of the modern age.

not to know..., paraphrase, Aristotle, *Metaphysics*, III.i.3.

That is why Lipsius. Joest Lips (1547–1606), Flemish classical scholar, humanist, moral and political theorist, inspired by Roman stoicism and the writings of Tacitus, of which he produced the first modern scholarly edition. He taught mainly at the universities of Leiden and Louvain and was the author of a vast correspondence and other writings among which *De constantia* (1584) and *Politicorum sive Civilis Doctrinæ libri sez* (1589), which in the present text is referred to as *Politica* for short. Its first edition was eventually placed on the Index of the Sacred College, though Naudé did have access to it.

Timons and. Timon the Misanthropist, Greek philosopher of the 5th century BC, who turned his personal losses and the misfortunes of his homeland into hatred of humankind. He became the butt of many satirists, and his name was used as a metaphor for misanthropy, that Naudé seems to have favoured.

Page 12

without being well informed. Naudé renders this phrase in Greek by the word ἀπαιδευτώς. His command of ancient Greek is questionable, and the scattered Greek words in the text are mere decoration, meant to impress the innocent only.

followed by Saint Thomas. If the above discussion about Aristotle was inspired by Schoppe's *Pædia Politices*, the long quotations attributed to St Thomas Aquinas are a verbatim transposition from the *Pædia* (pp. 33–40 of the 1663 Helmstadt edition). Alessandro Piazzi, the editor of the 1992 Italian translation of Naudé's *Political Considerations*, has identified the quotations as actually coming from Pietro d'Alvernia's *Politicorum continuatio*, Book V, ch. 11.

Page 13

Machiavelli and Cardan. Niccolo Machiavelli (1469–1527), Florentine author, political theorist, historian, civil servant, military strategist and diplomat, best known for his political treatises *The Prince* and *Discourses on the First Decade of Tito Livy*, both completed by 1515. Schoppe's *Apologia Machiavelli* is likely to have influenced Naudé's opinions of Machiavelli. Jerome Cardan (1501–1576), Italian physician, mathematician, astrologer and versatile author. His *Book of My Life* (ET 1930) has become as famous as Cellini's *Autobiography*. Naudé was a very keen collector of his writings, and published Cardan's autobiography in France in 1644.

strikes everything..., paraphrase, Claudian, *Against Eutropius*, I. 182-183. Marginal note: 'Claudian'.

as did Tarquin. Lucius Tarquinius Superbus (2nd half of the 6th c. BC), last king of Rome, who according to tradition, reigned between 534 and 510 BC as absolute despot and put to death a number of senators.

Thrasybulus and Periander. The legend of Periander's advice to Thrasybulus to eliminate those standing too tall is reproduced twice in Aristotle's *Politics*: Book III, xiii, §17 and Book V, x, §13. Thrasybulus (6th c. BC) was tyrant of Miletus. Periander (d.586 BC), tyrant of Corinth, considered one of the Seven Wise Men of Greece, was a firm and effective ruler, represented as a cruel despot in much of the ancient Greek literature, probably under the influence of the Corinthian nobility whom he treated harshly.

Page 14

just as religion..., Seneca, *On Mercy*, II,v.1. Marginal note: 'Lib.2.c.5.'

nothing befits..., Seneca, *On Mercy*, II.v.4.

King Epiphanes. The Seleucid king Antiochus IV Epiphanes (215-164 BC) was also known as Epimanes, meaning the Mad, because of his alleged emotional instability. Otherwise, he was a successgful and popular monarch.

that Ramiro of Aragon. Ramiro II the Monk (d.1154), king of Aragon between 1134 and 1137, was a monk and bishop-elect of Barbastro at the time of his election to succeed his brother Alfonso I. Eventually, he crushed a revolt of the nobles, but abdicated in 1137.

a king of Great Britain. That is James I (1566-1625), the first Stuart king of England, given his full name in *Addition*, ch.I, p. 12 (1630 Paris edition).

was looked upon..., the quotation is in Italian and probably from *Dieci Libri di Pensieri diversi* (1620) by Alessandro Tassoni. Marginal note: 'Tassoni lib.7.cap.4.' F.C.-D. has located the source on p. 206 of a 1646 edition printed at Venice. Italian poet, political writer and critic, Tassoni (1565-1635) is best known for his mock-heroic, satiric poem *La Secchia Rapita*, 1622 (ET: *The Rape of the Bucket*, 1825).

Henry III, so much. It is almost impossible to recognize King Henry III of France (1551-1589), son of Catherine de Medicis, in this characterization. He did indeed give up the throne of Poland but only to assume that of France left vacant by the death of his brother Charles IX.

Page 15

Pope Sixtus V to say. Sixtus V (1530-1590), Franciscan monk, pope between 1585 and 1590, was one of the founders of the Counter-Reformation. He rehauled the central administration of the Church (which remained substantially the same until the Second Vatican Council of 1962-1965), and in the sphere of international political relations, assumed the difficult task of balancing Spain against France to avoid the supremacy of the former, while also trying to contain the spread of Protestantism.

Monsieur de Villeroy. Nicolas de Neufville, Lord of Villeroi (1542–1617), secretary of state of Henry IV the Great (1553–1610), after long service under Catherine de Medicis and her sons, Charles IX and Henry III.

did not prevent Masson. Jean-Papire Masson (1544–1611), French historian, college professor and deputy general-prosecutor, wrote in Latin and published a series of works on the history of France from Roman to contemporary times, as well as others on ecclesiastical history. Marginal note: 'In Episcop. Rom.'

happened to Celestine V. Celestine V (c1209–1296), a Benedictine hermit, practising a rigorous ascetism, founded the Celestine order of monks, and was in his eighties when in 1294, he accepted to become pope in order to aleviate the critical situation of the Church without a pope for two years. Lacking administrative and diplomatic abilities, he resigned five months later to avoid endangering the Church any further. He was the first pontiff who had the courage to abdicate, although many, among whom Dante, considered his gesture an act of cowardice.

Paolo Giovio, as he talks. Paolo Giovio (1483–1552), Italian historian who wrote mainly in Latin, was made bishop of Nocera in 1528, wrote a contemporary history of Florence (1550–1552) and a sequence of lives of famous men, while also becoming himself a famous early art collector. Marginal note: 'Libr. de piscib. Rom.'

Adrian VI who had..., Adrian VI (1454–1523), the only Dutch pope, elected in 1522, met with the hostility of Italian bishops alongside that of the Protestants and the Turks, which prevented him from achieving much in the reorganization of the Roman Church. Giovio's sarcasm reflects the irritation felt by the Italians for anyone who was not one of them, no matter the real qualities of the individual concerned.

than Peter Martyr. Pietro Martire d'Anghiera (1457–1526), Milanese nobleman, ultimately chaplain at the Spanish court of Ferdinand II of Aragon and Isabella I of Castile, author of a collection of 812 letters, reflecting the political life of his time (1488–1526) and a history of the Spanish explorations, *On the New World*, published in 1530. According to F. C.-D., the quotation is from Book XXXV, epist. 753, p. 435, col. I, of the 1670 Amsterdam edition of his collection of letters.

Page 16

certainly, a sound mind..., free quotation from Seneca, *Epistles*, XXVII, 8, or *Letters to Lucilius*, III.28.8. Marginal note: 'Plaut. in Trinum.' has been placed too high by the typesetter, as it refers to the subsequent quotation which is from Plautus.

as Seneca says. Lucius Annaeus Seneca (c4BC–65AD), Iberian-born Roman philosopher, statesman and tragedian, disseminator of a kind of Stoicism that emphasized social duty and inner tranquillity.

the sage man..., paraphrase, Plautus, *Three Bob Day*, Act II, 363.

Alexander put his mind. Alexander III the Great (356–323 BC) king of Macedonia, expanded the Hellenistic world to India in the East and Egypt in the South, in a time-span of six years.

Caesar undertook. Gaius Julius Caesar (101–44 BC), Roman statesman and general, elected consul in 59 BC, conquered Gaul and unleashed the Civil War of 49–45 BC, then assumed the title of dictator but was assassinated in the Senate on 15 March 44 BC.

Two shepherds, Romulus and Tamerlane. Romulus, the legendary founder of Rome. Tamerlane (c1336–1405), Central Asian Turkic conqueror who eventually expanded his dominion over the territory between Mongolia and the Mediterranean Sea. He died on the expedition to conquer China.

Muhammad wanted. Muhammad (c570–632 AD), founder of Islam and of the Arab empire, unfortunately died before his followers embarked upon their advance beyond the Arab peninsula.

which Juvenal teaches. Decimus Junius Juvenalis (c60–c127AD) one of the most important Roman satiric poets, who mainly dealt with life in Rome, its follies and corruption. Phrases from his works have become widespread sayings still in circulation, such as 'who will guard the guards themselves?'

ask for a stout heart. The complete sentence is 'ask for a stout heart that has no fear of death': Juvenal, *Satires*, X, 357. Marginal note: 'Satyr.10'.

mean to enchase. The Rome edition uses the verb *enchaster*, which becomes *enchasser* in the 1667 edition.

Oh what a contemptible. Seneca, *Natural Questions*, I, Pref.,5. Marginal note: 'In procem.nat.quæst.'

like some god..., ancient Greek expression, which Naudé quotes in Latin, affirming the intervention of a divinity or supernatural creature that descends upon the stage by means of some machinery to give a happy ending, however implausible, to a tragic situation.

Page 17

slow to make..., Horace, *The Art of Poetry*, 164.

which befit..., paraphrase, Sophocles, *Tyro 1 and 2*, Fragments, 664: 'old age and the wear of time teach many things'.

The poet.... This long sentence is replaced by Dr King in his 1711 translation by the following paraphrase: 'for Youth, that is optima quaeque dies, etc., as Virgil and Seneca call it, has the Epithet of *Best* because the mind is tractable, and the Time fitted for Labour, and proper to be exercised in fitting studies.'

the best of our days..., Virgil, *Georgics*, III, 66–67. Marginal note: 'Virgil.3.Georg.'

why the best..., Seneca, *Epistles*, 108.27. Marginal note: 'Epist. 109', corrected in the 1667 edition to '108'.

not having bound..., Horace, *Epistles*, I.i.14. Quotation ommitted by Dr King from his 1711 translation.

Plutarch and Plato. Plutarch (c46–c120 AD), Greek moral philosopher and a priest of Apollo's temple at Delphi. Plato (428–348BC), Athenian philosopher, founder of the Academy, a centre for the systematic pursuit of philosophical and scientific research.

Homer and Virgil. Homer, presumably Ionian bard of the 9th century BC, to whom *The Iliad* and *The Odyssey* are attributed. Publius Vergilius Maro (70–19 BC), Roman poet, author of *The Æneid* and of bucolic poetry, a supporter of Augustus. Nonetheless, in his *Apology*, Naudé presents himself as Virgil's defender and devotes a whole chapter (XXI) to him. Actually, Plato was of little use to

Naudé, as was Homer, while Aristotle was more important to him than he wants to admit. His quotations are good evidence in this sense. Among the moderns, Lipsius, Botero, Campanella, Clapmar, Schoppe and Bodin were as important as Charron.

Page 18

but the BOOK OF ST ANTHONY. A rather surprising confession on Naudé's part. Is he referring to *The Life of Anthony of Egypt* by Athanasius (c293–373 AD), bishop of Alexandria, who describes Anthony's psychic struggles from which he emerged as a sane and sensible father of monachism, that is, of vita contemplativa? It may also be an indirect reference to his own struggles with the temptations of the flesh and political ambitions, and so a roundabout admission of his preference for vita contemplativa to the vita activa.

without intent. Dr King drastically condenses the text from here to the end of the paragraph, omitting the quotations in the process.

of Petronius who. Petronius Arbiter (d.66 AD), Roman man of letters, author of the *Satyricon*, in which he depicts the society of the 1st century AD, and is now considered the first European novel. A friend and victim of Emperor Nero, he was condemned to death by suicide, having been denounced as a participant in a plot against the emperor.

young man, you talk..., Petronius, *Satyricon*, 3. Marginal note: 'Init. Satyr.'

a *fine* mind. The quotation also appears in Naudé's *Addition à l'histoire de Louys XI* as coming from Seneca, 'epist. 107'. Actually, it is from Menander, *Sententiae singulares*, 557. Justus Lipsius uses it in his *Two Books of Constancy*, II, iv, 38–39.

while I am still. The segment from here to **I shall exert myself** is edited out by Dr King in his 1711 translation.

it is worthwhile..., paraphrase, Horace, *Epistles*, I.i.32. The 1667 edition adds: [Horat.1 Ep.1].

the good man Aratus. Aratus (c315–c245 BC), Greek poet, best known for his didactic poem on astronomy, *Phænomena*, over one third of which is a versification of a prose work on astronomy by Eudoxus of Cnidus (c390–340 BC).

Page 19

Celsus, who. Celsus (1st c. AD), Roman encyclopædist and medical writer.

Dioscorides was a soldier. Dioscorides was the name of several physicians and botanical writers. One of them, Pedacius, a physician, was the author of a work entitled *Materia Medica*, posterior to the Elder Pliny.

Macer, a senator. Æmilius Macer (d.16 BC), wrote poetry on birds, snakes and medicinal plants. A friend of Ovid's, he is mentioned by the latter in his *Tristia*, IV.10.33–34. A work, still extant and entitled *Æmilius Macer De Herbarum Virtutibus* dates however only from the Middle Ages.

Hippodamus himself. Hippodamus of Miletus (5th c. BC), Greek architect and town-planner, whose treatise is analyzed by Aristotle in his *Politics*, II, viii.

can infer and draw all kinds of conclusions. Here Naudé refers to the widespread rational doctrine of the mechanistic universe,

which in its popular form, was reducing knowledge about the world
and nature to a handful of principles, accessible to anybody interested. The mechanistic doctrine was built on a basis provided by the
Greek atomic materialism, and the research in mathematics and
anatomy of Renaissance Italy, in particular.

as Pliny says. See the Elder Pliny, *Natural History*, xxxv,50.

what the king..., Plautus, *Three Bob Day* Act II, 207–208.
Marginal note: 'Plaut.' The quotation also appears in *Bibliographia
Politica*, p. 182 of the Bosco edition.

Briefly to conclude. Dr King edits out Naudé's text from here to
the end of the chapter, replacing it by a paragraph summarizing his
stance when dealing with such risky matters.

since Cato, since Curtius..., Palingenius, *The Zodiac of Human
Life*, Book II 'Taurus', 448–450. Marginal note: 'Paling. in Tauro.'

together with Propertius: *I ascend...*, Sextus Propertius (c55–16
BC), Roman elegiac poet; the quotation is from his *Elegies*,IV.10.34.

Page 20

there are so many people. What Naudé does here is to try and
legitimize plagiarism and the theft of intellectual property in a way
that was still the norm at the time, though in decline, by invoking
the need of continuity in the advancement of knowledge, which he
considered to be a natural process. It is interesting to note in passing
that Naudé does exactly what he denies doing and what he criticizes
others for doing. In that way, he tries to divert attention from his
own shortcomings and from the fact that he is not the original writer
he claims to be.

the servile herd, Horace, *Epistles*, I.xix.19.

the frogs used to sing..., Virgil, *Georgics*, I, 378.

What Clapmarius says. Arnold Clapmar (1574–1604), German
jurist and political writer, professor of public law at the University
of Altdorf, won fame by his successful brokerage between the city of
Nuremberg and its princely neighbours. His main work, *De arcanis
rerumpublicarum libri sex* [Of Secrets of State in Six Books], was
dedicated to the City Council of his native Bremen, and published
there in 1605, with over six reprints between that year and 1665.
What Naudé criticizes Clapmar for is exactly what he does himself in
the *Political Considerations*. Was he jealous of the success scored by
Clapmar's book at the time?

as Bodin remarked. Jean Bodin (1530–1596), French political
theorist and economist, best known for his *Six Books of a Common-
weale*, 1577 (ET 1606), and his *Method for the Easy Comprehension
of History*, 1566 (ET 1945). In passing it may be remarked that
Naudé never mentions Bodin's concept of sovereignty.

Many have dealt..., Bodin, *Method*, ch. VI: 'Types of Government in States', p. 154 of the ET.

Page 21

these discourses..., free rendition of Plato, *Republic*, II. 378a.
Marginal note: 'Libr. de Repub.'

Campanella held it. Tommaso Campanella (1568–1639), Italian
Dominican monk, one of the pioneers of the New Science or the Age
of Reason, natural scientist, philosopher, politician, theologian and
poet, a contemporary of Giordano Bruno, Francis Bacon and Sarpi, and

Galileo's great friend. Best known in the English-speaking world as the author of the utopian treatise, *The City of the Sun*. Here Naudé alludes to Campanella's power of concentration which touched on the prodigious, and his remark also makes plausible the allegations of Campanella's talent for self-hypnotism.

Du Bartas would. Guillaume de Salluste, Lord of Bartas (1544–1590), Huguenot nobleman, counsellor of Henry of Navarre, authored a long epic poem with didactic intent, *La Semaine* (1578), more successful in England, where it was translated and published in 1605, under the title *Divine Weekes and Workes*, with several reprints.

Agrippa himself. Heinrich Cornelius Agrippa von Nettesheim (1486–1535), German medical doctor, lawyer, theologian, expert in occult sciences, for a time secretary of the Holy Roman Emperor, authored among others a major work on cabbalism, *Occulta Philosophia*, as well as *De Incertitudine et Vanitate Scientiarum et Artium* (1530), a pioneer work on the new scepticism, published in an English translation in 1569 as *Of the Vanitie and Uncertaintie of Artes and Sciences*.

never imagine myself a Nero or a Busiris. Originally, Lucius Domitius Ahenobarbus, Nero (37–68 AD) was the fifth Roman emperor, remembered for his unstable character during the second half of his rule. His memory was systematically denigrated by order of Emperor Trajan (53–117 AD, ruled from 98 on). Busiris, mythological king of Egypt, son of Poseidon and the daughter of Epathus, another legendary Egyptian king, who during a famine, was advised by a Cypriot seer to sacrifice a foreigner to Zeus each year. Eventually, Heracles, arriving from Lybia, was caught to that end but managed to burst his ties and kill Busiris. The name may also be an earlier Greek corruption of the name of the Egyptian god Usire, later changed into Osiris. Relatedly, 'Busiris' became the name of a city in the middle of the Nile Delta in ancient Egypt, that had a great temple dedicated to Isis, where seasonal festivals with sacrifices and passion plays were held in her and her husband Osiris's honour, as mentioned among others by Herodotus in his *Histories*, Book II, 60–63.

they gave their advice..., likely to have been transcribed from Lipsius's *Politica*, IV.xiii.1. Nonetheless, the attribution to Nero is incorrect, as the quotation may be traced back to Cicero, *Letters to Atticus*, II.i.8.

Chapter II

Page 22

a selection and a triage..., see Lipsius, *Politica*, I.vii.22–23. Naudé reproduces the definition only partially and in French instead of Latin, emphasizing the selection and omitting the understanding of the matter or issues in question, as a necessary condition, as well as the spheres of action involved, that is the private and the public, about which Lipsius is very clear: 'as the understanding and choosing of what is to be sought or avoided, both in private and in public.'

sagacious planning..., Lipsius, *Politica*, IV.xiv.6–7. Rendered in faulty Latin, with one change in the order of things: Naudé puts the interest of the kingdom before that of the king.

bribery and deception. Lipsius, *Politica*, IV.xiv.1.

Page 23

as Charron says. See Charron, *Of Wisdom*, III.iv.2 (p.1171 of the 1729 ET). Marginal note: 'Lib.3 c̈ö 2.'

make use of finesse..., paraphrase of a widespread age-old saying to be found in Arisophanes's *Wasps*, for instance, as well as in Erasmus, *Adages*, I.ii.28.

Louis XI, the wisest. Louis XI (1423-1483), king of France, who gained the fame of duplicity by the ways he used to consolidate royal power at the expense of nobles and neighbours.

whoever does not..., in *Addition*, Naudé uses this saying as its leitmotif (ch.ii, p.32 and ch.iii, p.64 of the 1630 edition), and attributes it to Charles VII. He might have taken it from Papirus Masson's book on Louis XI, IV, p.33. Lipsius quotes it in *Politica*, IV.xiv.2, and Botero in his *Reason of State*, V.5, p.104 of the ET. It may be noted that both these latter books were brought out in 1589. Botero, however, attributes it to Seneca.

Page 24

and Emperor Tiberius. Tiberius Claudius Nero Caesar (c42 BC-37 AD), Roman emperor (14-37 AD), succeeded his adoptive father Augustus to the principate.

of all the virtues..., Tacitus, *Annals*, IV.71. Probably quoted by Naudé from Lipsius, *Politica*, IV.xiv.2.

if one cannot..., Cicero, *Letters to Friends*, I.9.21. Likely to have been reproduced from Lipsius, *Politica*, IV.xiii.2. Marginal note: 'Ciceron. e lib ii ad Lentul.'

what Cicero calls. Marcus Tullius Cicero (106-43 BC), Roman barrister, orator and statesman, author of several philosophical treatises and a vast correspondence, always seeking the right balance in public matters.

to win the hearts..., Cicero, *Moral Obligation*, II.v.17. Likely to have been reproduced from Lipsius, *Politica*, IV.xiv.3.

taught by the politicians. In France, at least, there were two categories of people that were given this name. The first, made up of moderate Catholics, the opposite of the *dévots* and the *religiose*, and whose leaders belonged to the nobility, was more concerned with the peace of the realm and of their homesteads than with the salvation of their souls, thus putting the welfare of the commonwealth before waging war for God's sake. They formed a third party in the conflict between Catholics and the Huguenots, in the last three decades of the 16th century. The second category was broader and much looser, made up of peripatetic scholars and humanists who promoted the peaceful resolution of conflicts in Europe, on the basis of a realistic appraisal of situations. What the two categories had in common was the tendency of distinguishing between religion and politics and the desire for peace through an equilibrium of forces, at a time when political theory and public law based on natural law were at a very early stage of conceptualization.

secrets of imperium. Tacitus, *Annals*, II.36. The correct Latin phrase in Tacitus is *arcana imperii*.

Page 25

a thick book on the secrets. Actually this is not a description of Clapmar's book, which in its 1624 edition in octavo has only 240 pages, including the index. Rather it fits Federico Bonaventura's tome, 667-page thick in quarto, published at Urbino in 1623 under the title *Della ragion di stato e della prudenza politica*, with its material organized on the basis of Book V of Aristotle's *Politics*.

in Livy, Sallust, Ammianus Marcellinus. Livy, full name, Titus Livius (c59 BC-17 AD), Roman historian, author of a patriotic history of Rome from inception to the year 9 BC, in 142 books, only 32 of which have survived; Sallust, full name, Gaius Sallustus Crispus (c86 -c34 BC), Roman statesman and political historian, author of two monographs, *Conspiracy of Catiline*, and the *Jugurthine War*, as well as of a *History of Rome* in five books, of which only fragments have survived; Ammianus Marcellinus (c.330-395 AD), military man of Greek origin and last important Roman historian who continued the work of Tacitus by writing the history of the later Roman Empire to 378 AD, *The Chronicles of Events*, of which only the last 18 books survive, covering the years 353-378 AD.

in the way... . The rest of the sentence starting from here is omitted in Dr King's ET.

as Marbod the Poet. Marbod of Rennes (c1035-1123), French cleric, writer and teacher and bishop of Rennes, author of numerous lives of saints, didactic poems, satires and a *Book of Gems* (c1090) on the medical and magical properties of precious stones, knowledge of which was to be confined only to a few.

what is communicated..., F. C.-D. identified the quotation on page 9 of a 1539 Cologne edition of *De gemmarum*, etc. Marginal note: 'Libr. de Gem.'

Page 26

of Festus Pompeius. Sextus Pompeius Festus (2nd or 3rd c. AD), Roman lexicographer, author of an abridged edition of Marcus Verrius Flaccus' *De verborum significatione* (On the Meaning of Words).

Virgil: *I will speak...,* Virgil, *Æneid*, I.62. Marginal note: '*Æneid.I.*'

to honour you,... Virgil, *Æneid*, IV.442.

Horace: *neither wine...,* paraphrase, Horace, *Epistles*, I.xviii.37.

here is Lucan. Marcus Annæus Lucanus (39-65 AD), nephew of Seneca, poet with republican leanings, author of the historical epic, the *Civil War* also known as *Pharsalia* for the vidid description of the battle at that place, the single major Latin epic poem that is free of the intervention of gods. Jealous of his talent, Emperor Nero began to persecute him, a fact that made Lucan join a conspiracy to assassinate Nero. On the discovery of the plot he was compelled to commit suicide.

Nature has kept secret..., Lucan, *Civil War*, X.295-298.

Page 27

Augustus, intent on. Naudé got it all wrong here. Gaius Octavius, later known as Octavian (63 BC-14 AD), while as Rome's first citizen claimed at the end of civil war to reverse to the old republican institutions, introduced instead an authoritarian rule, and had the Senate reduced from 1,000 to 800 and then to 600 members. He himself came to be known under the changed name of Augustus, and later still, of Caesar Augustus, a step towards deification.

Maecenas and Agrippa. Gaius Maecenas (c70-8 BC), Roman diplomat and patron of letters, adviser of Octavian in his early days.

Marcus Vipsanius Agrippa (63-12 BC), early companion of the future emperor, he distinguished himself as admiral of Octavian's first fleet, helped him defeat his rivals, and became his second in command, actively participating in the defence and the administration of the empire.

to whom he was in the habit..., paraphrase, Dio Cassius, *Romaika*, LII.1.2. Dio Cassius (c150-235 AD), Roman administrator and historian who wrote a history of Rome in the last years of the republic and the early empire, in Greek. Marginal note: 'Libr.53.'

in Suetonius' *Julio* **that.** Gaius Suetonius Tranquillius (c69-c122 AD), Roman biographer and antiquarian, author among others of *The Lives of Caesars* and *Concerning Illustrious Men*. Here Naudé refers to Book I, 'The Deified Julius', of *The Lives of the Caesars*. According that text, however, only Cornelius Balbus is described as 'familiarissimus Caesaris' (LXXXI,2), while Quintus Paedius, one of Caesar's three grand nephews, is mentioned solely in connection with Caesar's last will, by which he is bequeathed only a fraction of Caesar's estate, the largest part going to Gaius Octavius, the future Octavian (LXXXIII.2).

after Lysander's victory. Lysander (d395 BC), Greek military and political leader; the victory is that which he scored for Sparta at the end of the Peloponnesian War. The establishment of the oligarchy of the Thirty Tyrants at Athens (404 BC) was his doing, as were the decarchies in the cities allied with Athens. What Naudé talks about is but legend.

the Six Procurators. The original function of the procurators was the administration of the endowments of the Church of St Mark, its upkeep and decoration, as well as the supervision of its chaplains, but their duties expanded, to include the administration of wills and the guardianship of minors and the insane. Alongside the dogeship, the elected procurators were the only dignitaries who enjoyed life-tenure. Their number increased from one in the 12th century to four in the 13th century, but after they ceased to draw a salary, their number increased to nine. Despite the fact that they were then expected to receive only divine awards, their life-tenure assured them a great influence in the Commune.

Cassiodorus say: *it is...*, Flavius Magnus Aurelianus Cassiodorus (c490-c585 AD), Roman civil servant, historian, statesman and monk, author among others of *The Variae* in twelve books, containing 468 official letters and documents which he composed in the name of the Ostrogothic kings of Italy and *Institutions of Divine and Secular Literature*. Marginal note: 'Libr.8.epist.10.' F. C.-D. has identified this and the quotation below in a 1668 Geneva edition of Cassiodorus' *Opera Omnia*, Book viii, letters 10 and 9 on p. 272.

of Theodoric. Theodoric the Great (c454-526 AD), Ostrogothic king of Italy (493-526).

he would confer.... Marginal note: 'Lib.8.ep 9.'

Page 28

had Charles IX. Charles IX (1550-1574) Second son of Henry II of France and of Catherine de Médicis, king of France from 1560, had his mother as regent, and remained under her domination for the rest of his life.

St Bartholomew's Day massacre. Originally meant to cover a failed assassination attempt on the life of the Huguenot leader, Admiral Gaspard de Coligny, regarded as a threat to the Catholic party led by the Queen Mother and the Guises, the massacre of French Huguenots in Paris on 23 August 1572 went out of hand and spread to the provinces. Oficially the Royal Court presented it as a pre-emptive action against a Huguenot plot to seize power. Modern estimates put the number of fatalities to 3,000 in Paris alone.

the deaths of the seigneurs of Guise. Henry III (1551-1589), king of France from 1574, took the opportunity offered in December 1588 by the assembly of States General at Blois to have the Duke of Guise and his brother Cardinal of Lorraine assassinated; they had been at the head of the league of Catholics intent on deposing him as they had considered him too lukewarm a defender of the faith.

following Tacitus. See Tacitus, *Annals*, II.36. The Latin term is *flagitia imperiorum*, while Clapmar uses *flagitia dominationis* to designate the permanent abusive disregard of public law and the misuse of liberties that characterize the rule of tyrants. Naudé's criticism is meaningless.

what Justus Lipsius. See Justus Lipsius, *Politica*,IV.xiii.2. Marginal note: 'Ciuil.doctr.lib.4.c.13.' From the accuracy of both the marginal note and the quotation one may infer that Naudé had access to the first edition of Lipsius's book, placed on the Index soon after its publication, because the passage on Machiavelli was edited out in subsequent, revised editions.

saintly man says..., marginal note: Basi. in Prouerb.' Allusion to Basil the Great, Saint (329–379 AD), bishop of Caesarea, one of the founders of the Greek Church and of monasticism, author of *Letters*, and of works on canon law, theology and monasticism. The quotation has been transcribed from Lipsius, *Politica*, IV.xiii.2. See also Basil's *Homilies in Proverbs* in Migné, *Collection of the Greek Fathers*, XXXI, cols.409 and 412.

Page 29

Gaspar Schioppius wrote. Gaspar Schoppe (1576-1649), German philologist, publicist and politician, converted to Catholicism in Prague in 1598. Ardent supporter of the League and the Papal cause, he is the author of several works such as *Grammatica philosophica* (1628) and *Paedia politices* (1623), in which he is as critical of the Jesuits as he is of the Protestants, while his little book on Machiavelli remained in manuscript. For a time he was suspected of heresy and arrested, but eventually he retired to Padua, and there Naudé visited him in old age.

letting the wretched..., Virgil, *Eclogues*, II.58-59.

it is foolish..., Juvenal, *Satires*, I.17-18. Marginal note:'Satyr.I.'

I saw Salmoneus..., Virgil, *Æneid*, VI.583.

Psapho, who was. Psapho was a Lybian, who intent on being considered divine, caught birds and trained them to say 'Great God Psapho'. The saying 'Psapho's birds' was used about someone who had achieved fame by some novel method. Erasmus claimed to have found it in *Philosophumena* (29.4) by Maximus Tyrius, a Sophist of the 2nd c. AD.

Heracleides Ponticus gave orders. Heracleides Ponticus (c390-c322 BC), Greek philosopher and astronomer, best known for being the first to suggest the rotation of the Earth and to attribute the apparent motion of Venus and Mercury to their revolving around the

Sun. He also studied supranaturalistic and cataclysmic phenomena to prove the existence of gods, divine retribution and reincarnation.

Empedocles, on the other hand. Empedocles (c490–430 BC), Greek philosopher, physiologist, politician and poet, anticipated the modern law of the conservation of energy. Although very few fragments of his writings survived, not the same may be said of the legend that he was a self-styled god who flung himself into the volcanic crater of Mount Etna to convince his followers of his divinity.

Page 30

Romulus, who in order. See Plutarch's *Lives: Romulus*, xxvii.5–7. The story also appears in Naudé's *Apology*, xii, p. 244.

Eager to be thought..., Horace, *Art of Poetry*, 464–466. Marginal note: 'Horat. de arte Poët.'

No one to this day..., Deuteronomy, 34,6–7. Marginal note: 'cap.34.'

what Diogenes Laërtius. Diogenes Laërtius (3rd c. AD), Greek author of the first surviving compilation on the history of philosophy: *Lives, Teachings and Sayings of Famous Philosophers.* For the references to Pythagoras see II, 323–331 and 335–337 in the Loeb Classical Library edition.

the golden thigh of Pythagoras. Pythagoras (c580–c500 BC), Greek philosopher, mathematician and founder of a religious brotherhood, who migrated to Southern Italy in c532, and there at Crotona, established his ethical and political academy. The association with Numa Pompilius (7th c. BC) is part of a forgery dating from the 2nd c. BC. About his thigh see Plutarch, *Lives: Numa*, viii.5(65).

what Hercules did. Heracles, Latin Hercules, legendary Greek hero, adopted not only by the Romans but also by the 16th and 17th centuries classicists, all of whom added to and amplified his incidental feats.

Page 31

as did Socrates, Plotinus, Porphyry, Brutus, Sulla and Apollonius. Socrates (c470–399BC), Athenean philosopher, known through the works of Plato and Xenophon. It was the 'mystical' character attributed to him and the 'voice' which he had been hearing from childhood, that interested those delving into the occult during Naudé's time. Plotinus (205–270 AD), the philosopher who revived Platonism in the Roman Empire, and whose own religion was a quest for a mystical union with the Good by the exercise of pure intelligence. Nevertheless, it was for his interest in the occult that his writings came to be sought in the post-Renaissance age. Porphyry (c234–c305 AD), was Plotinus' disciple and biographer, who edited the latter's collected works, the *Enneads*, and wrote exclusively on philosophy, religion, philology and science. Probably Lucius Junius Brutus (6th c. BC), a freedom-loving Roman who is held to have been the founder of the Roman republic, sacrificing his own sons for the cause. Lucius Cornelius Sulla (138–78 BC), Roman general and dictator, who called himself 'Felix' in the aftermath of various military victories, and suddenly resigned after carrying out a series of administrative reforms to strengthen the republic in its last century. Apollonius of Tyana (1st c. AD), a Neo-Pythagorean who became a mythical figure through the dissemination of a hagiographical biography of his, written on imperial command to counteract the influence of Christianity upon Roman civilization. For this issue of occultism, see also Naudé's *Apology*, III, p.166.

Pico della Mirandola, Cecco of Ascoli. Giovanni Pico della Mirandola (1463–1494), Italian scholar and Platonist philosopher, the first to use Kabbalistic doctrine in support of Christian theology. Best remembered for his disquisition *On the Dignity of Man*. Cecco d'Ascoli, real name Francesco Stabili (1257–1327), Italian writer, poet and astrologer, professor at the University of Bolognia, was eventually accused of heresy, tried, sentenced and burnt at the stake.

Hermolao, Savonarola, Nifo, Postel. Barbaro Hermolao (1454–1493), scholar and philosopher, Venice's ambassador to the Papal court, was banished by the Council when granted the patriarchate of Aquileia by Pope Innocent VIII. Girolamo Savonarola (1452–1498), Florentine Dominican monk, vicar of San Marco convent in Florence, church and political reformer. Agostino Nifo (c1473–c1538), Italian thinker, author of a work entitled *On the Intellect and Demons*, later, of a *Treatise on the Immortality of the Soul Against Pomponazzi*, and a plagiarized version of Machiavelli's *Prince*, published under the title *On Skill in Government*. Guillaume Postel (1510–1581), French linguist and orientalist, travelled widely in the Orient, taught Greek, Hebrew and Arabic at the Royal College in Paris. Undergoing a religious crisis, he gave up teaching to travel to Rome and join the Jesuits, convinced that his rationalistic approach to the Advent of Christ would be found acceptable, only to be imprisoned by the Inquisition. Managing to escape, he took refuge in Venice where he functioned as hospital chaplain and spiritual adviser of a certain visionary nun known as Mother Joan [Mère Jeanne]. After another journey in the Orient to collect books and a temporary stay at Basel, Postel returned to Paris where he rejoined the nun but his preaching and visions caused public outrage and he was forced to quit Paris once more, travelled to Venice via Vienna where he was regarded as a madman. Ultimately a serene old age brought him the indulgence of the brothers of the religious community of Saint-Martin-des-Champs, his last refuge.

mentioned by Arbatel. Arbatel, a revealing angel, mentioned in *Arbatel of Magic* [De Magia Veterum], printed at Basel in 1575.

under the name of Agrippa. See note on p.129. It may be added that his stormy and peripatetic career was propitious for such commerce. He was active from Spain to Italy, France and Central Europe and not only within the Catholic Church. He went teaching at the universities of Dôle and Pavia, was appointed orator and public advocate at Metz where he was denounced for defending a prosecuted witch, was banished from Germany for quarrelling with the Inquisitor of Cologne and imprisoned in France for criticizing the Queen Mother. The impetus he had added to occultism and the study of magic not only survived him but made of his name a seal for apocriphal writings.

Marsilio Ficino and Giordano Bruno. Marsilio Ficino (1433–1499), Florentine philosopher, theologian and linguist. Giordano Bruno (1548–1600), Italian philosopher, astronomer, mathematician and occultist. He became interested in Averroism and magic while a student at Naples, then joined the Dominicans, and to escape excommunication fled to Rome and then to Geneva where he became a

Calvinist, was persecuted, and had to flee to Paris, and in 1583 went to London as the guest of the French ambassador to Elizabeth's court. His lectures on Copernican astronomy aroused the hostility of the Oxford dons, and his mordant criticism of English habits and narrow-mindedness forced him to leave England in the suite of the out-going French ambassador; but he had to flee Paris too, lectured at Frankfurt though excommunicated by the Lutherans, wrote books on mathematical and natural magic, and on the atomic structure of matter. Invited to Venice, Bruno was denounced to the Inquisition and extradited to Rome, where after a summary trial, he was burnt as a heretic.

had played the impostor. Marginal note:'Reuchlin.lib.de Cabala.' Johannes Reuchlin (1455-1522), classical scholar, philologist, humanist and political adviser, revolutionized Hebrew studies by his *On Fundamentals of Hebrew*, and promoted the scientific study of classical Greek. He was the German representative of Renaissance Platonism to which he adduced Kabbalistic elements.

the stories of Numa, Zamolxis and Minos. Numa Pompilius (c700 BC), second of the seven kings who ruled Rome before the Republic, credited with the formulation of the religious calendar and the earliest religious institutions. Son-in-law of the Sabine king Titus Tatius, he was elected after and interregnum of one year, and according to tradition, by his reforms he pacified the Romans who had perpetuated Romulus' bellicose streak. Plutarch drew a portrait of his reign in his *Lives*. Zamolxis or Zalmoxis or Selmoxis, Thracian mythical deity, mentioned by Herodotus in his *Histories*, IV.94-97. Minos, legendary ruler of Crete, son of Zeus and Europa, a personification of the continent. As a powerful and fair ruler, he was associated with religion and ritual.

Adam has been governed. Naudé gives here a partial list of the preceptor angels from the Jewish Kabbala. The current spelling has been adopted for the names of the angelic counselors whenever Naudé's differs.

but let the Jew Apella...., Horace, Satires, I.v.100. A contemporary of Horace, Apella was a Jewish freedman who was legendary for his credulity.

Scipio was not admired..., Livy, *Roman History*, XXVI,19. Marginal note: 'Libr.6.'

Page 32
Vespasian had a special art..., Titus Flavius Vespasianus (9-79 AD), Roman emperor (69-79 AD). However, the description refers to Mucianus, another commander with rhetorical talents, who with his troops swore loyalty to Vespasian newly proclaimed emperor by his soldiers. Paraphrase, Tacitus, *Histories*, II,80. For Vespasian's deportment, see Tacitus, *Annals*,III.55. Marginal note: 'Annal. lib.3.'

Corbulo is described. Cnaeus Domitio Corbulo (d67 AD), Roman statesman and general, conqueror of Armenia, was forced by Nero to commit suicide because one of his nephews had been implicated in a plot against Nero.

drawing attention..., paraphrase, Tacitus, *Annals*, XIII.8.

princes must reign..., paraphrase, Tacitus, *Annals*, IV.40.

esteem and opinion..., source not identified. Marginal note: 'Lib.3 de vtilit.'

when insatiable..., source not identified. It is an obscenity rendered in Latin in the Rome edition, and positioned in the middle of the page with spaces around. Naudé seems to have relished it. In his 1711 ET, Dr King edits the quotation as follows: 'in their pursuit of unlawful Pleasures'. Other times, other mores.

by Bouchet or by Chaudière. Probably Guillaume Bouchet (c1513-c1593) French writer and printer at Poitiers, author among others of a collection of table-talks on the burghers of Poitiers, entitled *Serées* (1584). Claude Chaudière (b1516), French printer at Reims.

entered a brothel..., Juvenal, *Satires*, VI.121. Marginal note: 'Iuuenal.'

Page 33

which nothing..., incorrect simile. See Pliny the Elder, who wrote that asbestos was fire-resistant (*Nat. Hist.*, XXXVI.xxxi.139).

But the secret. Marginal note: 'Trigault.' Niklaas Trigault (1577 -1628), Flemmish Jesuit monk and missionary, worked in China and Europe. Among his most important works is a history of the Christian missions in China (1615) and a history of the most memorable events that happened in the Indies (FT 1609).

mentioned by Hippocrates. See Hippocrates, *Airs, Waters, Places*, §14. Marginal note: 'Libr.de aere.loct.& aq.'

tardigrada, carrying..., see Pliny the Elder, *Natural History*, XV. Apelles (4th c. BC), Greek painter and court painter of King Philip II of Macedonia and his son, Alexander III the Great.

Page 34

recounted by Mocquet. Jean Mocquet (b.c1575), French royal apothecary, travelled in Africa, and in Guyana, allegedly on assignment to gather 'rarities' for the royal collections, then undertook a tour of the world, the result of which were six books of travel accounts accompanied by illustrations. It is Naudé's error to attribute the immolation of wives to the Caribs, when in fact Mocquet associated the custom with the Indians, as F. C.-D. has found out in a 1635 edition of Mocquet's *Voyages*, pp. 294-295.

who would stretch..., source not identified.

practised by Denys, the tyrant of Syracuse. Dionysius the Elder (c430-367 BC), tyrant of ancient Syracuse, who by his military actions and ruthless policies made Greek Sicily the main power in Southern Italy.

Page 35

the comic poet Alexis. Alexis (c375-c275 BC), Greek writer, originally from Magna Grecia, was one of the foremost Athenian authors of a low form of comedy that succeeded that of Aristophanes. From a prolific output of 245 plays, only a thousand lines survive. Aristonicus of Anagyrus, son of Nicophanes, is known to have been of Demosthenes' party and to have proposed in the assembly that a golden crown be conferred on the latter, according to Plutarch, *Moralia: Lives of the Ten Orators*, VIII (Demosthenes). Naudé's Latin quotation has not been identified.

too far from..., Apparently the quotation comes from Pompeius Festus, *Collectana priscorum verborum*, n.p.,n.d., article: 'Equus', according to F. C.-D.

while on my part... . all the rest of the sentence starting from here is edited out by Dr King in his 1711 ET.

Xenophon in his PRINCE. Xenophon (c434–c355 BC), Greek general, historian and essayst. The work referred to must be the *Cyropaedia.*

Isocrates, Synesius and. Isocrates (436–338 BC), Athenian rhetorician and teacher, whose writings, mostly orations, are an important source of information on the political and cultural life of his day. Synesius of Cyrene (c370–413 AD), Neoplatonic philosopher and Christian prelate, later bishop of Ptolemais in Lybia; author of *Letters* and *Egypt or on Providence.*

Page 36

by Marnix, Ammirato, Paruta. Philips von Marnix van Sint Aldegonde (c1540–1598), Dutch Reformist theologian, politician, diplomat, burgrave of Antwerp, translator of the Bible into Dutch and author among others of a treatise *On the Education of Princes and Children.* Scipio Ammirato (1531–1601), Neapolitan cleric, man of letters and libertine, eventually attached himself to Cosimo I, Grand Duke of Tuscany, while writing about Tacitus, the history of Florence, about the noble families of Naples, and later, on the Florentine noble families. He is also the author of *Discourses addressed to various princes to prepare them against the power of the Turk* (1598), in Italian. Paolo Paruta (1540–1598), Venetian dignitary, diplomat, man of letters and historiographer, who among others wrote *Of the Perfections of Political life in three books* (1579), in which he defined the goal of politics as the enjoyment of the fruits of peace.

Remigio Fiorentino, Zinano, Malvezzi and Botero. Remigio Fiorentino, real name Nanni Remigio (1521–1581), Dominican monk, known for his charitable, scholarly and poetic works, editor of the complete works of St Thomas Aquinas and author of a *Discourse on civil and criminal matters as treated by Greek and Latin historians* (1560). Gabriele Zinano (b1564), Italian soldier, courtier, man of letters and politician, wrote such books as *The Divided Secretary in seven books* (1625), *The Councillor* (1625) and *Of the Reason of State in twelve books* (1626). Virgilio, Marquis of Malvezzi (1599–1654), Italian jurist, diplomat and historian, wrote among others *Moral and Political Considerations on the Life of Romulus* (1645). Giovanni Botero (1540–1617), Italian cleric, secretary of Cardinal Borromeo at Milan and of the Duke of Savoy in Rome, later tutor of the Duke's children in Madrid. His work *Of the Reason of State* (1589) has been widely disseminated.

the ragione di stato..., this is Botero's definition. See his *Reason of State,* ET p. 9.

we, with reason, maxims of state. Here again Naudé plays with the terms: he seems to give up the 'coups d'état' for 'maxims of state' for no obvious reason.

we see Emperor Claudius. Tiberius Claudius Drusus Nero Germanicus (10BC–54AD), nephew of Emperor Tiberius, historian and Roman emperor (41–54 AD), who eventually died poisoned by the very niece whom he married against the law, or rather by changing the law himself.

she a woman in the..., Tacitus, *Annals,* XII.3. Marginal note:

'Libr.12.'

Page 37
how much it went...,paraphrase, Tacitus, *Annals*,IV.53. See also Clapmarius, *De Arcanis*,IV.ix.139. Marginal note: 'Tac.lib.4.Annal.'

nobody should act..., wrong attribution and altered contents. The quotation, used also by Botero, comes from Tacitus, *Annals*, I.6. There it refers to the authority falling into the hands of *one man* and not of 'one people' as Naudé has it. Marginal note:'lib.2.dec.5.'

Page 38
with the Grand Seigneur. Pope Alexander VI (1431-1503) carried on negotiations with the Ottoman Sultan ('the Grand Seigneur') when threatened by France and in his attempts to bring Venice under his control. On the other hand, Francis I (1494-1547), king of France, concluded an alliance with the Turks in 1522 or thereafter, against Emperor Charles V, during the pontificate of Pope Paul III.

in Guicciardini. Francesco Guicciardini (1483-1540), Italian historian, diplomat and statesman, author of a monumental *History of Italy*, and also of *Ricordi*, maxims and observations on politics and social life, as well as of a *History of Florence*.

oh, if that corner..., Horace, *Satires*, II.vi.8-9. Marginal note: 'Horat.'

Aldus Manutius thought. Aldus Manutius the Younger (1547-1597), Venetian publisher, classical philologist and author, ultimately was called to Rome by Pope Sixtus V to superintend the Vatican press. F.C.-D. identified the passage in his *Discorsi politici sopra Livio*, III, Rome, 1624, p. 3f. Marginal note: 'Discorso 3.'

Valerius Maximus said. Valerius Maximus (1st c. AD), Roman historian and moralist, author of *Nine Books of Memorable Deeds and Sayings* (c31 AD), intended as a text-book for use in rhetoric schools, popular in the Middle Ages and beyond. An English translation of it was published in 1678.

Hannibal whose prowess..., Valerius Maximus, *Memorable Doings and Sayings*, IX.2.ext.2.

Page 39
those fine counter-claimants. The French throne was claimed by King Phillip II of Spain for his daughter Isabella Clara Eugenia (1566-1633), whose mother and Philip's third wife had been Elizabeth of Valois, daughter of King Henry II of France.

the Ethiopians. See Botero, *Reason of State*, IV.4 for a different version.

the Council of the Discoli. Did Naudé mean 'di Scuole', that is the Council of the Guilds? Because 'discolo' is the Italian for scapegrace. In the ET of Bodin's *Method*, ch. VI 'Types of Government in States', subsection 21: 'Form of Government of Lucca', it has been translated as 'the College of Censors at Lucca', ed. cit., p.244.

ut sint excessus..., See Tacitus, *Annals*, XIV.44. The contents of the quotation as such may also be detected in Pietro Andrea Canonhiero's *Dell'introduzione alla politica*, etc. (1614), for instance, in his definition of reason of state: 'un necessario eccesso del giure comune per fine di publica utilita' (p.574). See Meinecke, *Machiavellism*, New Haven, 1957, pp. 118-120.

Page 40

it strikes..., source not identified.

Goddess Laverna. An ancient Italian deity associated with the nether world and which the Romans came to regard as the protectress of thieves, as their dealings were connected with darkness.

grant me escape..., Horace, *Epistles*, I.xvi.61-62. Marginal note: 'Horat.'

Count of St Pol. Louis of Luxemburg Count of St. Pol (1418-1475), Constable of France under King Louis XI, was accused of connivance with King Edward IV of England and the Duke of Burgundy, tried for treason and beheaded.

Marshal de Biron. Charles Duke of Biron (1562-1602), Marshal of France, active supporter of King Henry IV, but thinking himself unrewarded for his services, conspired with the Duke of Savoy and Spain against France. For that he was sentenced to death and beheaded in the yard of the Bastillle prison.

of the Marquis d'Ancre. Concino Concini (d.1617), Italian adventurer, born in Florence, together with his wife Leonora Galigai exerted a great influence upon Marie de Médicis, the Queen Mother, who created him Marquis d'Ancre and Marshal of France. His personal greed and political incapacity aroused the displeasure of France's grandees. Eventually, on the advice of his council, Louis XIII consented to his removal. He was stabbed to death in the yard of the Louvre.

under Isabella. Naudé uses the Spanish equivalent of Elizabeth to name the queen of England.

of Maion under William. Maion of Bari, admiral of the Norman king of Sicily William I the Bad, was at odds with the court's barons who convinced the king that Maion was plotting against him, and consequently the king had him assassinated in November 1160.

Spurius Mellius, Roman knight. Sentenced to death on the accusation of aspiring to kingship. See Livy, IV.xiii, and Cicero, *In Catilinam*, I.3.

of Sejanus and Plautian. Lucius Aelius Sejanus (d31 AD), prefect of Emperor Tiberius' household guard, became chief administrator of the Roman Empire, was eventually arrested on suspicion of intended usurpation and executed. Sejanus is mentioned alongside Spurius Mellius by Clapmar in connection with the Valerian Law in his *De arcanis rerumpublicarum*, IV.xix., p.158 of the 1624 edition. Fulvius Plautianus, commander of the imperial guard and father-in-law of Emperor Caracalla (211-217 AD), was executed by order of the latter on the charge of conspiracy against the imperial dynasty.

or Henry VIII set his kingdom. Dr King omits this reference to Henry VIII and his conflict with the Pope in his 1711 ET.

Charles of Burbon sacked. Charles III, Duke of Burbon (1490-1527), Constable of France under King Francis I, largely responsible for the French victory over the Swiss at Marignano (1515), yet eventually lost the king's favour. When the latter moved to confiscate his lands, Charles of Burbon entered the service of Emperor Charles V, but when his German-Spanish army was not paid, he attacked Rome and although he was killed during the first assault, his troops captured and sacked the city (1527).

Page 41

Clovis, the first Christian king. Clovis I (465-511 AD), king of the Franks, who ultimately by his conquests became the sole monarch of the entire Gaul.

the good man Savaron. Jean Savaron (1550-1622), French magistrate and historian. He wrote against duels and masks, about the sovereignty of king and kingdom, and one year before his death, published a book entitled *Of the Sanctity of King Clovis*.

made use of Provost l'Hermite. Tristan l'Hermite, counsellor of Louis XI, king of France (1461-1483), created Grand Chamberlain by the latter who employed him on diplomatic missions.

secret assassination of Lignerolles and Bussy. Philibert, Lord of Lignerolles, gentleman of the King's chamber was assassinated in Anjou in 1571 by a group of nobles, apparently on the king's order. Naudé might have got his information from de Thou's *History*, L.ii, according to F.C.-D. Louis of Clermont of Bussy d'Amboise tried to profit by the chaotic situation in the wake of St Bartholomew Massacre, but his attempts vexed his protectors who complained to the king about his immorality. The king advised Count of Montsoreau, one of the deceived husbands, to defend his honour, and so Bussy lost his life in an ambush set by the count. By choosing such examples, Naudé betrays a lack of political discrimination.

and Louis the Fair. That is Louis XIII, also called 'le Juste' (1601-1643), whose court Naudé hoped at the time to join in a more substantial role than the token position of court physician.

intervention in the Valtellina. Important Alpine valley on the river Adda, north of Milan, disputed by the Swiss and the Duchy of Milan, important communication zone between Spain and Austria, which Richelieu made every military effort to free from Spanish occupation and so cut communication between Spain and the Hapsburg Empire.

as Villani says. Giovanni Villani (c1275-1348), Florentine chronicler and harbinger of Humanism, was involved in the social and financial life of his town, and authored a *cronica* or *Storia fiorentina*, a universal history in twelve books, seen from the vantage point of Florence but which he failed to complete as he fell victim to the Black Death of 1348. F. C.-D. identified the quotation in a 1559 edition of Villani's *History* printed in Venice, Book VI. xxxvii, p.127.

Celestine's prison. For Celestine see the note above. As regards the 'prison', it was Pope Boniface VIII, his successor, who did not allow him to return to his hermitage, and when Celestine tried to escape from his supervision, had him interned in the Furmone Castle where Celestine died.

the poison of Alexander VI. Pope Alexander VI (1431-1503), created cardinal by his uncle Pope Calixtus III, led the life of a wealthy Renaissance prince, patronizing the arts and fathering a number of children. He was elected pope in 1492. Embroiled in political manoeuvres of his own and of his children, he used intrigue as one of his weapons in his relentless pursuit of political goals and the aggrandizement of his family. It earned him Machiavelli's opprobrium and became a source of ceaseless gossip at Rome and elsewhere. It was he who concluded an alliance with the Turks in order to forestall the advance of the French into Italy.

attempt on Fra Paolo. Fra Paolo Sarpi (1552-1623), Venetian

monk of the Servite order, became its Provincial in 1579, yet is best known as state theologian during Venice's struggle with the papacy in defence of her political and religious autonomy, writing in support of the Republic. He is also the author of a *History of the Council of Trent* (1618). Sarpi refused to answer the summons to appear before the Roman Inquisition and on 5 October 1607, he was attacked on the street and stabbed, but survived to blame the Roman Curia for the incident; the charge however was never proved.

Page 42

Charles of Anjou. Charles I (1226–1285), king of Naples and Sicily (1246–1285), with papal help defeated Manfred, an illegitimate son of Emperor Frederick II, who had usurped the throne of Sicily, in the battle of Benevento in 1266. The Italian anti–papal Ghibellines invited Conradin, Duke of Swabia, king of the Romans and the last descendant of the Hohenstaufen dinasty, to recapture Sicily, as the legitimate heir. After a triumphant march through Italy, an overblown confidence in victory led to his defeat at the hands of Charles at Tagliozza in August 1268. Conradin fled to Rome and then to Astura in the hope of sailing to Sicily, but was intercepted and delivered to Charles who had him tried before a jury of his own choice at Naples that condemned him to death for treason to church and king. He was beheaded openly in the public marketplace. Consequently the action cannot be considered a coup d'état according to Naudé's definition. On the other hand **Frederic of Austria** has not been identified. It may be a misunderstanding on Naudé's part, as Frederick II (d1250), Holy Roman Emperor, king of Germany and Sicily, had been Conradin's grandfather, and himself excommunicated by the pope.

Sicilian Vespers. See Naudé's description of the event farther on in Chapter III, p. 61.

Henry VIII raised. Sentence edited out in the 1711 ET.

there was no man...,Marginal note: 'Il dialogo di Charonte.' The the dialogue is an anonymous work, a copy of which was found by F. C.-D. at the Paris Bibliothèque Nationale, bound with other works, n.l.n.d., but the quotation could not be identified in it. Could it have been taken from A. de Valdès, *Dialogo en que particularmente se tratan de las cosas occuridas en Roma el año MDXXVII*, Venice, 1545 (ET 1952)? The book was not accessible to me.

to the aid of Dom Antonio. Illegitimate son of King John III's brother, Dom Antonio, Prior of Crato, tried to resist Philip II's annexation of Portugal after the death of King Henry, and although he was acclaimed as Antonio I at Santarem, his endeavours ended in failure, and Philip II of Spain became Philip I of Portugal (1580–1598), as John III's nephew and husband of his daughter by his first marriage.

from Cardinal d'Ossat. Arnaud d'Ossat (1536–1604), French cardinal and diplomat of humble origins, who after the death of his master, the French bishop and ambassador Paul de Foix whose secretary he had been, assumed the initiative in the negotiations between King Henry IV and the Holy See. Successful, he was appointed state counsellor and made bishop of Rennes, though he continued to reside in Rome as Henry's diplomatic agent. More diplomatic successes scored for France won him a cardinalate. His *Letters*, published in Paris in 1624, served as model of diplomatic correspondence.

Page 43

saying that..., see Pliny the Elder, *Nat. History*, VIII.vii.18.

as John of Salisbury. John of Salisbury (c.1115–1180), Latinist, secretary to two English archbishops, one of them being Thomas Becket, himself later made bishop of Chartres, wrote a pontifical history (1163), as well as the *Metalogicon*, the first Western analysis of Aristotle's writings on logic and a pioneer appeal against specialization, and *Policraticus*, in which he affirmed the role of the church as the spiritual core of the body politic, against the life style of contemporary courtiers and administrators.

he did not want..., Marginal note: 'Polycrat.cap.3.lib.i.' See *Policraticus*, I.iv. in J.B. Pike, *Frivolities of Courtiers*, etc. Minneapolis, 1938.

they let Phidias. Phidias, (c490–430 BC), Athenian sculptor, painter and engraver, was charged by Pericles with the supervision of the artistic part of his vast building programme in Athens, author of the two most famous statues of Zeus and Athens, said to have set the image of those deities for eternity, though neither has survived. First accused by Pericles' enemies of theft of the gold meant for the statue of Athena Parthenos in 438 BC, he managed to exculpate himself from the charge, only to be accused again, this time of impiety for allegedly including his and Pericles' portraits on the goddess' shield, and imprisoned. It is believed now that he was exiled to Elis where he worked on his Olympian Zeus. The last years of his life remain a mystery, and what circulated about it in Roman times is only legend.

as Seneca says. Lucius Annaeus Seneca the Elder (c55BC–c39AD), Iberian-born Latin author of rhetorical exercises, gathered in separate collections which also contain anecdotal material on the life of the early empire. For his reference to Phidias and the treatment he received at the Elians' hands, see his *Controversiae*, 8.2.

Page 44

by that of Travail. Alphonse Travail (d1617), Huguenot officer converted to Catholicism, joined the Capucin order and was implicated in different actions and coalitions against Henry IV but survived him to be sentenced to death by the Paris Parliament on the accusation that he had tried to poison the Queen.

on the part of Chancellor Poyet. Guillaume Poyet (c1473–1548), French lawyer and royal counsel, acted as diplomatic negotiator and became Chancellor as the protégé of Constable Montmorency. Eventually he was made to pay for all his intrigues and injustices by imprisonment and a considerable fine, after Montmorency had lost royal favour.

the philosopher Bigot. Guillaume Bigot, philosopher and physician, found a destructive challenger to his access to Francis I, king of France (1515–1447), in Pierre Castellau, bishop of Macon. After Bigot was nominated by the king to lecture at Paris University, Castellau accused him of belonging to the 'Peripatetics'.

Reboul's death. Huguenot secretary of Marshal Buillon (1555–1623), fired by his master and excluded from his church by its consistory, changed religion and began producing lampoons against the Protestants. Winning the protection of the Secretary of State Villeroy

(1542-1617) and of Cardinal d'Ossat, he went to Rome to collect a reward for his conversion but was turned down. To repay the refusal, he wrote a biting satire against the papacy, only to be subsequently hanged for heresy.

the imprisonment of Abbot Du Bois. Georges Du Bois (d.1628), Celestine monk with oratorical talents, was granted a temporary suspension from his monastic obligations, to take part in the war of religion on the King's side and under his lay name. The war over, he returned to his religious order, attacked the Jesuits holding them accountable for the assassination of Henry IV, but was sent to Rome by the Queen to escape local persecution. There, however, he was arrested by the Inquisition and imprisoned at Castel Sant'Angelo for the rest of his life.

of Perron, to Monsieur de Sully. Jacques Davy Du Perron (1556-1618), erudite Normand nobleman, confidant of Charles IX, reader to Henry III, and servant of Henry IV, worked for the latter's conversion, became Cardinal in 1604 and a member of the Regency Council in 1610. Maximilien of Béthune, Baron of Rosny and Duke of Sully (1560-1641), Huguenot, trusted supporter and minister of Henry IV, contributed to the economic and administrative rehabilitation of France in the aftermath of the wars of religion. His career came practically to an end with the assassination of Henry IV in 1610. Never converting to Catholicism, he spent his retirement writing his *Memoires*.

to Monsieur de Luynes. Charles D'Albert, Duke of Luynes (1578 -1621), falconer and favourite of King Louis XIII who made him Constable of France despite his military incompetence, played an influential role as the king's first minister after the death of Concini, opposed Richelieu's nomination to the cardinalate and as long as he lived Richelieu considered him a liability.

and allow... . In the 1711 ET Dr King replaces the rest of the sentence by the following: 'and proceed to the following chapter'

Chapter III

Page 45

I come now... . Here is another instance of Naudé's effort to string different, independent notions together as if they were deriving from one another, in a logical sequence. What should also be remarked is his awareness of the versatility of things and the double meaning of actions.

Telephus' spear. Telephus, legendary king of Mysia whose wound caused by Achilles' spear was healed by a plaster made of the rust of the same spear.

Diana of Ephesus. Diana (or Artemis in Greek), goddess of wild nature, proverbial for her wrath, had a temple erected for her at Ephesus in about 550 BC, which was considered one of the Seven Wonders of the World, rebuilt in 356 BC, and ultimately destroyed by the invading Goths in 262 AD. As Roman deity, Diana absorbed the identities of Selene and Hecate (Greek deities) and became known as Diana *triformis*, but not as a double-faced Janus-like deity, as Naudé wants to represent her.

were I as lucky..., source not identified.

those mentioned by Charron. See Charron, *Of Wisdom*, III.2, pp. 1023-1025 of the 1729 ET. Charron mentions only three conditions:

necessity, defensive use, and third, moderation and discretion in their use. By delating, Naudé makes five rules out of the three. Marginal note: 'lib.3.cap.2.'

by frauds and tricks..., paraphrase, Aristotle, *Politics*, 1304b and 1313a.

and do you want it... . All this sentence is taken from Lipsius, *Politica*, IV.xiii.1.

Page 46

it is characteristic..., commonplace. Source not identified. The idea may also be found in Cicero, *Of the Nature of Gods*,III.xiii.33.

it is against nature..., Cicero, *Moral Obligation*, III.vi.30. Marginal note: '3.de offic.'

where corrosive... .the rest of the sentence starting from here is translated by Dr King as follows: 'for by the Application of a Caustick only nothing is effected, but to leave a Rancour behind it.'

he is always doing his duty,... paraphrase, Cicero, *Moral Obligation*, III.vi.31. Marginal note: 'Ibid.'

salvation of the people..., Roman public law maxim, part of the *Law of Twelve Tables*.

it is expedient..., see *John*, XI.50 and XVIII.14. The words are Caiphas', the high priest of the year. The quotation is in Latin in Naudé's text.

no delay is..., Juvenal, *Satires*, VI.221. Marginal note: 'Claudian.'

Page 47

vile seems to us..., source not identified.

habit is a many-time..., commonplace, source not identified.

induction,.. . This last part of the sentence has been edited out in the 1711 ET.

by Claudian to Emperor Honorius. Claudius Claudianus (c370–c404 AD), last major poet of the Roman classical tradition, though a Greek-speaking Alexandrian, came to Rome where he gave up his native tongue to reveal a mastery of Latin. Flavius Honorius (384–423 AD), Roman emperor in the West from 393 AD, during a period in which Rome was plundered by the Visigoths and the Western Empire was overrun by barbarian invasions.

will you be content..., paraphrase, Claudian, *The Fourth Consulship of Honorius*, 402–403. Marginal note: 'de4. Consul.'

let him feel..., paraphrase, Suetonius, *Lives of the Caesars*, IV.xxx.1.

which teaches..., Claudian, *Panegyric on the Consulship of Mallius Theodorus*, 224.

Page 48

I would call cruel..., Seneca, *On Mercy*, II.iv.3. Marginal note: '2. de clem. cap. 3.' (corrected to 'cap 4' in the 1667 edition).

the prince be slow..., Ovid, *Letters from the Black Sea*, I.ii.123–125. Naudé's incorrect attribution is omitted in the 1711 ET.

or a sick man... . The segment from here to the end of the sentence has been edited out in the 1711 ET.

let it be added...add it to mine, this segment has been edited out in the 1711 ET.

145

Page 49

prudence shows..., Palingenius, *Zodiac*, Book VI 'Virgo', 572. Marginal note: 'Palingen.in Virgine.' Dr King does not translate the quotation.

Charron suggests four or five.... See Charron, *Of Wisdom*, III. ii., pp. 1034-1035 of the 1726 ET. Marginal note: 'liu.3.cap.2.'

only fleetingly, Naudé uses the phrase *à la Sfugita*.

I shall develop. In chapters I and II, Naudé attributed this procedure wrongly to Clapmarius, criticizing him for it. But it is Naudé who went on eliminating the distinction between maxims and coups.

Page 50

one must concede..., Livy, I, Preface, 7. Marginal note: '1.4. decad.1.'

Queen Semiramis. For her birth, infancy and change of dress, see Diodorus Siculus, II.4.1-5 and II.6.5-6. Naudé got it wrong about her alleged change of sex and about Ninus' identity. Diodorus portrays him as Semiramis' husband while her son by him was called Ninyas, for whom she acted as regent after her husband's death. About her end, see Diodorus Siculus, II.20.1-2. It is quite possible that behind that name is hidden the historical figure of Sammu-ramat, queen regent of her son Adad-nirari (811-782 BC), and on whom many god-like attributes were heaped along the centuries.

her garment covered.... Marginal note: 'Iust.initio.' I had no access to the works of Marcus Junianus Justinus (3rd c. AD), Roman historian, author of a summary of the history written by Pompeius Trogus (1st c. BC), *Historiae Philippicae*, dealing with the ancient kingdoms of Assyria, Persia, Macedonia and the Hellenistic monarchies. F.C.-D. mentions as source: 'Justin, *Hist. Philippicæ*, 1.ii.3.'

Cyrus, who founded. See also Herodotus, *Histories*, I.108-112. F.C.-D. refers to Justin, op.cit., I.iv.2.

Page 51

whence Sidonius. Sidonius Apollinarius (c431-c484 AD), courtly poet, senator, and late in life, bishop of Clermont (in modern Central France), was author of letters and poems.

the great Alexander..., Sidonius, *Panegyric on Anthemius*, I. 121-122, only the name of Augustus is replaced in Naudé's text by 'Romanus'. The legend is reiterated by Plutarch, *Lives: Alexander*, II.4.

the goddess Diana. The legend is related by Cicero, *The Nature of Gods*, II.27.69, and Plutarch, *Alexander*, III.3.

greet him as the son..., See Quintus Curtius, *History of Alexander*, IV.vii.25-27, also Plutarch, *Alexander*, XXVII.6, and Diodorus Siculus, XVII.51.1ff. Marginal note: 'Iustin.I.ii.'

paid to Jason. Jason of Pherae, ruler of Thessaly, early 4th century B.C.

no other name..., F.C.-D. has identified the source in Justin, op.cit., XLII, iii, 5.

revealed that cure to him. See Diodorus Siculus, XVII.103.4-8, also Quintus Curtius, IX.viii.20-28.

following Callisthenes' remonstrances. Callisthenes of Olynthus (c360-328 BC), Greek historian and nephew of Aristotle, was appointed to write about Alexander's Asiatic expedition. Later, he was accused of conspiracy against Alexander, and either executed or left to die in prison.

Page 52

it is in order to rule..., source not identified.

As for Romulus. See Plutarch, *Lives:Romulus* and *Numa*,IV.12.

by the deceit with the vultures. Omitted in the 1711 ET.

with the help of his nymph. See Plutrach, *Numa*, IV.1-2.

by what fortune..., paraphrase, Virgil, *Æneid*, Vi.781-782. Marginal note: 'Virgil.'

from a republic into a kingdom. The error was corrected in the 1667 edition.

madness of Junius Brutus. Lucius Junius Brutus (late 6th c. BC) presumably a historical figure to whom the foundation of the Roman republic is attributed by his ousting the despotic king Tarquinius Superbus from Rome. It is said that he was elected to the first consulship soon after, and that he sentenced his two sons to death for plotting to restore the Tarquins.

genuine secret of imperium. Here Naudé uses the Latin *arcanum imperii,* as used by Tacitus, where Clapmar might have used 'arcanum dominationis' if by his actions Brutus pursued his personal aggrandizement.

Page 53

we remember, we..., Livy, I.ii.7. Marginal note: 'apud Liuiīo lib.2.'

Indeed, as. Marginal note: 'Postellus & aly.' F. C.-D. refers here to Postel's *Alcorani seu Legis Mahometi et Evangelistarum concordiae liber*, etc. Paris, 1543, especially pp. 67-70, and *De Orbis Terrae concordia libri quatuor*, n.p.,n.d., especially, L.iii. I did not have access to any of Postel's writings.

his secretary Abdala Ben-Salon. In Bell and Watt, *Introduction to the Qur'an*, Edinburgh, 1970, p.37, one comes across the following story: among those employed for writing down the revelations was Abd-Allāh ibn-Abī-Sarh who was struck with awe at the description of the creation of man while Muhammad was dictating to him the passage beginning 23:12, and when Muhammad paused after the words 'another creature', exclaimed 'blessed be God, the best of creators'. Muhammad told him to write that down as part of the revelation, fact which aroused doubt in the secretary who gave up Islam and went back to Mecca. When the latter was conquered, Abd-Allāh was one of the proscribed but was pardoned at the intercession of Uthman.

Page 54

but the earth..., paraphrase, Petronius, *Poems* im *PLM*, 86.13.8. Marginal note: 'Petron. in epigram.'

it is no lesser virtue..., Ovid, *Art of Love*, II.13-14.

Page 55

who take pleasure..., source not identified. The quotation appears also in Naudé's *Apology*,XV, p.298, in connection with Agrippa of Nettesheim

as Aesculpaius had done. Asklepios, in Greek, god of medicine, son of Apollo and of the nymph Coronis. Hippolytus was a lesser god in Greek mythology, whose name suggests that he was trampled by horses.

with Pasquier's impressions. Etienne Pasquier (1538-1615), French jurist and magistrate, loyal servant of the monarchy, was the author of a systematic encyclopaedia, *Recherches de la France* [Inquiries about France].

Page 56

Paolo Emilio doesn't say. Paolo Emilio (1460-1529), Italian-born historian, appointed canon to the Paris Notre-Dame Cathedral church by King Louis XII, was the author of *De rebus gestis Francorum* [On the History of the Deeds of the Franks].

as of a powerful machine. In the sense of a war machine.

descendants of Clodio. What we have here is a family quarrel for the reintegration under the strongest ruler of a fragmented territorial administration, the result of the division of the patrimony among numerous heirs, all of whom had Merovech as their common ancestor.

make Scipio say. Publius Cornelius Scipio Aemilianus (c185-129 BC), Roman magistrate, best remembered for his destruction of Carthage in the Spring of 146 BC and for the conquest of Spain.

if by slaughter..., Horace, *First Book of Letters*, Epistle I, 32.

enlarged by Charlemagne. Also known as Charles I the Great (742-814), king of the Franks and later, Emperor of the West.

under Charles VII. Charles VII of France (1403-1461), king of France who succeeded in chasing the English from France and in consolidating the administration of his kingdom, although his last years were plagued by the revolts of some of his nobles.

admitted as such by Justus Lipsius. Incorrect attribution on Naudé's part.

Page 57

du Bellay Langey. Guillaume du Bellay, Lord of Langey (1491-1543), French soldier, diplomat and writer, author among others of an *Abridgement of the Early Times of the Gauls and of France*, and of *Instructions on the Facts of the War*.

du Haillan in his. Bernard de Girard, Lord of Haillan (1535-1610), French diplomat and historiographer, author of a *General History of the Kings of France from Pharamond to Charles VII*, and of *On the State and the Success of the Affairs of France*. In the 1711 ET his name is spelled 'Haillot'.

what Monsieur Duke of Nevers. Louis Gonzaga, Duke of Nevers (1540-1595), Italian-born French courtier and military man, author of *Memoirs*. F.C.-D. has identified the long quotation in his *Traicté des causes et raisons de la prise des armes*, etc., of 1590, dedicated to Pope Sixtus V, pp. 34-35.

Page 58

that was remarked. F. C.-D. has located the quotation that follows at the Bibliothèque Nationale in Paris, in a collection of pamphlets bound together and bearing the title, *Deffense pour le roi de France tres chrestien*, Paris, 1543, on the backside of page 34, as the reply to a letter sent by a German secretary to a servant of the most Christian King.

their compatriot Antonio Perez. Antonio Perez (1534-1611),
secretary of King Philip II of Spain, became a fugitive, after years of
intrigue with all the parties at the court and beyond to consolidate
his position. Eventually, he only riped the king's displeasure for
having induced him to consent to the murder of Don John's secretary
as alleged plotter of the king's overthrow. When the Aragonese
refused to surrender him to the Inquisition, Philip II sent a Castilian
army into Aragon, while Perez flew to France. There, and in
England, he spent the rest of his life blackening the character of
Philip, but once the latter was dead, Perez ceased to enjoy any
prestige and influence that his previous connection with the Spanish
king had given him, and ultimately died in poverty in France. His
Relationes [Records], published in 1598, knew several editions.

Page 59

as reported by Tacitus. See Tacitus, *Annals*, XIV.42-45. Marginal note: 'l. 4.Annal.' Cornelius Tacitus (c56-117 AD), Roman orator, magistrate, author, and historian of imperial Rome. He began by
writing a biography of his father-in-law, Julius Agrippa, Roman
governor of Britain (78-84 AD), then a description of the Roman
frontier zone of the Rhine, *Germania*, reserving the years of leisure
from imperial service to the writing of *The Histories*, covering the
period between 69 and 96 AD, and the *Annals of Imperial Rome*,
which covered the interval between 14 and 68 AD, that is from the
death of Augustus to that of Nero. His writings, along those of
Plutarch, his contemporary, were used as the groundwork of much of
the 16th-and-17th-century political theory in Western Europe.

gentleness and clemency..., paraphrase, Cicero, *Moral Obligation*, I.xxv.88. Marginal note: 'i.Officior.' The quotation may also be
found in Charron, *Of Wisdom*, III.2, p.1040 of the 1729 ET.

Page 60

in the case of Bessus. Bessus (d.c329 BC), satrap of Bactria and
Sogdiana under Darius III, king of Persia, murdered the latter after
several defeats at the hand of Alexander the Great, and assumed the
kingship as Artaxerxes IV, continuing to resist Alexander. Eventually, he was captured and executed for regicide.

Ferdinando Pinto claims. Fernão Mendes Pinto (c1510-1583),
Portuguese adventurer and author of *Peregrinacion*, in which he described his experiences and impressions of Asian civilizations. There
is an ET by M.S. Collins, published in 1949 under the title *The
Grand Peregrination*.

and so provision..., Pseudo-Sallust, *To Caesar*, I.6.1. Marginal
note: 'Salust. ad. Cæsar.'

as it is defended..., paraphrase, Juvenal, *Satires*, II.47-47. Not
translated into English in the 1711 ET.

ulcers that have..., Claudian, *Eutropius* II, 13-14, 16-18. Marginal note: 'Claudian.3. in Eutrop.'

Page 61

which Mithridates. Mithridates VI Eupator (c132-63 BC), king
of Pontus, greatly expanded his realm by conquering the territories
round the Black Sea. Eventually, he came into conflict with the

Romans, as he decided to expel them from Asia, following their interference in his policies of partition. In 88 BC he organized a general massacre of the Roman and Italian residents in Asia. The number of victims varies with the different sources. The war with the Romans was waged on and off until his ultimate suicide at Kerch in Crimeia in 63 BC.

hatched by Prochytes. Naudé's spelling of the name of John of Procida makes apparent his access to a copy of an anonymous chronicle in the Sicilian dialect, as the source of his story about the Sicilian Vespers revolt: *Rebellamentu di Sichilia lu quale Hordinau e Fichi pari Misser Iohanni in Prochita contra Re Carlu.* John of Procida (b1210), an eminent physician born in Salerno, became the personal physician of Frederick II, king of Sicily and Germanic Emperor, who rewarded him with various lands, including the island of Procida. After Frederick's death, he entered the usurper Manfred's service, and was appointed Chancellor of the Realm. When Manfred was defeated by Charles of Anjou, Pope Clement IV recommended him to the victor, but as John had joined Conradin, Frederick II's gradson and claimant to the throne of Sicily, who was later defeated and executed by Charles, he took refuge first at Venice, then in Germany, but from there, moved to Barcelona with two of his sons before 1275. That he was implicated in the revolt of 1282 is part of the legend.

Something similar happened. The incident on the Isle of Magna is related once more in Chapter IV, on page 90, where the name of the city is changed to Acosta and its story is attributed to Garcias ab Horto, who also figures among the authors listed in Naudé's *Bibliographia Politica.* The region in which it took place must have been that of the present-day Mumbay. More interesting, however, is that by the dates which Naudé gives to the incident, we may approximate the time when he himself was at work on the *Political Considerations.* On page 90 he gives 1613 as the year of the revolt, while on page 61 he writes about the same thing as having happened 'less than twenty years ago', and by adding them up we come with 1632 as the approximate time of Naudé's writing his own book, which also corroborates René Pintard's dates.

the death of Captain Charry. Laurent de Charry (d1563), French soldier under the command of Monluc, Marshal of France, distinguished himself in the battles against the Huguenots. When entrusted by Catherine de Médicis with the organization of the core of the King's French guard, he came against the opposition of his military superior, the colonel-general of the infantry, who eventually had him assassinated in Paris.

assassination by Poltrot. Jean de Poltrot (c1537-1563), French Protestant of noble birth, assassinated Francis Duke of Guise at the siege of the city of Orleans, during the French wars of religion.

made him withdraw from Meaux. In a pre-emptive attempt against Catherine de Médicis' presumed hostile intentions to arrest them, the French Huguenot leaders organized a revolt and tried to seize the king by surprise at Meaux, in September 1567, thus starting the second religious war in France.

The affair was in the works. That is the preparations for getting rid of the Huguenot leaders, who were themselves nobles with republican aspirations, considered by some a challenge to the monarchy as

an institution. Originally planned as the assassination of Admiral
Gaspard de Coligny, one of the Huguenot leaders, as a way of putting
an end to the religious war, it turned into a retaliatory massacre
when the assassination attempt failed, which involved the crowds not
only in Paris but in the other main cities of France. Began on 23
August 1572, it lasted until the beginning of October of that year,
only to lead to the renewal of the hostilities between Catholics and
Huguenots.

Page 62

For were it to have been carried out. Naudé's is one of the
many interpretations of the threads from which the plot and its
consequences were woven. In his detached narrative he had a prede-
cessor who inspired him and from whom he drew not only the
necessary courage but also lines of text. He was Marin le Roy de
Gomberville (1600–1674), who in 1620, published *Discours sur les
vertus et les vices de l'histoire* [Discourse on the virtues and vices
of history]. Gomberville had neither condemned nor praised the massacre but justified its cause while at the same time acknowledging
the mistakes in the execution of the coup with their calamitous
consequences. That Naudé had access to that publication is attested
by the fact that he transcribed from it at least the passage starting
from: **'the latter had been tried'** and up to: **'praise that action'**, and
paraphrased the comparison with the surgeon's procedure and
Monsieur de Thou's opinion of the event. I did not have access to
Gomberville's book, but the quotation from it, reproduced by Etienne
Thuau in his work on reason of state is relevant. See the footnote to
page 329 of Thuau's *Raison d'État et Pensée Politique à l'époque de
Richelieu*, Paris, 1966.

and Monsieur de Thou. Jacques–Auguste de Thou (1553–1617),
French statesman, historiographer and bibliophile, author of memoirs
and of a chronicle of his times in five parts, written in Latin and as
impartial as it was then possible, starting from the last years of King
Francis I to 1607, of which only the first four parts were printed in
his lifetime. An ET in two volumes was completed between 1724 and
1734.

verses by Statius. Publius Papinius Statius (c45–96 AD), Roman
epic and lyric poet of the Silver Age of Latin literature, author among
others of a long epic poem, the *Thebaid* and of an unfinished one, the
Achilleid, about the early years and education of Achilles. The quotation that follows could not be identified in any of his works.

Page 63

we read in Plato. Marginal note: '5.de Rep.' Actually, paraphrase, Plato, *Republic*, III.389b.

Page 64

Coutras, Saint–Denis, Moncontour. Battlefields in the wars of
religion between Catholics and Protestants in France.

the inhabitants of Caesarea. See Josephus, *Jewish War*, II.457.

that in Pliny. See Lipsius, *Of Constancie in Two Books*, II,xxi
and xxii, from which most of the examples are taken. ET 1939,
c1594.

every great example..., Tacitus, *Annals*, XIV.44. Marginal note:

'Annal.14.'

Page 65
    the mind is less irritated..., Horace, *Art of Poetry*, 180.
    Beza's HISTORY. Theodore Beza (1519–1605), French lawyer and
minor Latin-language poet, underwent a conversion after a serious illness and went to Geneva in 1548, to join Jean Calvin. There, as the
latter's assistant, he became a theologian and administrator, and after
Calvin's death in 1564, the leader of the Calvinist Reformation
centred on Geneva. The work mentioned by Naudé is *Ecclesiastical
History of the Reformed Church in the Kingdom of France* (1580).
While Calvin was still alive, Beza travelled back to Paris for an
œcumenical colloquium, and was retained at court by the Queen
Mother for a time, to help pacify the Huguenots.

Page 66
    had no better way. See Aristole, *Politics*, 1314b and 1315a.
    Zoroaster from Oromasis. Transcribed from *Apology*, VIII, p.198.
Naudé uses a corruption of Oromasdes, the Greek form of Ahura
Mazdā, the wise lord, who according to tradition, appointed Zoroaster
to preach the truth. See Plutarch, *Lives: Alexander*, xxx.3.
    the Trismegistos from Mercury. Actually Hermes Trismegistos
[the Thrice Great], was the Greek name given to the Egyptian god
Djhowtey [Thoth], presumed inventor of writing and author of the
Hermetic Writings, a collection of dialogues on astrology and other
occult sciences, as well as on theology and philosophy, dating from
the first three centuries of our era. Mercury was the Latin name
given to the Greek Hermes.
    Charondas from Saturn. Saturn or Saturnius, Roman god of sow-
ing, was equated with Cronos, the Greek god of agriculture. 'Charondas' is a corruption of Cronos.
    Lycurgus from Apollo. Lycurgus, legendary lawgiver of Sparta,
who according to different traditions, was active either in the 10th
or the 7th century BC.
    Draco and Solon. Draco (c7th c. BC), Athenian lawgiver, alleged
author of a first comprehensive written code, prescribing harsh punishments even for petty crimes. Solon (c630–c560 BC), Athenian
statesman, poet and legislator, who repealed all Draco's laws save
that about murder, and introduced a more humane administration.
    Muhammad from angel Gabriel. Reference previously mentioned
in *Apology*, III, p. 164.
    the Mosaic religion..., See Campanella, *Aforismi Politici*, 62,
p.112, in the 1941 Firpo edition. What Campanella wanted to convey
here is the rather close link between law and religion in a political
entity, link that disappeared in such cases as the Jews' with the
destruction of their state in the 1st century AD, but reaffirmed itself
and continued in the renewed form of the Christian political entities.
Marginal note: 'in aphoris.polit.'
    It may have given to Cardan. Rather to Lipsius, *Politica*, IV.2,
with his concept of religious prudence. As already seen, the role of
civic religion in social relations is traceable to Aristotle.

Page 67
    love is by far more..., paraphrase, the Younger Pliny, *Letters*,

I.8. Marginal note: '8.epist.'
  in **Tavannes' MEMOIRS**. Guillaume de Saulx, Lord of Tavannes
(1553-1633), French soldier, attached to the royal cause, after an
impressive military record, retired to his estate where he wrote
*Memoirs of Events in France and the civil wars between 1560 and
1596 (1625)*.
  he went broke. Naudé uses the Italian expression *al verde*.

Page 68
  Centaurs stabled..., Virgil, *Æneid*, VI.286.
  Monsieur Marescot. F.C.-D. identified the quotation in the 1599
Paris edition of the physician Marescot's book entitled *Discours véri-
table sur le faict de Marthe Brossier de Romorantin prétendue
démoniaque*, p.6.

Page 69
  It is from Cayet. Pierre-Victor-Palma Cayet (1545-1610), French
historian and controversialist, Huguenot converted to Catholicism, was
involved in the controversies aroused by the wars of religion, wrote
a history of the civil wars of 1589 and 1604, and compiled a nine-
year chronology of events from 1589 to 1598. Marginal note: 'Hist.
Sept.'
  The reason on which Charron. See his *Of Wisdom*, III,iv.2, p.
1171.
  in virtue of the Valerian Law. The text of the law was most
likely transcribed by Naudé from Clapmar's *De Arcanis*, IV.xix, p.
158 of the 1624 edition. There, the reference is given as 'I. 6. D.',
that is from the *Digest*, which is the collection of passages from the
writings of Roman jurists, arranged according to subject matter, compiled on the initiative of Emperor Justinian, and published in 533
AD when they were given statutory force. The mentioning of Ulpian,
the Roman jurist and pretorian prefect (d228 AD), in connection with
the law was in this case simply a diversion on Naudé's part.

Page 70
  The execution of Parmenio. See Arrian, *Anabasis of Alexander*,
III.xxvi.
  of William Maion of Sicily. It is hard to decide whether one is
faced here with a typographical or an editorial error. Actually, Maion
was killed on the order of William, as already said above in Chapter
II, p. 38.
  to whom Antonio de Leve. Navarre-born Spanish general of Emperor Charles V, appointed governor of Milan, won fame fighting the
French and the Turks, and participating in all of Charles V's military
campaigns. The French hated him and spared no effort in denigrating
his merits.
  his colleague Cesare Fregoso. Scion of the Genovese noble family
of the Fregosi, supported by the French, Cesare was appointed envoy
of the French king Francis I to the Ottoman Court but disappeared on
his way to Turkey through the Milanese, which at the time was
under the Spanish authority. The occurence renewed the French-
Spanish hostilities in 1542.
  even one of our bishops. Marginal note: 'Belcar.lib.22.' François
Beaucaire de Péguillon, known as Belcarius Peguilio (1514-1591),

bishop of Metz (1555-1568), was deprived of his see by his relation
and former pupil, Cardinal Charles of Lorraine, for his unpopular
ideas, inspired by the decrees of the Council of Trent. He wrote a
history of France in Latin, *Historia gallica*, covering the period
between 1462 and 1566, which was published in folio at Lyon in
1625. F. C.-D. found his commentary on the event on p. 720 of a
later edition, printed at Lyon in 1642.

Page 71

reported by Noel Conti. Or Natalis Comes (d1582), Italian man
of letters and prolific author; among his works are a *Book of Elegies*
(1560) and *Universal Histories of His Times* (1572), both written in
Latin. F.C.-D. located the quotation in a 1612 edition of the *Universal History*, p.65.

Moreover Cardinal George of Hungary. György Martinuzzi, originally Juraj Utiesenovic, but popularly known as 'Brother George'
(1482-1551), became a Paulist friar after a short career in the
military. He was a close adviser of King John Zapolya of Hungary
and then guardian and regent of his son John Sigismund. He concluded an agreement with the Austrian Emperor Ferdinand, but as
he also tried to placate the Turks by resuming the payment of
tribute, was suspected of double-dealing by the Emperor and assassinated.

that Wallenstein was assassinated. Albrecht Wenzel von Wallenstein (1583-1634), one of the most famous military commanders of
his era, was twice generalissimo of Ferdinand II, the Holy Roman
Emperor, during the Thirty Years' War, but lost the latter's confidence and was deposed by him. Ferdinand ordered Wallenstein's
capture and liquidation at the hands of English and Scottish
mercenary officers at Eger, on 25 February 1634. In Naudé's time
Wallenstein's assassination weighed as heavy or even heavier than
the Massacre of St Bartholomew in Europe's political life as it affected the whole continent. Naudé too found it worthy of mention in his
Political Considerations in 1638, while he was re-editing his manuscript for eventual publication.

That Burgomaster La Ruelle. Sebastian La Ruelle was mayor of
Liège in 1630 and 1635. He tried to preserve the city's neutrality in
its precarious position between the Hapsburg claims and the French
opposition, but was assassinated in 1639 on suspicion of French
collusion.

did not want to except his own son. Allusion to the end of Don
Carlos (1545-1568), prince of Asturias, son of King Philip II and
Maria of Portugal, heir to the Spanish throne, who conspired against
his father in the Low Countries, was arrested and eventually died in
prison.

You may indeed..., Sallust, *The Conspiracy of Catiline*, LII.4.

upon the person of Luther. Martin Luther (1483-1546), German
founder of Protestantism and the 16th-century Christian Reformation.
Luther, however, could not have been present at the Augsburg Diet
of 1530, because at the time he was officially an outlaw.

Alas, how many stretches..., Lucan, *The Civil War*, I.13-14.

Page 72

religion has..., Lucretius, *On the Nature of Things*, I.83.

the death of over a million. Marginal note: 'Bodin & autres.' The 1667 edition omits 'over' from the text.

religion can persuade..., Lucretius, *On the Nature of Things*, I. 102. It was a popular quotation among the sceptics, such as Montaigne (*Apology for Raymond Sebond*) and Charron.

Luther came to Augsburg. That was the personal interview of 1518 with Tommaso de Vio, Cardinal Cajetan (1468–1534), general of the Dominican order, renowned Thomist and papal legate in Germany. Cajetan had been charged in 1517 to bring Luther back to the Roman fold which he failed to do.

his adversaries, Ecchius, Cochlaeus, Sylvester Prierias. Johann Eck (1486–1543), a scholar from Ingolstadt with a weakness for disputation, who became involved in the controversy round Luther's ninety-five theses. Johannes Cochlaeus (1479–1552), German humanist and leading Roman–Catholic opponent of Martin Luther. Sylvester Prierias (1456–1523), Dominican theologian assigned by the Pope to combat Luther in the matter of the ultimate authority of the papacy over man's relation to God.

Page 73

since Ferrier took. Arnaud de Ferrier (d1585), French Protestant jurist and president of the Paris Parliament under Henry II, openly opposed papal authority as the king's envoy at the Council of Trent; then, on the run to avoid Catholic retaliation, he was offered the chancellorship by the King of Navarre, but preferred to stay out of the limelight for reasons of personal safety.

gold passes..., Horace, *Odes*, III.16.9–11. Marginal note: 'Ode 16.1 3.'

and the Benedictine Barnes. Robert Barnes (1495–1540), a prior of the Austin Friars at Cambridge, where he came to be persecuted for his reformist ideas. He took refuge at Wittenberg and there formed an enduring friendship with Martin Luther. Henry VIII and his chief minister Thomas Cromwell used him in diplomatic negotiations with the Lutherans on the Continent to bolster their drive to acknowledge the king as head of the Church of England. After Cromwell's downfall in June 1540, Barnes was burnt for heresy.

with Jan Hus and Jerome of Prague. Jan Hus (c1372–1415), ordained priest and preacher, Rector of Prague University, and the most important 15th-century religious reformer, agreed to attend the Council of Constance in 1414, if granted safe conduct. Within a month of his arrival, however, Hus was arrested and imprisoned in a Dominican monastery, then tried for heresy, convicted and burnt at the stake. Jerome of Prague (c1365–1416), Bohemian theologian and philosopher, continued his studies at Oxford where he was exposed to the thinking of the English reformer John Wycliffe. He returned to Prague and as university professor there spread Wycliffe's teachings. In April 1415 he went to Constance secretly to defend Hus before the Council, but was unsuccessful. As he was making ready to leave Constance, Jerome of Prague was arrested, imprisoned, and after a year, tried as a relapsed heretic and sentenced to be burnt at the stake.

the martyrs' blood..., Prudentius, *Crowns of Martyrdom*, 7.9.

Page 74

the Dominican friar who. He was Jacques Clément who at a time when regicide was lent the semblance of a noble action, got access to the presence of King Henry III and wounded him mortally on 1 August 1589.

the learned mathematician Regiomontanus. Johann Müller (1436–1476), better known as Regiomontanus, the Latinized form of his birthplace, German astronomer and mathematician, identified the comet which two centuries later was named after Halley, did pioneer work in trigonometry and algebra, and was summoned to Rome by Pope Sixtus IV to advise on the reformation of the Julian calendar. Later, he was appointed bishop of Regensburg but died before he could assume that office.

on the part of Gregory XIII. Ugo Boncompagni (1502-1585), pope from 1572, expert in canon law, taught jurisprudence, attended the Council of Trent, was made Cardinal in 1565 and sent as papal envoy to Spain. He promoted Church reform in conformity with the Trent decrees, investigated abuses of ecclesiastics, founded colleges and seminaries, among them the Gregorian University, placing the Jesuits whom he patronized in their charge. He celebrated the Massacre of St Bartholomew with a Te Deum in Rome, initiated the Index Librorum Prohibitorum, and with the help of astronomers and mathematicians, corrected the Julian calendar, established in 46 BC by Julius Caesar, and issued the Gregorian calendar in 1582, yet his building programme and political ventures exhausted the papal treasury with serious consequences for the Papal States. The reputation of poisoner must have been construed by his enemies who could not appreciate his support of the Jesuits and his reformist acts. Besides, Pope Gregory could have nothing to do with Regiomontanus' violent death as he himself was born after the event.

crime of George Trabzon's children. George of Trebizond (1396–1486), Byzantine humanist and Greek scholar and polemist, contributed substantially to the cultural enrichment of Italian Renaissance. He had come to Italy from the Black Sea city as a youth. His hurried translations of Aristotle, Plato, Ptolemy and of other works on astronomy, as well as of the Greek Church Fathers allowed for errors and linguistic deformities that aroused the fierce criticism of other scholars, and eventually, forced him to leave Rome in 1453. A radically revised Latin grammar and a work on rhetoric, however, redeemed him later in the eyes of his critics when he returned to Rome in 1466.

their fellow citizen Loredan. Pietro Loredan (d1439), Venetian nobleman and admiral, later general of the Republic, was a popular hero who ensured Venice's trade supremacy in the Mediterranean and dominant power in northeastern Italy. Apparently he found a bitter competitor in the Doge Francesco Foscari for the dogeship in 1433. Ultimately Loredan was murdered in Venice in 1439, his death being attributed to the doge's son, Jacopo Foscari. Marginal note: 'libr. 6.'

the Argonauts who did not. The incident is recounted by Plutarch in his *Precepts of Statecraft*, 819D.

Page 75

for a man..., Horace, *Epistles*, II.i.13–14. Marginal note: 'Horat. od.1.lib.2.'

that the Duke of Ossuna. Here Naudé combines two stories into one. Pedro Tellez y Giron, Duke of Ossuna (1579-1624), Spanish courtier and dignitary, viceroy of Sicily and subsequently, of the Kingdom of Naples, fought against Venice's naval supremacy in the Adriatic, and then went on to hatch a plot againt the city itself, when suddenly he was recalled, imprisoned and left to die in detention. The Spanish ambassador to Venice, though, was the Marquis of Bedmar who very likely encouraged the foreign mercenaries, gathered in the city at the end of the naval war, to join in his subversive scheme. The Venetian Senate became aware of the moves and asked the Spanish king to recall Bedmar, but without advancing any specific charges. In that way, by its silence, the Senate allowed the world to suspect the worst and so discredit Spain.

    let no god..., Horace, *The Art of Poetry*, 191-192. Marginal note: 'epist. ad Pis.' which in the 1667 edition is replaced by 'De arte poetica'.

    extreme remedies..., paraphrase, Publius Syrus, *Sententiae*, C 5. Lipsius uses it in his *Politica*, IV.ix.2.

Page 76

    of whom the mathematicians..., source not identified. It is interesting to note that by 'mathematicians' is here meant astrologers; it was the time when mathematics, astronomy and astrology still went along together.

    the artifice of a Montecuculi. Sebastian Montecuculi, Italian count and courtier who accompanied Catherine de Médicis to France, was later appointed cupbearer to the dauphin. During a journey along the banks of the Rhone, the latter asked for something to drink, and Montecuculi offered him a cupful of fresh water. Four days later, the dauphin, son of King Francis I, was dead, and Montecuculi was as a result arrested and quartered at Lyon in 1536.

    It was found..., source not identified.

Chapter IV

Page 77

    it has been established..., Boethius, *Consolation of Philosophy*, II.iii.17-18.

    all things die..., Sallust, *The Jugurthine War*, Preface, 2[3].

    there is nothing immortal..., source not identified.

    the powerful families. That is the Hellenistic families sprung from the successors of Alexander the Great, the diadochoi.

    are we surprised..., marginal note: 'Rutil.in itiner.' The quotation is not in the text as we have it of Rutilius Namatianus Claudius, *Itinerary of His Return Journey* (417 AD).

    now a cornfield..., source not identified.

    Do you see that Byzantium..., Justus Lipsius, *Two Books of Constancie*, I.xvi.

Page 78

    as did the Swiss. Reference to the Helvetic Confederation, the result of a long process of alliances, territorial expansion and armed struggle, beginning in the last decade of the 13th century, and which acquired formal recognition as a sovereignty by the Treaty of Westphalia in 1648.

    *the inhabitants of Lucca.*The city acquired its independence for the price of 100,000 florins in 1369.

the Dutch and the Genevans. Reference to the United Provinces of the Netherlands, or for short, the Dutch Republic, made up of the mostly Calvinistic Northern Netherlands, and the result of an agreement of January 1579, known as the Union of Utrecht. Somewhat earlier, and more exactly in 1536, the citizens of Geneva proclaimed their city a republic, having embraced the Reformation initiated by Jean Calvin. Subsequently Geneva became known as the 'Protestant Rome', and received further recognition of sovereignty by the Treaty of Saint-Julien of 1603.

As we discern..., source not identified.

Gracchus, Sertorius and Spartacus. Gaius Sempronius Gracchus (153–121 BC), Roman magistrate and eventually tribune of the people, scion of an aristocratic family holding high office, was together with his elder brother among the first to confront the social and political crisis experienced by Republican Rome. He introduced reforms that affected all the spheres of social life, including the redistribution of land. Quintus Sertorius (c123–72 BC), Roman statesman and military commander, found himself in revolt against Sulla and the constitution he had imposed in Rome. Spartacus (d71 BC), a Thracian by birth and Roman deserter, sold as a slave, became leader of the Gladiatorial War (73–71 BC) against Rome.

Sulla, Marius, Pompey. Lucius Cornelius Sulla (138–78 BC), Roman general and dictator in the last century of the Republic. Gaius Marius (c157–86 BC), Roman general and politician who towards the end of his life seized Rome and had some of his enemies executed. Gnaeus Pompeius Magnus (106–48 BC), general and statesman of the late Roman Republic, associate and later opponent of Julius Caesar, gifted administrator of the eastern provinces of the Republic.

the furies of the Triumvirate. Triumvirate to organize the state, title given to a group, made up of Mark Anthony, Lepidus and Octavian, Julius Caesar's adopted son, in 43 BC, for five years, and renewed in 37 BC. The protracted military confrontations between the Triumvirs led to the foundation of the Principality under Octavian who added 'Augustus' to his name.

the fate of the Roman Empire..., source not identified.

Page 79

Cosimo and Lorenzo de' Medici. The most famous representatives of the Medici family of merchants and bankers of Florence: Cosimo (1389–1464), posthumously declared Pater Patriae (Father of the Homeland), was a passionate builder and collector of books and manuscripts, as well as a supporter of sculptors, painters and scholars, found himself at the head of a hereditary principate, although without official title or legal right. His grandson Lorenzo, the Magnificent (1449–1492), became, as Guicciardini wrote, 'a benevolent tyrant in a constitutional republic', and that under the appearance of a simple citizen. Lorenzo emulated his grandfather's interest in the arts and the letters, despite the decreasing resources of the Medici bank.

the study of the insentient..., Horace, *Odes,* I.34.1–3. Marginal note: 'Ode.31.1.1.'

until I go on..., paraphrase, Lucretius, *Of the Nature of Things,* I.932.

I have come to you..., paraphrase, Paul, *Romans* 15,20.

the kings Almasur and Miramolin. Al-Manşūr, Hārūn ar-Rashīd and al-Ma'mūn, the three Abbāsid caliphs who between 750 and 833 AD raised the Muslim Empire, that extended from the Western Mediterranean to India, to a new level of power and cultural development. The first was the third Abbāsid caliph and grantfather of Hārūn who is best remembered as the romanticized character of the epic of *The Thousand and One Nights*. According to Jacques Prévot, Miramolin or Miramamolin was the generic name given to Muslim rulers by the West, in the Middle Ages.

Page 80

as in all things..., paraphrase, Seneca, *Epistles*, 106. See Botero, *Reason of State*, V.5, pp.103-104 where the discussion refers to military qualities and their connection with the study of letters.

And as Archimedes. Archimedes (287-212 BC), Syracusan mathematician, physicist and inventor.

who is he that..., paraphrase, Cicero, *Philippics*, III.1.2. Marginal note: 'Philippic.5.'

that of Epicurus. Epicurus (341-270 BC), Greek philosopher who advanced an atomistic theory as the basis of an ethically oriented philosophy.

see what big rivers..., source not identified. It is a commonplace which in a less poetic form may be found in Cicero, *The Supreme Good*, V.21: 'the beginnings of all things are small.'

an overlooked spark. See Lipsius, *Politica*, VI.iii.2.

it is by neglect..., paraphrase, Quintus Curtius, *History of Alexander the Great*, VI.iii.11.

Count Julian's daughter. After 754 AD, tales began to be circulated by Latin and Arab writers not least about a Count Julian, 'Byzantine governor of Ceuta', and his daughter Florinda who was violated by King Roderic, deed that determined Julian to assist the Arabs in their advance into Spain. Actually, Roderic, the Visigoth duke of Baetica, proclaimed king in 711 AD, was soon after defeated by a coalition of his counter-claimant to the throne and the Muslims of North Africa.

that the Aetolians. For these examples and others see Lipsius, *Politica*, IV.v.5.

Page 81

slow and hesitant..., *Exodus* 3.1. Marginal note: 'Exod.3&4.'

but sent them..., paraphrase, *Exodus* 8.

looking for the asses..., see *1 Samuel* 9,3-4. Marginal note: 'I. Reg. cap.11.'

who tended the sheep..., paraphrase, *1 Samuel* 16,11. Marginal note: 'cap. 17.' The quotation is left out in the 1711 ET.

from Holophernes' persecution. Holophernes, general of the Chaldean king Nebuchadnezzar II (c630-562 BC), was killed in his sleep by Judith at the gates of Bethulia, the city he had been besieging.

but struck him down..., *Judith* 13,16. Marginal note: 'Iudith.9.'

disappointment of two monks. Martin Luther had been an Augustine friar, indeed, but not Jean Calvin (1509-1564). A Frenchman converted to Protestantism, he had been bestowed two ecclesiastical benefices early in his childhood by his local bishop in order to finance his studies. Calvin's father had been the bishop's secretary. Calvin returned those benefices at the time of his conversion when he also left Paris and eventually settled at Geneva. In Paris, he studied the humanities (MA) and then read law at Orléans. His interest in theology developed only at the time of his conversion.

at times the strong lions..., See Quintus Curtius, *The History of Alexander the Great*, VII.viii.5. for the same idea more laconically conveyed. Naudé's version has not been identified.

Page 82

through the paulette. The paulette was an annual tax or fee which the judiciary and the fiscal officers were paying to the king to secure continuity in office. It was introduced in 1607, and was so called after the name of Paulet, the first general farmer to collect the tax.

Page 83

one must have a close knowledge. See Lipsius, *Politica*, IV.v.1 and also Tacitus, *Annals*, IV.33.

Those who have given. The populace was generally held in great contempt by the politicians, and in that Naudé closely follows Lipsius, *Politica*, IV.v.2-15, Charron, *Of Wisdom*, I.lii.1-2, (pp.530-540 of ET), and Botero, who all found precedents in Sallust, Tacitus and Cicero, to mention only them. Campanella, a direct victim of the mob, was nonetheless working for the physical and material redemption of the populace.

the judgement of the common...,Palingenius, *Zodiac*, XII 'Pisces', 573. Marginal note: 'in Piscib.'

enraged, the mob..., Palingenius, *Zodiac*, IX 'Sagitarius', 641. Marginal note: 'in Sagit.'

here the mores of the mob..., Probably taken from Lipsius, *Politica*, VI.iii.2., but originally coming from Sallust, *The Conspiracy of Catiline*, 37[3].

shifty of temper..., Probably taken from Lipsius, *Politica*, IV.v.11, but originally from Sallust, *Jugurthine War*, 66.

Page 84

human affairs..., Seneca, *On the Happy Life*, II.1-2. Marginal note: 'de vita B. cap.1.§2.'

that which is solid. Persius, *Satires*, V.25.

we are saved if..., source not identified.

when David George. Dutch actor and painter (1501-1556), joined the Anabaptists, and later had to flee from the Netherlands to avoid religious persecution and settled in Basel where he got involved in the controversies surrounding Servetus and the death penalty inflicted on him at the instigation of Calvin, with dire consequences for himself and his family.

fanatical taylor. Reference to the Anabaptists who took refuge from the Netherlands into the Westphalian city of Münster where they established a communistic theocracy in 1534, under the leadership of Jan Mathijs and John of Leiden (Jan Beuckelson), who ruled as king. A year later, the local bishop was able to regain control of the city, John was caught, tortured and put to death. The irregular way of life that went on during John's theocracy seriously discredited the whole Anabaptist movement. Whether he had been a taylor or not I cannot say.

When Father Domptius. Figure not identified.

Rosicrucian brothers. The Rosicrucians were a sect of illuminati of German origin that became widespread in Europe in the 17th century, combining a variety of religious and occult beliefs and practices. Naudé had published a pamphlet about them early in his publicistic career, in which he also gave a list of authors whose writings had, in his opinion, the approval of the Rosicrucians, but which in fact were highly representative of the Renaissance Hermetic tradition. So Naudé the bibliographer and colporteur of rare-to-find and forbidden books also made his debut with this pamplet, *Warning about the Rosicrucian Brothers*, Paris, 1623.

Page 85

stories about Melusine In the French folklore, Melusine was the daughter of a fairy who could partly change into a snake.

Lullist. Follower of Ramón Lull or the Blessed Raymond (c1232–1315), Franciscan friar, born at Palma de Mallorca, writer and philosopher, who dedicated his life to the conversion of Muslims and Jews and pagan Tartars with a view to the complete reunification of mankind through Christianity. In his writings he sought to re-establish the unity of truth between philosophy and theology, starting from the Neoplatonic realism and adding a close familiarity with the writings and convictions of contemporary Jewish and Muslim authors. Among his works are the early *Ars Magna* (c1274), later revised and expanded under the title of *General Art* [Ars Generalis Ultima], *The Tree of Science* (1296), and what may pass for the first philosophical-social novels, *Blanquerna* and *Felix*.

When a Peter the Hermit. Peter the Hermit (c1050–1115), French preacher, the main propagandist of the First Crusade to which he rallied miscellaneous bands that caused considerable disorder across Europe, ultimately to be annihilated by the Turks.

When told jokingly... . This whole sentence is edited out in the 1711 ET.

raised their voices..., Acts 14,7–20.

Sejanus *is being dragged...*, Juvenal, *Satires*, X, 66–67. Marginal note: 'Iuuenal. Satyr.10.'

is incensed and..., Horace, *Art of Poetry*, 159–160. Marginal note: 'ad Pison.'

Page 86

always wavering.... Marginal note: 'de vita B cap.28. F.C.-D. found the quotation in a 1602 Paris edition of Seneca's *De vita beata* [On the Happy Life], I, 28, p.337. The 20th-century edition available to me had only the beginning of ch. 28, the rest being considered lost.

religion is what freins..., Palingenius, *Zodiac*, VII 'Libra', 896–899. Marginal note: 'In Libra.'

nothing moves..., paraphrase, Quintus Curtius, *History of Alexander the Great*, IV.x.7. Marginal note: 'Q.Curt. lib. 4.'

Page 87

who feign their fighting.... Marginal note: 'epist. 13.lib.2.

Unable to verify.

the priests of the god Canopus. Canopus was the name of a town while the name of the god was Osiris. Whether the error is Naudé's or that of his source is impossible to establish.

last chapter of Daniel. See *Daniel* 14. The *Book of Daniel* became part of the *Apocrypha* in the Protestant bibles.

who draw their profit..., Livy, IV.xxx.9-10, Marginal note: 'Liuiusl.4.'

Page 88

Giacomo Bussolari was for a time. Giacomo Bussolari (d.c1359), Augustine friar, turned preacher, preceded Savonarola in turning Pavia, his native city, into a morally reformed place, and by the patriotism which he inspired, kept the besieging Milanese at bay for three years, after which he was thrown into jail where he died.

Giovanni of Vicenza. Dominican monk (d1260) who by his preaching succeeded in bringing peace to north-eastern Italy for several months in 1233.

about the last, Machiavelli. Paraphrase. Machiavelli, *Discourses*, I.xi. See also Naudé's *Apology*,III, p.165. Marginal note:'sur T.Liue.'

it was by its means that the Sufi Ismail. The whole story had already been included in Naudé's *Apology*, III, having been taken from *Le Nouveau Cynée* by Emery Crucé, p. 102 of the 1623 edition. Naudé wants to give the impression that he had the information from Lipsius, which is not the case. Sufi Ismail I (1487-1524), shah of Iran, religious leader and founder of the Ṣafavīd dynasty, converted Iran from Sunni to the Shia sect of Islam. The name 'Treschel Cuselbas' might be a corruption of 'Kizilbash' (the Read Heads), a Shi'ite group led by his father, and which remained loyal to him after his father's death. I had no access to Crucé's book.

a certain Calender. Dr King translates Calender by 'fortune teller'; of Greek origin, it is a noun which may be translated as 'proclaimer', although Naudé treats it as the name of an individual person.

that can reverse..., See Cicero, *Letters to Atticus*, V.xiv.2.

Page 89

Vespasian gathered people. Titus Flavius Vespasianus (9-79 AD), Roman emperor (69-79 AD), the first emperor to come from an equestrian family, he carefully built up an extralegal authority by resorting to divine portens and other related practices.

father Jesus Maria. According to F. C.-D., it is the pseudonym of Thomas Busten (1549-1619), religious missionary who went to Goa in 1579, and spent the rest of his life at the mission there.

than that of Prague. Reference to the Battle of the White Mountain near Prague in 1620, in which the Protestant forces were defeated, the city lost its status of capital, its Bohemian noblemen were executed and the process of Counter-Reformation was given free rein.

for whom Heaven combats..., source not identified.

as if he were Topiltzin. Two of the chronologies of the Toltec Empire list Topiltzin as ruler between 885 and 959 or 923-947, respectively. He was also given the name of a deity, Quetzacoatl.

sent by Viracocha. Creator god of the pre-Inca and Inca peoples, cultural hero and ultimately divine protector of the Inca emperors, with a temple of his own.

Page 90
in connection with Acosta. The incident has already been mentioned on p. 61, only there the name of the city is Corme.
the report of Garçia ab Horto. Twice mentioned by Naudé in his *Bibliographia Politica*, Garçia ab Horto (16th c.) was a Portuguese botanist who travelled to India as the physician of the Portuguese viceroy.
Orpheus, holy messenger..., Horace, *Art of Poetry*, 391–393. Reproduced from Naudé's *Apology*, IX, p.215. Marginal note: 'Horat. ad Pison.'

Page 91
fortune follows..., paraphrase, Cicero, *Tusculan Disputations*, II. iv.11. Marginal note: 'T. Liuius.'
by Demosthenes' eloquence. Demosthenes (384–322 BC), Athenian statesman, leader of the democratic faction and Greece's greatest orator, opposed to Macedonian supremacy, but committed suicide as his fortune faltered.
Pericles too. Pericles (c495–429 BC), Athenian statesman and general who made of his city the leading power in Greece. He was deposed during the 431 BC war with Sparta, but reinstated during the intervening crisis, only to die soon afterwards.
Ephialtes' fine way. Ephialtes (d461 BC), Athenian leader of the democratic faction opposed to Sparta and promoting power for the common people, succeeded in securing its domination in the Popular Assembly. His radical measures, however, aroused the opposition of the aristocrats and led to his assassination.
by Godfrey of Bouillon. Godfrey of Bouillon (c1060–1100 AD), Duke of Lower Lorraine and a leader of the First Crusade, became 'protector of the Holy Sepulchre' and de facto ruler of Jerusalem.
John Gerson, who came. John of Gerson (1363–1429), theologian Chancellor of Paris University, led the conciliar movement for Church reform during the Great Schism of the Western Church, playing a leading role at the Council of Constance in 1415. He opposed Jean Petit, professor at the same university, who defended tyrannycide as justified and implicitly the assassination of Louis, duke of Orléans, by the men of John the Fearless, duke of Burgundy. The Council, however, refused to condemn Petit explicitly, and instead condemned the Bohemian reformer Jan Hus for heresy. Gerson, on his part, was prevented from returning to France by the duke, and had to seek refuge in Germany until the latter's death in 1419. On his return, he settled at Lyons.

Page 92
father Giacinto da Casale. Giacinto da Casale Monferrato (1575–1627), after reading law, science and the humanities, became a Capuchin monk and set on reforming his religious order. Moreover, he assumed the role of a politician by his efforts to discourage war among princes and preserve a balance of power between them.
furious battle of Marignano. Fought ten miles southeast of Milan for two days (13–14 September 1515), during Francis I's first Italian

campaign in alliance with Venice. It resulted in victory over the Swiss allies of the Milanese, who suffered heavy losses, and the recovery of the Duchy of Milan by the French.

to a heretic king. That is Henry III who by his concessions to the Huguenots, his extravagant lifestyle and the prospect that the Huguenot Henry of Navarre would inherit the French crown increased the Catholic opposition against him. The latter organized itself as the Holy League and stirred up the people of Paris against the King on the Day of the Barricades (12 May 1588). Henry III in turn allied himself with the king of Navarre to be able to fight the opposition, thus exacerbating the hatred of the League. About a year later, he was stabbed to death by a fanatical Jacobin friar who had gained admission to his presence.

Boucher, Rose, Wincestre and many. Jean Boucher (b1548), taught at Reims University then at the Sorbonne where on winning his doctorate in theology, was appointed lecturer of theology and curate of the Parisian parish church of Saint-Benoît. He took an active part in the revolt against king Henry III, promoting regicide, but had to flee Paris when the royal forces reoccupied the city, to find refuge at Tournai, under Spanish occupation, where gradually his fury was redirected against the Jesuits and the Calvinists. Guillaume Rose, theologian of a noble family, became chaplain and preacher of Henry III, and later bishop of Senlis. However, he joined the League and took a strong position against the king, justifying regicide in a way similar to Boucher's. About Wincestre, Naudé seems to have gathered his information from Cayet's *Chronology*, as he preached revenge for the assassination of the Guise brothers at Blois on 23-24 December 1588. Dr. King preferred the spelling 'Wincester'.

that Montauban might not. Both the towns of La Rochelle and Montauban had been Protestant enclaves that were eventually defeated and ransacked by the royal troops of Louis XIII.

had not minister Chamier. Daniel Chamier (d1621), French Protestant theologian, professor of theology at Montauban, died during the siege of the town by the Royal soldiers.

Page 93
Campanella intended to become king. Not exactly, Campanella was no John of Leiden, although he was the main factor of the failed popular rebellion against the Spanish occupation of Calabria in the Summer of 1599.

your brother Aaron..., Exodus 4,14-15. Marginal note: 'Exodi cap. 4.'

Behold I have..., Exodus 7,1-2. Marginal note: 'cup. 7.'

whose tongue is..., Virgil, *Æneid*, XI, 338.

Venus that changes..., See Horace, *Odes*, IV.iv.34

Page 94
it is one and..., Virgil, *Eclogues*, VIII, 80-81. Marginal note: 'Virg.ecloga 4.'

rejoice as a thousand..., Horace, *Epistles*, I.vi.19.

Messierus de Luynes. A Provençal family, the d'Albert de Luynes counted among its members soldiers, clergymen and politicians, the most famous being Charles (1578-1621), Constable of France and favourite of King Louis XIII.

of Jansen against. Cornelius Otto Jansen (1585–1638), Dutch theologian and reformist of Roman Catholicism, was rector of the University of Louvain and bishop of Ypres. He became the head of a Catholic religious movement that expanded mainly in France, Italy and the Low Countries under the name of Jansenism, centred on the problem of the reconciliation of divine grace and human freedom.

Page 95

as Father Paul the Hermit. That is, Paolo Sarpi.

all evils are..., paraphrase, see Lucretius, *On the Nature of Things,* I. 83 and 102.

which Pope Leo heaped. Leo I the Great was bishop of Rome between 440 and 461 AD, and witnessed the disintegration of the Roman empire, yet he devoted himself to the suppression of heresy, corruption and disunity in favour of a Church under papal supremacy. The letters in question were addressed to the Eastern Roman Emperor Theodosius II (401–450 AD) and his sister Pulcheria, about the Council of Ephesus and its manipulated decisions about Christ's hypostatic nature. See Leo's letters 44 and 95 in the Fathers of the Church Series, Vol.34, Washington DC, 1963.

what Mariana. Juan de Mariana (1536–1624), Spanish Jesuit, theologian and historian who because of his liberal mind was imprisoned and forced to do penace while his *Seven Treatises* on moral and political subjects were banned by the Inquisition. Nor was his legitimatization of regicide under certain conditions well received by his superiors. His *General History of Spain in Thirty Books* (1592–1605) written in Latin and translated into Spanish by himself is an anecdotal history that combines legend with fact.

he will show..., marginal note: 'lib.6.c. 5.'

Then, referring... . The whole sentence, including the quotation, is edited out in the 1711 ET.

they put on the pretext..., marginal note: 'cap. 6.'

the best is to conceal..., marginal note: 'cap. 7.'

it was Boniface VIII. Benedict Caetani (c1240–1303), pope between 1294 and 1303, though impulsive and short-tempered, did not incite the two brothers one against the other, but intervened in the conflict between the kingdoms of Naples and that of Aragon over the island of Sicily, when it seceded from the Neapolitan king, disregarding papal overlordship.

but there was so much..., marginal note: 'lib.51. cap.1.' It is changed to :'Book 5 c2' in the 1711 ET.

Page 96

but it was done..., marginal note: 'lib. 25.cap. ult.'

and make use of it as a drug. The idea does not originate with Karl Marx, but was widely circulated in the 16th and the first half of the 17th centuries.

such things should not..., Palingenius, *Zodiac,* VII 'Libra', 879–880. Marginal note: 'Paligen. in Libra.'

things timely..., paraphrase, Ovid, *Remedies of Love,* 131–132.

Page 97

One such occasion. See Tacitus, *Annals,* I.27–28.

it is a stratagem..., See Livy, I.xxvii.5–11 and xxviii.1–6. This incident is also mentioned by Frontinus, *Stratagems*, II.vii.1 and by Machiavelli in *Art of War*, IV.2, among others.

in appeasing the commotions..., Tacitus, *Annals*, I.29.

what chance presents..., paraphrase, Tacitus, *Annals*, I.28.

men have been..., source not identified. The quotation is edited out in the 1711 ET.

Thus we read that. Columbus' incident is narrated in Diego Mendez, *Account of the Fourth Voyage of Columbus (1502-1504)*. See his *Four Voyages of Christopher Columbus*, tr. J.M. Cohen, Baltimore, 1969, p.316.

Page 98

it does not attain..., paraphrase, Valerius Maximus, *Memorable Deeds and Sayings*, VIII.3, Preface. Marginal note: 'Val Max. 1.7. cap.3.' See also Charron, *Of Wisdom*, III, 2, p.1022.

Chapter V

Page 99

the first to set in motion. The Thomist notion of primum mobile was reactivated in the 16th century as a basic principle of a universal ecumenism.

To that, however. Naudé's counter-argument is at first sight contradictory and at a closer look, utterly hostile to monarchy as an institution, which makes me think that the book was not meant for Louis XIII after all.

God covers..., commonplace; source not identified.

he is said to be..., paraphrase, Cicero, *In Defence of Cluentius*, xxxi.84. Marginal note: 'Cicero pro Cluentio.'

Velleius Paterculus has remarked. Velleius Paterculus (b.c19 BC), Roman historian, soldier and political figure, authored a compendium of Roman history from the origins to year 29 AD.

great tasks..., Velleius Paterculus, *History of Rome*, II.cxxvi.1-2. Marginal note: 'lib. 2.'

the prince who assumes..., Tacitus, *Annals*, XII.5. Marginal note: '12. Annal.'

Page 100

as Euripides says. The quotation in Greek letters that follows could not be identified.

a prince grows wise..., source not identified. The idea, however, appears in Plato, *Laws*, 710d, and is resumed in Plutarch, *Moralia: That a Philosopher ought to Converse with Men in Power*.

had the Sieur de Chièvre. William of Croy, Lord of Chièvre (1458-1521), after changing parties twice, was eventually entrusted with the education of the future Emperor Charles V who later on appointed him his first minister.

were Count Dunois. John of Orléans, Count of Dunois (1403-1468), illegitimate son of Louis Duke of Orléans, fought the English at the side of Joan the Maid of Orléans and helped in the surrender of Normandy and of Guienne to the French king, for which he was rewarded with the military grade of lieutenant general, and later, appointed Grand Chamberlain of the king.

Louvet, President of Provence. Favourite of the French king Charles VII, was president of the Chamber of Accounts at Aix. An unscrupulous politician, he profitted by his position to enrich himself. Eventually Charles VII was constrained to dispense with his services.

Tanneguy du Chastel and a Count Dammartin. Tanneguy Du Chastel (c1368-c1458), Breton warlord, later Provost of Paris, apparently did not refrain from dispatching those who opposed his politics, ultimately obliging the king to remove him from office. Antoine de Chabannes, Count of Dammartin (1408-1468), took part in the war against the English and distinguished himself at the siege of Orléans. Under Charles VIII, he was appointed governor of Paris and Ile-de-France, the surrounding region.

witness Cardinal Balue. Jean Balue (c1421-1491), son of a modest family, joined a monastic order, and became secretary of state of Louis XI who later imprisoned him between 1469 and 1480 for having revealed some of the king's secrets to Charles the Bold, Duke of Burgundy.

Philip de Commynes. Philip of La Clyte (1445-1509), born at Comines in Flanders and brought up at the Burgundian court, became squire of Charles the Bold, took part in several military expeditions, was made the Duke's counsellor and sent as envoy to England, Brittany and Spain. His greatest diplomatic feat was his negotiated agreement between the Duke and King Louis XI, which persuaded the latter to win Commynes over to his court as confidential adviser and chamberlain. Commynes also served on and off his successors, Charles VIII and Louis XII. His *Memoirs* (1524), despite many errors of fact and ommissions, is one of the most important works on the history of those times.

his physician Jack Coictier. Jack Coictier (d.c1490), President of the Paris Chamber of Accounts and hack doctor of Louis XI, would play on the king's fears and superstitions in order to enrich himself, but as the blackmail gradually lost its effects, the physician was sent away

with Cardinal Briçonnet. William Briçonnet (1445-1514), Superintendent of Finances under Charles VIII, he played important roles also at the court of Louis XII, his successor. A widower, he took holy orders, and ultimately became cardinal, and on the orders of Louis XII, began a campaign against Pope Julius II.

with Cardinal d'Amboise. George d'Amboise (1460-1510), son of the chamberlain of two kings and ambassador to Rome, he became chief minister of King Louis XII, in which quality he carried out important reforms of the administration and the judicial system, and helped organize the king's expedition against Milan.

with Admiral d'Annebaut. Claude d'Annebaut (d1552), Marshal and Admiral of France, was used by King Francis in all his military campaigns in Italy, Flanders and Champaigne.

with Constable Montmorency. Anne Duke of Montmorency (1493-1567), Marshal of France, one of the main councillors of Henry II, was fatally wounded in a clash with the Huguenots at Saint-Denis.

Cardinal Birague. René of Birague (1507-1583), Milan-born French statesman, chief lord justice then chancellor, he was apparently one of the instigators of the Massacre of St Bartholomew, took holy orders under Henry III and was made a cardinal in 1578.

Monsieur d'Épernon. Jean Louis de Nogaret de la Valette, Duke of Épernon (1554-1642), a favourite of Henry III, who created him duke and later appointed him colonel-general of the army. After the death of Henry IV (1610), Épernon promoted the regency of Marie de Médicis but was soon replaced on the Queen Mother's Council by Concini.

πολλοῦ βασιλέως..., corrupt quotation. It looks like an attempt to translate into Greek Naudé's Latin paraphrase of a passage from a Latin translation of Xenophon, *Cyropaedia*, VIII.ii.12. Marginal note: 'lib.28.pæd.' Dr King changed it to: 'Book 13 Cyropaed.'

Page 101

and the triumvirate. That is the cooperation between Sully, Villeroy and Sillery. Nicolas Brulart, Marquis of Sillery (1544-1624), diplomat and chancellor (1607-1624).

there cannot be..., source not identified.

Messalina's death..., Tacitus, *Annals*, XII,1.

Page 102

about Emperor Galba. Servius Sulpicius Galba (c5BC–69AD), had been Roman Emperor for seven months after Nero, when he was assassinated by the Praetorian bodyguards.

Galba's easiness..., Tacitus, *Histories*,I.12. Marginal note: '6hist. li.5.'

about Clement VII. Giulio de' Medici (1478-1534), a weak and vacillating man at a time when Charles V and Francis I were fighting in Italy over the domination of Europe, Henry VIII wanted to divorce Catherine of Aragon and Charles of Bourbon went on sacking Rome.

every time..., quotation reproduced in Italian in the original, source not identified.

if he relies on one minister only. The way in which Naudé fawns on Richelieu here betrays his original intentions about the dedicatee. After Richelieu's death, he became hostile to the Cardinal's memory.

as Vegetius. Flavius Vegetius Renatus (4th c. AD), Roman military expert, author of a most influential treatise on military organization and tactics, *The Military Institutions of the Romans*. For the criteria of recruitment and related issues see Book I of that work.

Page 103

counselling minister and the executive minister. In this categorization Naudé closely follows Lipsius' *Politica*, Book III.

it is more to you..., Livy, XXIV.viii.17–18. Marginal note: 'lib. 24.'

Thersites cannot claim..., Juvenal, *Satires*, IX.30–31.

an Appius was. Claudius Appius (mid-5th c. BC), Roman patrician who helped codify Roman law.

Cleon had no understanding. Cleon (d422 BC), first plutocrat of stature to play an important part in Athenian politics, after the death of Pericles, his political enemy. Cleon advocated an offensive strategy in the Peloponnesian War and extreme measures against the defeated.

Philopoemen had no idea. Philopoemen (c252-182 BC), general of the Achaean League, born in Arcadia, crushed the Spartans as a result of the introduction of new, heavier armour and phalanx tactics in the military formations which he was leading.

Diomedes was good only. Diomedes, a Greek legendary figure, was the commander of eighty Argive ships in the Trojan War, and one of the most respected leaders.

to appoint to each function..., source not identified.

because the Roman Empire..., Livy, IV.3. Marginal note: 'T. Liuius lib.4.'

Page 104

virtue is not denied..., likely transcribed from Lipsius, *Politica*, II.iii.2. Paraphrase, Seneca, *On Benefits*, III.18.2. Marginal note: 'in epistol.'

they do not despise..., Tacitus, *Germany and Its Tribes*, §8. Marginal note: 'de morib. Germ.'

wisdom often hides..., paraphrase, Cicero, *Tusculan Disputations* III.xxiii.56. Cicero in turn quoted it from an unassigned fragment of a play by the Roman comic poet Caecilius Statius (c219–166 BC).

Had not Matteo Palmieri. Matteo Palmieri (1405–1475), Florentine dignitary, historian, prior and diplomat.

defending Ramus against Charpentier. Pierre de la Ramée (1515–1572), French humanist, mathematician, philosopher and logician, professor of mathematics at the Paris Royal College, was killed during the Massacre of St Bartholomew. Jacques Charpentier (1524–1574), King Charles IX's physician, was an open adversary of Ramus whom he attacked in his speeches and in print, ultimately accused of having instigated Ramus' assassination.

and Ximenes. Francisco Ximenes de Cisnero (1436–1517), Spanish prelate, statesman and religious reformer, was confessor of Queen Isabella of Castile. Later, he was made Cardinal and Grand Inquisitor and served as regent and virtual prime minister of Castile, after the queen's death.

whose noble birth..., paraphrase, Saleius Bassus, *Panegyricus in Calpurnium Pisonem*, 10.

Page 105

La Noue a soldier. François de la Noue (1531–1591), French Huguenot gentleman and military commander, changed camps more than once. Henry IV appointed him lieutenant-general of his army. His memoirs, *Political and Military Discourses*, were published at Basel in 1587.

even a kitchen gardener..., see Aulus Gellius, *Attic Nights*, 2.6.9, quotation included as a proverb in Erasmus, *Adages* I.vi.1.

Tiberius entrusted..., paraphrase, Tacitus, *Annals*, IV.6. Marginal note: 'Tacit.4.Annal.'

made use of Granvelle. Antoine Perrenot de Granvelle (1517–1586), born in Franche-Comté, at the time when it was a Hapsburg dominion, became minister of King Philip II of Spain, and cardinal in 1561.

Francis I of Trivulce. Giangiacomo Trivulce (1448–1518), Milan-born Marshal of France, one of the best generals of King Charles VIII, who went on to serve under King Francis I.

Henry II of Strozzi. Piero Strozzi (1510–1558), Florentine who entered the service of King Henry II, and ultimately became Marshal of France.

grey hairs are..., commonplace, source not identified.

an extraordinary virtue..., paraphrase, Cicero, *Philippics*, V. xvii.47. Marginal note: 'Philipp.5.'

the examples of Joseph and David. Joseph, son of Patriarch Jacob by Rachel, was sold by his brothers to a party of Ishmaelites, was carried to Egypt where he obtained a high place in the Pharaoh's kingdom, as told in the *Book of Genesis* 37–46. David (d962 BC), second king of Israel, who began his public life as aide at the court of Saul, the first king of Israel, but later, he had to flee for his life, because his fame as a warrior had stirred up Saul's jealousy. See *1 Samuel* 18–20.

Hephaestus and Papirius. Hephaestus, god of fire, originating in Asia Minor, became the divine smith and patron of craftsmen in Greece and in central Italy where occasionally he was represented as a beardless younger man wearing a short, sleeveless tunic and a round, close-fitting cap. Sextus Papirius, legendary Roman pontiff to whom is attributed the collection into one corpus of all the Roman laws from before the Republic.

it was on the advice of his father-in-law. See Exodus XVIII,17–26.

Louis XI thought. Actually that was not the case, because Louis XI (1423–1483) not only reinstated his father's ministers but the war launched against him by the League of the Public Weal, made up of malcontent princes, ended by the dissolution of the League.

to a good mind..., paraphrase, Menander *Remarkable Sayings*, 557, likely to have been transcribed by Naudé from Lipsius, *Two Books of Constancie*, II.iv.38–39.

capable of innovating..., paraphrase, Quintus Curtius, *History of Alexander*, IV.i.30. Marginal note: 'Curtius lib.4.'

they are dismayed..., Cicero, *In Defence of Roscio Comoedo*, 11, 31. Marginal note: 'Cicero pro Roscio.'

Emperor Alexander made use. See Aelius Lampride, *Sacred History of Alexander Severus*, 18.32.4. Marginal note: 'Lamprid. in eo.'

Cardinal Richelieu has been. Armand-Jean du Plessis (1585–1642), was actually recalled from a forced exile in the papal city of Avignon where he had been whiling away his isolation writing theological tracts.

given by Xenophon. Xenophon (c430–c355 BC), Athenian historian, philosopher and general, a pupil of Socrates', led the retreat of the Greek mercenaries of the Persian prince Cyrus back to Greek land, after the latter's death, expedition which he described in his book, *Anabasis*. He saw service under a Thracian prince and later, under the Spartan king Agesilaus II and was present at the Battle of Coronea when Agesilaus defeated a Greek coalition including Athens, a fact that led to his banishment from Attica. Xenophon took residence at Sparta and settled near Olympia, on an estate granted to him by the king. Later on, he moved to Corinth when Sparta's glory began to wane. Following the conclusion of an alliance between Athens and Sparta against Thebes, his banishment was revoked and he was able to spend the last decade of his life at Athens, promoting a policy of peace for all the Greeks.

Oribasis elevated Julian. Oribasis (c325–403 AD), Greek physician attached to Emperor Julian. He also had the merit of having collected the writings of the ancient physicians.

Apolophanes was head. According to Polybius, *Histories*, V.56.

1-9 and 58.3-10, Apolophanes was a native of Seleucia and physician to Antiochus the Great (223-187 BC), king of Syria, and enjoyed much authority as the latter's political adviser.

Stephanus was sent. Stephanus, noted physician, sent by Emperor Justinian I (483-565 AD) to intercede with Persian king Chosroes for the city of Edessa. See Procopius, *History of the Wars*, II, xxvi. 31ff.

and Olivier le Dain. Flemish-born favourite of Louis XI, was groom of the chamber and barber of the king, made Count of Meulan, and eventually governor of Saint-Quentin. Sent on a diplomatic mission to Burgundy, he incurred the derision of the Ducal court by his extravagant behaviour. After the king's death, the regent Anne of Beaujeu had him hanged in 1484 to appease popular hatred.

Page 106
and Monsieur Miron. Marc Miron, Catherine of Médicis' physician, was used by Henry III in the negotiations with the Duke of Guise who at the head of the League forces was occupying Paris in the Spring and Summer of 1588. His son Charles became Archbishop of Lyons and delivered the funeral oration at the obsequies of King Henry IV.

the great talent..., paraphrase, Plautus, *The Captives*, I.ii.62. Marginal note: 'in Capt.'

I do not know..., paraphrase, Petronius, *Satyricon*, 84. Marginal note: 'Petron.'

to carry the prize..., Plautus, *Amphitryon*, Prologue, 78. Marginal note: 'Plaut.'

But their nakedness. The sentence ironically summarizes what would happen to Naudé when Mazarin's library, which he had managed, was liquidated, and soon after, at the Swedish court, where he was turned into an object of derision and humiliation, shortly before his death.

Page 107
dressed as Hippias of Elis. Hippias of Elis (5th c. BC), Sophist philosopher of great versatility, although of his ample work only a few fragments have survived. The comparison with Hippias is omitted in the 1711 ET.

Ask for a stout..., paraphrase, Juvenal, *Satires*, X.357-362.

Chancellor L'Hospital. Michel de L'Hospital (c1505-1573), French lawyer, statesman and humanist, Chancellor of France, contributed to a governmental policy of tolerance towards the Huguenots and was one of the initiators of the group of Politiques in France. Nonetheless, when the civil war broke again in September 1567, he lost favour with the regent Catherine de Médicis, and as a result, he asked to be released from office and allowed to retire to his estate.

Page 108
like that of Epictetus, Socrates. Epictetus (c55-c135 AD), Stoic philosopher, primarily interested in ethics, born in the Northwest of Asia Minor, was a slave freed by Emperor Nero but chased out of Rome together with other philosophers by Emperor Domitian. His teachings were collected by his pupil Arrian into two books,

Discourses and the *Manual*. The latter is a summary of his doctrines in the form of aphorisms. Socrates (c470-399 BC), Athenian thinker who concentrated his attention on analyses of human conduct and character, on the basis of an original theory of the soul, whence his notorious command: 'know thyself'. He wrote nothing, and it is from Plato's and Xenophon's works that one learns about his personality, method and ideas. Indicted for corruption of the young and impiety, he accepted the death sentence and drank the cup of hemlock.

Brutus, Cato. Marcus Junius Brutus (85-42 BC), a Stoic and one of the leaders of the conspiracy against Julius Caesar. He had joined Pompey's senatorial army in the civil war, was pardoned and appointed to high office, but unreconciled to the dictatorship which had replaced the Republic, Brutus joined another conspiracy, organized by Gaius Cassius Longinus. Five months after Caesar's assassination, he left for Macedonia to gather a senatorial army against the Caesarian party led by Mark Antony. After an initial victory at Philippi, his army was crushed three weeks later. Realizing that the republican cause was lost, Brutus committed suicide. Admired by his contemporaries for his dignity and idealism, he might have in turn emulated Cato the Younger. Marcus Porcius Cato the Younger (95-46 BC), Roman statesman and general, great-grandson of Cato the Elder, was a staunch defender of the Roman Republic against the newer power-seekers, such as Julius Caesar. After Pompey's forces, which he had joined, were defeated, Cato saw to it that the men from what was left of his troops in Africa were safely evacuated from Utica. His mission completed, he stayed behind and committed suicide. Lucan in his *Civil War*, and Plutarch, among others, would present him as a model of virtue.

President Jeannin. Pierre Jeannin (1540-1622), French magistrate and state councillor, he was the signatory of the French-Dutch alliance in 1608 and of the twelve-year armistice between France and Spain.

straight in the eyes. Naudé uses the Italian expression 'oculo irretorto'.

I consider the best..., Tacitus, *Agricola* 19, likely to have been reproduced by Naudé from Lipsius, *Politica*, III.iv.15, although why Naudé attributed it to Pliny the Younger is impossible to answer.

that Cassius Blosius served. Cassius Blosius of Cumae, scion of a noble family from Campagna, Stoic tutor and close friend of Tiberius Gracchus, urged the latter to bring forward his agrarian law. Accused in 132 BC for his involvement in Tiberius Gracchus' schemes before the consuls, Blosius fled to Aristonicus, king of Pergamum, who was at war with the Romans. He commiited suice shortly after the Romans' victory. See Plutarch, *Lives:Tiberius Gracchus* VIII.xvii.20 about Blosius' end. Marginal note: 'Val. Max. l. 4.cap.7.'

Page 109
here I do not..., source not identified.

public good is..., Here Naudé makes a maxim out of the title of chapter vi, Book III of Lipsius' *Politica*.

for there where..., Palingenius, *Zodiac*, Book IX 'Sagitarius', 845-847. Marginal note: 'P aling.n Sagitt.' Mistakenly, it is changed to 'Scorp.' in the 1711 ET.

It is what Stilicho. Not a favourite of the chroniclers, Flavius

Stilicho (365-408 AD), of Germanic stock, commander-in-chief of the army, regent in the West of the Roman Empire, eventually became father-in-law of Emperor Honorius who ultimately put him to death on suspicion, fed by false rumours, that Stilicho intended to place his own son on the Eastern throne. Apparently Stilicho had persuaded the Roman Senate to pay Alaric a large compensation for his participation in a campaign for the annexation of Illyricum, which was cancelled before it started. The sum was large and depleted the treasury of the Western Empire.

Page 110

Pietro della Vigna. Pietro della Vigna (1190-1249), lawyer, imperial judge, high official in the Kingdom of Sicily, was accused of plotting against the Emperor, was blinded by the local Sicilian magistrates, and soon after, committed suicide in prison.

with Pope Alexander III. Here Naudé seems to mix up the Fredericks! Pope Alexander III (c1105-1181) was in conflict with Frederick I Barbarossa (c1123-1190) and not with his successor.

Cardinal Duprat fell. Antoine Duprat (1463-1535), lawyer, crown functionary, politician, Chancellor of France under Francis I, brokered the Concordat of 1515 between the king and Pope Leo X, afterwards took holy orders, was made cardinal in 1527 and later, papal legate in France. He negotiated the final treaty of Britanny's reunion with France.

credulity is more..., Cicero, *Letters to his Friends,* X.xxiii.1 (to Plancus). Marginal note: 'Cic. lib.1. epist.23.'

nothing that does not..., Seneca, *On Anger,* II.xxiv.2. Marginal note: Seneca de Ira.'

whoever readily believes..., Palingenius, *Zodiac,* Book III 'Gemini', 149.

The squeaking of..., Valerius Maximus, *Nine Books of Memorable Deeds and Sayings,* I.i.5. Marginal note: 'Val. Ma l.1.cap.10.'

whoever is..., paraphrase, Cicero, *The Supreme Good,* I.xix.63. Marginal note: 'Cicero 1. finibus.'

Page 111

nothing more..., paraphrase, Lucretius, *On the Nature of Things,* II.58. See also Naudé's *Apology,* XV, p.297.

by error of judgment..., source not identified. Marginal note: 'Paschas. de virtut.'

audaciously exclude..., source not identified.

whoever is entangled..., paraphrse, Quintus Curtius, *History of Alexander,* IV.x.7-8.

Lycurgus was held. See Plutarch, *Moralia: Ancient Customs of the Spartans,* 238D.

it is not such a terrible..., see St Augustine, *Christian Instruction,* II,xx.31 in the Fathers of the Church Series, Vol. 2, Washington DC, 1966. Marginal note: 'D. August. de Doctrina Christ.'

Lucullus was. Lucius Licinius Lucullus (c117-c56 BC), Roman general who as governor of Asia fought Mithridates, king of Pontus, and his son-in-law Tigranes, king of Armenia, defeating the latter in 69 BC. See also Plutarch, *Moralia: Sayings of the Romans,* 203A-B.

no more than Lucius Æmilius Paulus. See Plutarch, *Life of Æmilius Paulus,* V. 257c.

Page 112

let such insanity..., See Varro in the *Grammar of Marcellus Nonius*, 122. F. C.-D. identified the quotation in a 1601 edition of the existing works of Terentius Varro, printed at Leyden, p. 245. Marginal note: 'in Eumenidib.'

disliking to go..., Horace, *Epistles* I.xvi.52.

we have no solid..., source not identified. Quotation omitted in the 1667 edition.

as the Lesbian law. The phrase has become a metaphor for any flexible law, as the legislation on the Isle of Lesbos, had to accommodate its autonomy every time it managed to recover it through its history.

happy he who..., source not identified.

Page 113

imitate the god Vertumnus. Roman deity of uncertain origin, Vertumnus was the god of the changing year and its seasons, as well as of all sale transactions in Rome; the booksellers had their shops in the proximity of his statue.

my nature may..., Propertius, *Elegies*, IV.ii.21-22.

that often..., in French in the original. So it seems that Naudé got the quotation from Charron, *De la sagesse* [Of Wisdom], III.2. (p. 1036 of ET). The latter too refers it to Plutarch, who in turn attributes the saying to Jason, a Thessalian king; see Plutarch, *Precepts of Statecraft*, 818a1. Lipsius reproduces it in *Politica*, IV.xiv.8. Marginal note: "Liure de la curiosité.'

prudence and civil science...,see Aristotle, *Nicomachean Ethics*, 1141b 24. Marginal note: 'lib. 6 Eth.cap.8.'

as it orders..., see Artistole, *Nicom. Ethics*, 1168a 13.

had we but wisdom..., paraphrase, Juvenal, *Satires*, XV, 315.

Page 114

he does what..., paraphrase, Velleius Paterculus, *History of Rome*, II.xcviii.3.

Page 115

be concise..., Horace, *Art of Poetry*, 335.

think, he says..., Seneca, *Letters*, III.2-3.

discuss all things..., Seneca, *Letters*, III.2.

everyone wishes..., paraphrase, Livy, XXII.xxii.14. Probably transcribed from Lipsius, *Politica*, IV.xiv.1.

Page 116

do not seek..., F.C.-D. identified the source in a copy of Joannis Aurelii Augurelii, Ariminensis, Chrysopæia et vellus aureum, I, p.24, n.l.n.d., in the collections of the Bibliothèque Nationale in Paris. Marginal note: 'Augurel.'

fraudsters and traitors..., source not identified.

Do you wish..., source not identified. The whole quatrain, which is in French in the original, is omitted in the 1711 ET.

if you wish to see me..., Horace, *Art of Poetry*, 102.

why should I..., source not identified.

the wounds..., paraphrase, Isocrates, *To Nicocles*, VIII.28.

you cannot use me..., paraphrase, Aristotle, *Politics* 1314a 3.
the one whose ears..., Tacitus, *Histories*, III.56. Marginal note: 'Tacit. 3.hist.'

Page 117
it is a favour..., paraphrase, Plutarch, *Lives:Alexander*, XXXIX. 1. Marginal note: 'Seneca.' The text from here to the end of the sentence was edited out in the 1711 ET.
to please the princes..., Horace, *Epistles*, I.xvii.35. It is also quoted in Charron, *Of Wisdom*, III.xxx.
liberality is a sort...,paraphrase, Cicero, *In Behalf of King Deiotarus*, IX.26.
the most highly esteemed...,paraphrase. See Botero, *The Reason of State*, I.20, pp.20-30 (ET).

Page 118
Michael Angelo and Raphael of Urbino. Michelangelo Buonarroti (1475-1564), Florentine painter, sculptor, architect and poet. Raffaello Santi (1483-1520), painter born at Urbino, eventually became chief architect and superintendent of buildings at the papal court in Rome.
The day will come..., Dr King re-edited this whole versified finale to suit his own patron, and expanded the area of fame to include China, and 'Carolina and the distant West'.
provided Lachesis..., reverse paraphrase, Ovid, *Sorrows of an Exile*,V.10.45.
accept with good grace..., paraphrase, Virgil, *Æneid*, IV,128, IX.625, *Georgics*, I.40.

INDEX OF NAMES

Joseph, 105
Julia Agrippina, 36
Julian [Count], 80,89
Julian [Roman emperor], 105
Juno [deity], 19,38
Junius Brutus, 52
Jupiter [deity], 29,30,35,43,51,
    85,89,118
Justinian [emperor], 81,104,105
Juvenal, 16,17,107,113

Kish [Saul's father], 81

Lachesis [one of the Fates],118
La Noue [Francis de], 105
La Ruelle [burgomaster], 71
Laverna [Roman goddess], 40
Leo [Pope], 95
Lignerolles [Philibert], 41,44,61
Lipsius [Justus], 11,22,23,24,
    28,45,56,64,78,88
Livy [Roman historian], 25,31,
    37,50,97,103,115
Loredan [Pietro], 74
Lorenzo de' Medici, 79
Lorraine [scions], 63,100
Louis IX [saint,king of France],
    41
Louis XI [king of France], 23,
    40,41,57,100,105,110
Louis XII [king of France],
    100
Louis the Fair [XIII, king of
    France], 41,100
Louis [Duke of Orleans], 91
Louvet [Jean], 100
Lucan, 26,71
Lucius Aemilius Paulus, 111
Lucrece [Roman lady], 52,80
Lucretius [Roman poet], 72,79
Lucullus, 111
Luther [Martin], 40,57,58,71,
    72,73,98
Luynes [Charles de, Constable
    of France], 44,94
Lycurgus [Spartan legislator],
    66,111
Lysander [Spartan general], 27

Macer, 19
Machiavelli, 13,28,42,88
Maecenas, 27,100
Maion [of Bari], 40,70
Malvezzi [Virgilio], 36

Marbod [of Rennes], 25
Marescot [physician], 68
Margaret [of Valois, queen], 62
Mariana [Juan de], 95
Marnix [Aldegonde], 36
Mars [Roman deity], 52
Marsilio Ficino, 31
Marthe Brossier, 68
Martyr [Peter], 15
Mary Stuart, 40
Matteo Palmieri, 104
Mehmet II (Turkish sultan], 90
Melusine [fairy], 85
Mercury [Roman deity], 66,85,
    102
Merovech [Frankish king], 56
Messalina, 101
Metraton [angel], 31
Mettius, 47
Mettius Fuffetius, 97
Michael Angelo, 118
Minerva [deity], 66
Minos [legendary Cretan king],
    31,66
Miramolin, 79
Miron [Marc, physician], 106
Mithridates [king of Pontus],
    61,64
Mocquet [Jean], 34
Mondus [legendary character],
    87
Montaigne [Michel de], 3,16,
    17,105
Montecuculi, 76
Montluc [Bishop of Valence],
    92,95
Montmorency [Constable], 100
Moses, 30,31,66,80,93,105
Moses [Rabbi], 87
Muhammad, 16,53,54,66,88,89,
    98

Nebuchadnezzar, 80
Nero, 21, 100
Nestor, 93
Nevers [Duke of], 57,96
Nifo [Agostino], 31
Ninus [king of Assyria], 50,93
Noel Conti, 71
Numa [Pompilius], 30,31,52,66

Olivier le Dain, 105
Olympias [queen of Macedonia],
    51,52